A HISTORY OF MODERN ENGLISH COINAGE

A History of
Modern English Coinage

Henry VII to Elizabeth II

JAMES MACKAY

Longman
London and New York

Longman Group Limited
Longman House, Burnt Mill
Harlow, Essex CM20 2JE, England
Associated companies throughout the world

Published in the United States of America
by Longman Inc., New York

© Longman Group Limited 1984

First published 1984

British Library Cataloguing in Publication Data

Mackay, James
 A history of modern English coinage.
 1. Coinage – Great Britain – History
 I. Title
 332.4'042'0941   HG935
 ISBN 0-582-50311-6

Library of Congress Cataloging in Publication Data
Mackay, James A. (James Alexander), 1936–
 A history of modern English coinage.
 Bibliography: p.
 Includes index.
 1. Coins, British.   2. Coinage – Great Britain –
History.   I. Title.
 CJ2492.M32   1983   737.4942   82-8932
 ISBN 0-582-50311-6   AACR2

Set in 10/11 Linotron 202 Garamond Roman
Printed in Hong Kong by
Astros Printing Ltd

Contents

Preface

The modern coinage of England (and the United Kingdom since 1707) had its beginning in the late fifteenth century when realism replaced the stylised portraiture of the Middle Ages. The change did not come overnight, and traces of medievalism continued until the time of the early Stuart kings more than a hundred years later. This book spans a period of almost five centuries; from the fairly primitive hammered coins, confined to precious metal worth their face value, to the mass-produced base-metal coins of the present day. The economic crises, political changes and social upheavals of the past 500 years have all had some bearing on the coins yet the overall pattern of English coinage has been one of gradual evolution, reflecting the inherent stability and innate conservatism of the country.

The major part of this book is based on a series of articles which ran, under the title of 'Elizabeth to Elizabeth', in *Coin Monthly* from November 1977 to May 1980. I have taken the story back to the beginning of the Tudor period in order to trace the origins of modern coinage, and brought the story up to date. I am grateful to David Couldridge, editor of *Coin Monthly*, not only for permission to make free use of the articles from which this text has been condensed and extensively revised, but also for many of the illustrations. I should also like to thank the press office of the Royal Mint for additional information and illustrations.

James A. Mackay
Dumfries, January 1984

Acknowledgements

We are grateful to the following people for permission to use, and for supplying, photographs

Richard Bishop of Christie's; Peter Clayton of B. A. Seaby; David Could-ridge and Angela Latham of *Coin Monthly*; Tony Davies of Lubbocks (Numis-matists); and Graham Dyer of the Royal Mint.

CHAPTER ONE

Henry VII (1485–1509)

It is a gross oversimplification to state, as historians used to do, that the reign of Henry VII marked the end of the Middle Ages in England and the beginning of the modern period in English history, but in many respects this was true. Henry Tudor's defeat of Richard III at Bosworth on 22 August 1485 brought the disastrous Wars of the Roses to an end, but peace was only secured by Henry's marriage later in the same year to Elizabeth, eldest daughter and heiress of Edward IV whose brothers, the Princes in the Tower, had been murdered by order of Richard. The marriage was a dynastic union rather than a love match. Henry used matrimony as a form of diplomacy, linking his family to the ruling houses of Spain and Scotland through the marriages of his son Henry to Katherine of Aragon, and his daughter Margaret to the King of Scots.

Henry's reign lasted 24 years and was not without the internal dissensions which were the legacy of the civil wars. Among a succession of Yorkist conspiracies, the most serious were the rebellions in favour of Lambert Simnel (1486–87) and Perkin Warbeck (1494–97), but after the execution of Simnel and the Earl of Warwick in 1499 no further insurrections took place. Henry proved to be equally successful in avoiding foreign entanglements, apart from a half-hearted campaign against France in 1492. He repelled a Scottish invasion in 1496 and then secured his northern frontier by the union of the Thistle and the Rose, as the royal wedding of 1503 was romantically dubbed. He subdued the Irish who had provided Warbeck and Simnel with a power base, and showed no mean skill as a diplomat in maintaining good relations with the duchy of Brittany, the rulers of France and Spain, and the Emperor Maximilian, as well as the papacy.

During his relatively long reign, parliament met only seven times; during its second session it instituted the infamous Court of Star Chamber, initially for the correction of irregularities in justice but eventually employed by Henry as an instrument for curbing the power of the nobility. Significantly, parliament, when it did meet, was mainly concerned with the regulation of trade, wages, hours of labour and trading and manufacturing standards. Economically at least, this reign marked the watershed between the medieval sense of self-sufficiency at a parochial level and the development of trade at a national and even international level. Good relations with France and the Empire brought considerable commercial advantages. Trade with the Low Countries flourished, based largely on the export of a primary commodity – wool – and the import of finished goods and luxury products from the Continent. This trade had long existed but now England began importing the technology and the technicians to develop its own secondary industries.

Henry is best remembered for his attitudes towards money. Years spent in exile had probably inculcated habits of thrift and parsimony but Henry used his royal powers to accumulate money, originally for his own security against intrigue and insurrection, but latterly as an exercise in pure avarice. In the closing years of his reign he was personally unpopular because of the exactions of Empson and Dudley who revived ancient methods and developed new ways of extorting taxes. By the time of his death in 1509 Henry was reputed to be the richest prince in Christendom.

During this reign England, indeed, ceased to be a medieval, introspective little kingdom on the outer fringe of Europe, both geographically and intellectually. The radical movements in learning and the arts, known as the Renaissance, had been influencing the countries of the Continent for upwards of 50 years before they made themselves felt in England and even then the changes which they wrought only gradually took effect.

In the coinage these trends are graphically demonstrated. For the first four years of his reign Henry was content to continue the style and pattern of his predecessors, with no more than a perfunctory change in the name and mintmark. The pound existed solely as money of account, as it had done for centuries, the largest denomination of gold coinage being the angel, worth 6 shillings 8 pence or one-third of a pound. Coins did not bear a date, but had impressed on either obverse or reverse (and sometimes both) a device which corresponded with a period covered by a trial of the pyx, the ancient ceremony in which the fineness and weights of the coins were tested. As this trial took place at more or less annual intervals the mintmarks corresponded to well-defined periods which enable numismatists to date the coins fairly accurately.

The angel derived its name from the motif on the obverse, showing the Archangel Michael slaying the dragon. The reverse featured a galleon bearing a shield emblazoned with the royal arms and surmounted by a cross. Although this was a relatively new coin, introduced in the reign of Edward IV to provide payment of the standard professional fee by a single gold piece, it was thoroughly medieval in design. Moreover, the earliest angels of Henry's reign continued to bear Richard's name and can only be distinguished from the preceding reign by the mintmarks. On the reverse the monarch's initial appeared alongside the mast, and in some early examples this was shown as 'e' (i.e. Edward IV), but later amended to a Lombardic

Gold angel, highly regarded as a talisman or lucky piece. (*Christie's*)

'h' for Henry. The legend on the reverse of this coin read PER CRUCEM TUAM SALVA NOS CHRISTE REDEMPTOR (*By Thy cross, save us, O Christ, our Redeemer*) and explains why this coin was so highly regarded as a talisman or lucky piece. It was also associated with the ceremony of touching for scrofula or King's evil, a miraculous healing power which demonstrated the Divine Right of Kings, and explains why a high proportion of angels are in less than perfect condition, having been pierced for suspension round the neck of the sufferer. By 1489, however, the reverse had acquired a new motto, the Latin signifying *But Jesus, passing through the midst of them, went His way*, a quotation from Luke 4, 30. More importantly, the figure of the archangel cast off his medieval appearance about 1493, and emerged in a modern suit of Renaissance armour. At the same time the medieval Lombardic lettering, with its quaint mixture of rounded capitals and lower-case letters, gradually gave way to the square lettering then fashionable in Europe. The half-angel, or angelet, followed a similar pattern in its obverse and reverse designs.

Gold angel after 1493, now renaissance rather than medieval. (*Royal Mint*)

The silver coins at the beginning of this reign were just as conservative. The principal unit was the silver penny, struck in sterling (0.925 fine) quality and weighing 12 grains. Its obverse and reverse designs had remained virtually unchanged for 150 years. The obverse bore a full-face portrait of the king, boyish, clean-shaven and smiling, with a mass of curls cascading under an open crown. This portrait had been the same for centuries, irrespective of the age or physical attributes of the monarch. It was, in fact, a symbol of kingship rather than an attempt to portray the king himself. The reverse featured the long cross introduced by Henry III in 1247 with

Silver penny, an average day's wage. (*Peter Clayton*)

a view to preventing the dishonest clipping of the coins. In the interstices of the cross were groups of three pellets. While the obverse recited the king's name and title the reverse gave the name of the city where it was minted. In addition to the penny, which represented an average day's wage, there were its sub-divisions, the halfpenny and farthing, and its multiples, the half-groat and groat, worth twopence and fourpence respectively. Production of the silver coinage from the half-groat downwards was shared by the regal mint at London, two mints at Canterbury (regal and archiepiscopal), two at York (regal and archiepiscopal) and the ecclesiastical mint at Durham. Only the Royal Mint located in the Tower of London, however, had the privilege of minting groats and the gold coinage.

There was also a gold coin worth half a pound or ten shillings known as the ryal, but apparently confined to a brief minting in 1487 since surviving specimens are of the greatest rarity. This was a thoroughly medieval coin in appearance, having originated as the noble in the reign of Edward III. Its obverse, showing the king standing in a galleon, crowned and armed and hopelessly out of scale, is thought to have been inspired by the decisive victory of the English navy over the French at Sluys in 1346. Where previous ryals and nobles had an elaborate cruciform motif on the reverse the rare Tudor ryal had a much simpler and startlingly effective device showing the lilies of France in a shield superimposed on the Yorkist and Lancastrian roses, an allusion to the traditional claim of the English kings to the French throne and the union of the erstwhile warring factions. The claim to the French throne, a relic from the Angevin rulers of England, was also asserted in the recital of the king's name and titles which indicated in Latin, abbreviated

Gold ryal or ten-shilling piece. (*Peter Clayton*)

to some extent on the smaller coins, that Henry was king, by the grace of God, of England and France and Lord (DNS = *Dominus*) of Ireland.

The introduction of the sovereign

Henry was not content to follow the pattern of coinage laid down by his predecessors except in so far as it guaranteed continuity and stability. At the same time he kept a close watch on developments on the Continent where he had so recently resided in exile. In 1487 the Emperor Maximilian, acting as regent for his son Philip the Handsome, issued a large gold coin known as the *réal d'or* or *grote reaal*. This large coin was struck in response to the influx of gold from West Africa but it had overtones of political propaganda in its obverse, which showed the emperor crowned and enthroned in full majesty. Henry copied this two years later, when he introduced a new coin called the sovereign. For the first time England had a gold coin tariffed at the pound sterling. Both in its name and in its obverse design, this coin underlined the king's strong position. A full-length portrait of the monarch on the throne, holding sceptre and orb, and wearing a double-arched crown, was matched by the reverse motif of the concentric roses (the so-called Tudor rose) superimposed by a shield bearing the English royal arms, the fleur-de-lis and the three leopards in alternate quarters. The shield was surmounted by the new-style arched crown, which henceforward was regarded as a distinctly Tudor emblem. This magnificent coin weighed 240 grains of almost pure gold ($23\frac{3}{4}$ carat fineness), and is a reminder of a time when a grain or pennyweight of gold was worth just that – a penny.

Gold sovereign, introduced in 1489. (*Peter Clayton*)

The earliest sovereigns had an overall pattern of lilies in the field of the obverse, while the reverse had a cross fitchee mintmark. These coins are extremely rare nowadays, although the initial output is believed to have amounted to 50,000. A somewhat similar sovereign, without the lilies on the obverse, and a cinquefoil mintmark (1489) on the reverse, is believed to be unique. Later the obverse was considerably modified, the back of the throne raised and its sides ornamented with the greyhound of Richmond and the Tudor dragon. The reverse was also drastically altered, the crown being removed and the Tudor rose becoming much more elaborate. Later variants had obverses with a high-backed throne breaking into the legend round the circumference or a narrow throne with a portcullis emblem beneath the king's feet. Two unique pieces, struck on sovereign dies but twice or three times the thickness, are also known. It is thought that these double and treble sovereigns were piedforts intended as presentation pieces.

Changes in the silver coinage

More or less contemporaneous with the sovereign were the groats and pennies in which the open medieval crown was replaced by the new-style Tudor arched crown. The full-face portrait, however, continued in the medieval stylised form, as indeed did the portrait of the monarch enthroned on the gold coins. The detail of these Tudor crowns varied enormously as the reign progressed and their shape and decoration are further aids to the accurate dating of the coins, particularly on the large groats whose size permitted a greater degree of variation. The most startling departure from the medieval pattern, however, was the introduction of a sovereign-type penny about 1489–90. In this type a creditable attempt was made to reproduce the enthroned monarch design in the relatively confined space of the penny. This was accompanied by a new reverse, replacing the groups of pellets with an armorial shield superimposed on the long cross.

Silver sovereign-type penny. (*Peter Clayton*)

Up to this point the coinage of Henry VII was still essentially medieval in concept. Most of the existing denominations were to retain their medieval features right to the end of the reign, but in 1504 the first coin in a thoroughly modern idiom was introduced. This was the testoon or shilling weighing 144 grains and tariffed at 20 shillings to the sovereign or worth 12 pence each. This new coin, together with an issue of groats and half-groats, bore a profile of the king and, for the first time, an attempt was made to depict the monarch as he really was. Credit for this profile is given to Alexander Brugsal (Bruschella or Brussels) who, as his surname implies, was a native of Belgium, then a part of the Spanish dominions in the Netherlands. The first essays in the realistic portraiture of rulers had appeared a generation earlier in the large silver coins produced in Italy. The Renaissance

Silver testoon – prototype of the shilling. (*Peter Clayton*)

princes of Bologna, Bentivoglio and Savoy had set the pattern with *testoni* bearing lifelike profiles, and this example had been emulated by Pope Sixtus IV in his silver grosso and, surprisingly, by James III of Scotland in his groat of 1485. So far as Scotland was concerned, this experiment proved to be short-lived, and no further portrait coins were issued until 1526. It is remarkable that Henry was so tardy in emulating the realistic portraiture of his Scottish contemporary.

Alexander Brugsal had been appointed 'graver of the coinage irons within the Tower of London' in 1494, at a salary of £10 per annum, and he is thought to have been responsible for the later and more florid versions of the sovereign. He is generally credited with the engraving of the dies for the testoon, though it is equally possible that the work was executed by his deputy and (in 1509) successor, Sir John Sharp. The obverse inscription with the king's name and titles was executed in neat lettering of uniform appearance. The reverse marked a further departure from the medieval style. Since the total mintage took place in London it was no longer necessary to refer to this in the inscription. In place of the rather cluttered concentric circles with two inscriptions, there now appeared a single band of lettering, broken up by the elaborate bifurcations of the cross, but permitting an extensive Latin motto POSUI DEUM ADIUTOREM MEUM (*I have made God my Helper* – Psalm 54, 4). Variants of the testoon show the king's name as HENRIC(US), HENRIC VII or HENRIC SEPTIM.

The groats that accompanied this new coin are interesting in that they show a close affinity with the medieval full-face groats at first, but gradually they emerged with a bolder image and stronger lettering in the modern idiom. Half-groats followed a similar pattern but production was not confined to London. The half-groats minted at Canterbury (both regal and ecclesiastical mints) may be recognised by their mintmarks of a rose and martlet respectively. The same mintmarks were used by Archbishop Bainbridge at York, but his half-groats additionally showed two episcopal keys below the shield or the letters XB alongside.

The testoon appears to have been unpopular, judging by the relative scarcity of surviving specimens, yet the variety of inscriptions indicates the use of several dies, which would have been necessary if the output had been great. The emphasis during this reign continued to be laid on the groat as the most convenient form for the merchant classes in their daily transactions. The groat was, in fact, to remain the 'workhorse of the English coinage' during the ensuing reign. The other trend noticeable in the coinage of Henry VII was the gradual diminution of the importance and output of the ecclesiastical mints. At most, their activities were confined to the smaller silver coins and the Durham mint was closed down after the death of Bishop Fox in 1501, while it is evident, from the combinations of ecclesiastical and regal mintmarks, that the king shared the profits of the York and Canterbury mints from the closing years of the sixteenth century, an important stage in the centralisation of the coinage, as well as other aspects of power and privileges formerly enjoyed by the Church in England.

CHAPTER TWO

Henry VIII (1509–1547)

The third child and second son of Henry VII came to the throne on 22 April 1509. Born in 1491, he was suddenly propelled into the line of kingship by the death of his brother Arthur in 1502 and, at the same time, was forcibly betrothed to his late brother's wife, Katherine of Aragon. Both Pope Julius II and Archbishop Warham of Canterbury expressed doubts as to the validity of this union, but Henry had to accede to the wishes of his father and Ferdinand of Aragon who regarded England merely as a Spanish fief and his daughter as his resident viceroy. The marriage of Henry and Katherine did not take place, however, until shortly before his eighteenth birthday, a few weeks after his accession. The marriage lasted 24 years but ended in political, diplomatic and religious turmoil when Katherine failed to produce the desired male heir to the English throne.

Henry inherited political stability and economic prosperity. His secure throne freed him from the immediate necessity to take a personal interest in domestic politics, which he left to Archbishop Warham, while a full treasury gave him the money to indulge his varied but extravagant sports and amusements. Much has been made of Henry's wide range of interests and talents, very much in the mould of the Renaissance prince. He had a deep and abiding interest in the arts and the new learning, and had ambitions to make England a great sea power. He laid the foundations for the Royal Navy and the shipbuilding industry and the ill-fated *Mary Rose* was a splendid manifestation of this.

Unlike his canny father, however, he soon embroiled himself in foreign adventures, mainly as an ally (at times reluctantly) of his father-in-law against the rising might of France. Much of the blame for England's expensive foreign policy in the 1520s must be given to Cardinal Wolsey. For a time (1520–21) England actually held the balance of power between Francis I of France and the emperor Charles V, who had succeeded his grandfathers Ferdinand and Maximilian and thus united the might of Spain and the Empire. But as the power of the emperor grew he dispensed with his English ally. Henry turned his attention to domestic politics and competed with Wolsey whom he eventually ousted. The failure of his wife to produce a male heir precipitated the religious crisis of 1526, culminating in Henry's divorce of Katherine and his break with the Papacy seven years later. In this he was greatly assisted by Wolsey's successor, Thomas Cromwell. More importantly, however, Henry's tussle with Pope Clement VII made him realise that the Papacy was hardly worth conciliating and his personal power and prestige grew as the embodiment of a deep-seated resentment of the English towards papal jurisdiction and ecclesiastical privilege.

The abolition of the monasteries and the confiscation of church property not only brought Henry popularity but a much-needed influx of money, at a time when the wealth accumulated by his father was dangerously depleted. This windfall was reflected in the coinage of the period. More than at any time before or since the coins of this reign serve as a barometer of the national economy, affected not only by the king's extravagances but by factors which were outside his control. In 1509 Henry had inherited a well-filled treasury and a buoyant economy, and this is reflected in the coinage during the first seventeen years of the reign which remained virtually unchanged, even to the extent of retaining the portrait of Henry VII on the larger silver coins.

Henry VIII's first coinage comprised gold in the same mixture of modern sovereigns and medieval angels and angelets, struck in the same sizes and weights and tariffed at the same values. The silver coins also followed the identical pattern of the preceding reign, with profiles of Henry VII on the groat and half-groat, the sovereign-type obverse on the penny and a medieval full-face stylised portrait on the halfpenny. Only on the extremely rare farthing was any change discernible. In place of a portrait, which was hardly practical on such a tiny coin, there appeared a portcullis, badge of Henry's grandmother, Margaret Beaufort. It will be remembered that this had appeared at the foot of the last sovereigns of Henry VII. It was again used in the reign of Henry VIII as a mintmark, in 1523 the year in which these rare farthings were struck.

Extremely rare portcullis silver farthing. (*Peter Clayton*)

The only concession to the change of ruler was the inclusion of the Roman numerals VIII on the obverse of angels, angelets, groats and half groats. All of the other coins can only be attributed to Henry VIII by reference to their mintmarks. Since the pheon (heraldic arrowhead) was used on the last coins of Henry VII and the first of Henry VIII numismatists can only tell them apart by minute differences in the lettering. In the early part of this reign the angel was the most important gold coin, while the groat was the chief silver coin. As usual, production of groats was confined to London, with the exception of an issue in 1513–14 struck at Tournai during Henry's campaign in the cause of Spain against France. The Tower Mint produced a substantial amount of silver coinage in the period 1509–26 but in some years output dropped alarmingly. Only £180 worth of coins were minted in 1516, and only £64 in 1520, compared with £13,562 (1513) and £14,237 (1519). As coining tended to reflect the amount of bullion available, it shows tremendous fluctuations in the quantities of precious metal coming into England at that time. This was a period when the earlier influx of gold from West Africa was being augmented by both gold and silver from the Spanish mines in America. This led to inflation all over Europe, at a time when prices were rising steadily, wage rates were hardly keeping pace, and the value of goods and services led to an inordinate increase in the demand for coinage.

Output of coinage at the ecclesiastical mints was stepped up, and the episcopal mint at Durham revived. Canterbury produced half-groats, pence and halfpence, while production at York was confined to half-groats and at Durham only pennies were struck. The coins from these mints provide a rich variety of types, embellished with the initials of successive prelates and reflecting their rising status. Thus the cardinal's hat appeared on the coins of York after Archbishop Bainbridge became a prince of the church in 1511, while the Canterbury coinage was similarly decorated after Warham became a cardinal in 1516.

Second coinage, 1526–44

A coinage based on gold and silver, in which the intrinsic content was very close to the face value, was only possible in times of economic stability, when the value of one metal remained static against the other. In the 1520s, however, inflation in Europe gathered momentum and the increased output of the Spanish silver mines in the New World lowered the value of silver in relation to gold. England, being still on the fringe of Europe and tending to be somewhat behind the times, continued to use gold coins which were seriously undervalued, at a ratio of 1 : 12 whereas European gold and silver were in the ratio of 1 : 14.66. Inevitably English gold coins drained abroad, where merchants could gain the advantage of higher exchange rates in terms of silver. The situation became so desperate that foreign gold coins were actually being imported (at a premium, of course) for use as currency to fill the gap left by the English angels. The most popular of the Continental coins was the French *écu au soleil*, worth 4 shillings 4 pence.

In August 1526 the gold coinage of England was raised in value by 10 per cent. The sovereign was raised to 22 shillings, the angel to 7 shillings 4 pence and the half-angel to 3 shillings 8 pence, while the *écu au soleil* was re-tariffed at 4 shillings 6 pence. At the same time a coin of the same value as the *écu* was introduced and known as the crown of the rose, from its motifs — a crowned shield (obverse) and a rose embellished with the royal mono-

Gold crown of the rose, or rose crown. (*Peter Clayton*)

gram, lilies and lions (reverse). The king's name and titles appeared on the obverse, while the reverse had the curious Latin motto HENRIC RUTILANS ROSA SINE SPINA (*Henry, blushing rose without a thorn*). It was struck in the same weight (51 grains) and fineness (only 23 carat) as the French *écu*. It was obviously intended as a rival to the *écu* but its great rarity suggests that it was unsuccessful. Two points are notable about this coin. It was the first English coin to show the monarch's numeral in Arabic (8) instead of the conventional Roman (VIII) form. Secondly, it was the first coin known as a crown, though a large silver coin of this name did not appear for a further quarter of a century.

Clearly these reforms, instigated by Cardinal Wolsey, were not enough to combat inflation and the drain of good English coinage. In November 1526 more drastic measures were announced. The value of the gold coins was raised a further 2 per cent, tariffing the sovereign at 22 shillings 6 pence and the angel at 7 shillings 6 pence. The crown of the rose was replaced by a coin known as the crown of the double rose, from the principal motif of a Tudor rose surmounted by a crown, and as it was tariffed at 5 shillings sterling it immediately had the edge over the *écu*. Henceforward the *écu* and other foreign gold coins were regarded merely as bullion, to be taken to the Tower for recoining into English money. While the fineness of the sovereign and angel remained unchanged at $23\frac{3}{4}$ carat, the new crown was debased to 22 carat – henceforward known as 'crown' gold and the fineness which is used at the present day. As a compromise, however, yet another coin was introduced to fill the gap left by the re-tariffing of the angel. The professional and mercantile community still needed a coin worth 6 shillings 8 pence – one-third of a pound or half a mark – and this was now served by a coin

Gold crown of the double rose. (*Peter Clayton*)

Gold George noble – worth 6 shillings 8 pence or one-third of a pound, or half a mark. (*Peter Clayton*)

called the George noble. This coin may be regarded as something of an anachronism or a throwback to medievalism, with its revival of the old name and its obverse motif of a galleon with the Tudor rose amidships. Its reverse, however, showed St George slaying the dragon and thus provides an interesting forerunner to the silver crowns almost three centuries later which bore the same device. The George noble seems to have been little used, and surviving examples are very scarce. There was also a half George noble, of which only a single example is now extant.

The crown of the double rose, by contrast, proved immensely popular and underwent numerous minor variations in dies over the ensuing eighteen years. It was accompanied by a gold half-crown – not so plentiful, but still resulting in no fewer than five major die variants. The silver coins were reduced in weight, resulting in a penny of 10.66 grains, but the fineness remained the same. The opportunity was taken to replace the profile of Henry VII by one showing the young king clean-shaven. This portrait was soon out of date, because Henry began growing a beard a year later. The reforms of 1526 succeeded in attracting large quantities of bullion to the Tower and in the ensuing four years an annual average of £44,000 in gold and £65,000 in silver was coined there. Though output decreased after that it continued to be substantial for several years.

Silver halfgroat with clean-shaven bust. (*Royal Mint*)

The chief interest in the crown of the double rose lies in the sequence of initial letters which, in conjunction with the mintmarks, show the chronology of the issue. Early crowns bear the letters H (Henry) and K (Katherine). After the divorce in 1533 and Henry's remarriage to Anne Boleyn the letters are H and A, and this arrangement continued until Anne's execution in 1536. More elusive are those inscribed H and I (Jane Seymour) since Henry's third wife died in 1537, shortly after producing the long-desired male heir. The last of these coins were inscribed HR (Henricus Rex); later wives of the much-married Henry were not to be honoured in this way. To some extent a similar pattern may be discerned in the half-crowns. Both crown and half-crown are known in a rare variety showing the title of king instead of lord of Ireland (1542). This is also found on some of the later groats and half-groats and signifies Henry's assumption of this title, confirmed by an Act of the Irish parliament, in place of the title of lord which was dependent on the pope.

As with the first coinage, the silver in the second series reflects the activities of the three ecclesiastical mints. Exceptionally, groats were minted at York in the name of Archbishop Wolsey whose initials TW appear beside the shield, with his cardinal's hat below. These Wolsey groats belong to the period up to 1530 when Wolsey was dismissed from his office as chancellor and was summoned to London to face charges of treason. Had he not died on the way he would probably have faced the charge of unwarranted minting of groats, in addition to his other crimes. These groats were followed by a rare issue showing the voided cross mintmark of York, but omitting the initials TW. Half-groats were struck at Canterbury with the initials of Archbishop Warham (until 1532) and Thomas Cranmer, but it is the half-groats of York which exhibit the greater variety, successive issues showing the initials of Wolsey and Archbishop Lee, with the unmarked coins of 1530–31 from York when the see was vacant. Ecclesiastical pennies were minted in the names of Warham and Cranmer at Canterbury, and Lee at York, but the Durham pennies include several varieties bearing the initials of Wolsey as bishop before his elevation to the see of York. Unmarked Durham pennies of 1529–30 indicate the vacant see, followed by those struck by authority of Bishop Tunstall, with the initials CD (for Cuthbert Durham). The reverse legends also bore the names of the cities as before: CIVITAS CANTOR (*Canterbury*), CIVITAS EBORACI (*York*) and CIVITAS DURRAM (*Durham*). Halfpennies were minted in the facing bust type at London, Canterbury and York, but production of the portcullis farthings was confined to the Tower mint and these are exceedingly rare.

Third coinage, 1544–47

The monetary reforms of 1526, coupled with the windfall of the monastic property in the late 1530s, enabled Henry to withstand the ravages of inflation for a time, but his own personal extravagance, together with the high costs of expeditions against Ireland and the Scots and the subjugation of the last vestiges of feudalism in the north of England and the Welsh borders, inevitably placed Henry in dire financial straits. By 1540 he was resorting to the debasement of the coinage, a practice which was recognised in an indenture of May 1542 in which he authorised the reduction of fine gold from 23.75 carat to 23 carat and silver from the traditional 11 oz 2 dwt to the pound of metal, to less than 10 oz fine. This indenture was never published, but it seems likely that the Tower Mint was diluting the fineness of both gold and silver from then until 1544, but holding these debased coins in readiness for release when the time was right.

The new coinage was proclaimed in May 1544. The sovereign, which now bore Henry's full-length portrait, was reduced from 240 to 200 grains and 23 carat fineness. This was rapidly overtaken by sovereigns in which the king's portrait was reduced, the weight was reduced from 200 to 192 grains, and the fineness dropped successively to 22 and then to 20 carat. At the same time a half-sovereign of 96 grains was released. Both coins had an entirely new reverse, showing the crowned coat of arms supported by the English lion and the Welsh dragon. The ecclesiastical mints had been shut down following the confiscation of church property, but subsidiary mints at Southwark and Bristol were now established to cope with the recoinage. Angels weighing 80 grains and tariffed now at 8 shillings were minted in London, as well as half- and quarter-angels, all in 23 carat gold. Crowns and half-crowns, originally in 22 carat 'crown' gold but reduced to 20 carat in 1545, were also struck in weights of 48 and 24 grains respectively. These coins were likewise struck at Southwark and Bristol and may be recognised by their mintmarks: s or e (Southwark) or ws (initials of William Sharington, Bristol). The e mark of Southwark was the initial of the Latin form of the mintmaster's name John Yorke (*Eboracum*).

Third coinage gold sovereign. (*Peter Clayton*)

The debased silver of 1544–45 was, in fact, only 9 oz fine and comprised the testoon of 120 grains, with the corresponding half-groat, penny and halfpenny. In 1545–47 the five silver denominations were progressively debased to 6 oz and then to a mere 4 oz. The debased silver coins bore a facing bust of the king – portly, bearded and with an expression that ranges from the majestic hauteur of the first testoons to the jaundiced dissipation of the later versions. Smaller versions were used for the penny, which now abandoned the enthroned effigy, and the halfpenny, which dropped the last vestige of medievalism. On the groat and half-groat, however, the portrait

Silver groats (fourpence pieces) showing different busts. (*Peter Clayton*)

of the king was turned slightly to the right. The expression on the three busts used for the groats ranges from shrewdness, through cynical testiness to outright world-weariness. A new reverse was introduced for the testoon, a crowned double rose copied from the gold crowns, but the other silver coins retained the armorial or cruciform reverses of the earlier issues. The mints at the Tower and Bristol produced all five denominations, and Southwark produced all but the halfpenny, while temporary mints were reopened at Canterbury and York under regal supervision to strike the denominations from the groat downwards. The debased silver coinage of 1544–47 is still reasonably plentiful, testifying to the vast output of the mints and the tremendous profit which must have accrued to the king as a result.

CHAPTER THREE

Edward VI (1547–1553)

Henry's early death in his fifty-sixth year, on 28 January 1547, brought to the throne his son by Jane Seymour. Edward VI was not quite 10 years old and inevitably the government was entrusted to a council, with the Earl of Hereford (soon to become Duke of Somerset) as Protector of the Realm. Somerset pursued Henry's policies of religious reform and centralisation of government with a ruthlessness which his late master would have endorsed, but it provoked a great deal of unrest in the west country and East Anglia. The outbreak of hostilities with France again did nothing to alleviate the situation.

In Europe the influx of gold and silver from the Spanish Main continued to wreak havoc on the economies of Spain and the Spanish Netherlands and the enormous increase in the money supply pushed up prices everywhere. Not much of this Spanish gold and silver percolated down to England, but its inflationary side-effects did and this resulted in a continuation of the debased coinage. Although the merchants of Antwerp recognised Henry's last coinage for what it was, and immediately adjusted their exchange rates accordingly, the debasement had no immediate effect on the English domestic economy. The groat in one's pocket remained the same, in terms of purchasing power, since England was self-sufficient and imports had a negligible effect on market prices. Henry's currency policies could only work for a short time before economic Nemesis caught up with them. Further debasement in 1545–47 only accelerated the inflationary spiral and the council of regency was at a loss to know how to cope with it. They took the view that if they did nothing the problem might resolve itself, and therefore continued to mint coins in the base 4 oz silver standard, in the name of the late king, so that he would incur the blame.

The posthumous coinage continued for a period of four years. In this period coin production at the Tower Mint was largely in the hands of a French technician, Anthony Levers, and a group of French and Dutch die engravers and sinkers, though overall responsibility belonged to Henry Basse and his deputy, Robert Pitt.

Posthumous base coinage, 1547–51

It was recognised by the council that the debasement of the coinage by Henry was strongly deflationary but they realised that so drastic a remedy would bring its own long-term problems. An effort would have to be made to return to the old standards, but meanwhile the debased coinage was allowed to continue. In the end the council compromised, and this resulted in a curious dual system of debased coinage in Henry's name, alongside various attempts in Edward's name to raise the standards again. For this reason the debased coinage was deliberately produced with the minimum of alteration in the designs. Nevertheless the considerable output of debased coinage meant that subsidiary mints were involved, and this gave rise to the interesting but very complicated sequence of mintmarks during this period.

The main production of debased coins at the Tower was in the hands of Sir Martin Bowes (whose emblem, an arrow, was used in 1547–49) and Thomas Knight (who used an initial κ as mintmark). Across the Thames at Southwark, John Yorke continued to strike coins with his ε mintmark, but a third mint was established temporarily at Durham House under John Bowes, who used a bow mintmark. Coins minted in Bristol were marked ws (William Sharington) or τc (Thomas Chamberlain). The subsidiary mint at Canterbury continued until 1550 under William Tillesworth, who signed his coins with capital or lower-case τ. Other mintmarks which identify the debased coins as belonging to the posthumous period were the annulet and pellet (1547), lis (1547–48), grapple (1549) and martlet (1550–51), while a lis or rose was also used at Canterbury in 1549.

The posthumous coins comprised sovereigns (London and Bristol), and half-sovereigns, crowns and half-crowns (Tower and Southwark Mints). The silver coins consisted of testoons (mainly from the Tower but some from Southwark), groats, half-groats and pennies (the Tower, Southwark, Durham House, Bristol, Canterbury and York) and halfpence (the Tower, Canterbury and York). With the exception of a few groats bearing the lis mintmark, none of the York debased silver coins bore a mintmark. Stylistically the

Posthumous groats of Henry VIII and a Tower penny. (*Peter Clayton*)

posthumous coins showed a greater tendency towards the use of the more modern Roman lettering in place of the medieval Lombardic. While the half-sovereigns substituted a youthful portrait of the new king, three new busts of Henry were employed in the groats and some of the Tower pennies were given a three-quarter bust instead of the usual facing portrait. The inscriptions on these coins followed the pattern laid down in Henry's lifetime with one curious exception. The coins minted at Durham House had the reverse legend REDDE CVIQVE QVOD SVVM EST (*Render unto each that which is his own*), which is thought to be an allusion to the use of base silver for the posthumous coinage, acquired by melting down base testoons, but if this were so it seems odd that the same inscription was not used at the other mints.

First coinage, April 1547–January 1549

While the council dithered over ways of solving the economic and monetary problems inherited from Henry's reign, an attempt was made to issue coins in the name of the boy-king but two years elapsed before any improvement in the standards of fineness were achieved. In the interim, however, there was an issue of both gold and silver in the debased standards, but referring to Edward VI. The gold was confined to half-sovereigns, struck at the Tower and Southwark, as well as a very few half-crowns and crowns, though only one example of the latter appears to have survived. The coins retained the designs of the previous reign but were inscribed EDWARD 6 – a remarkable instance of the king's name rendered in English instead of the customary Latin form.

The base silver consisted of testoons, now known for the first time as shillings (though, of course, no inscription denoting this actually appeared on them), and confined to Durham House; groats struck at the Tower and Southwark, half-groats from the Tower, Southwark and Canterbury, pennies (Tower, Southwark and Bristol) and halfpence (Tower and Bristol). The obverse of these coins showed a right-facing profile of the young king, while the reverse depicted the royal arms superimposed on a bifurcated cross. In general, the inscriptions on these silver coins followed the pattern of Edward's predecessor, but an innovation was the Latin motto on the Durham House shillings TIMOR DOMINI FONS VITE (*The fear of the Lord is a fountain of life* – Proverbs 14, 27), a portent of the wide range of biblical texts which were to grace the later coins. Another innovation in the shilling, of even greater long-term importance, was the inclusion of the date, rendered in Roman numerals MDXLVIII (1548).

Second coinage, January 1549–April 1550

In January 1549 the council took the bold step of raising the standard of the gold coinage to 22 carat fineness and the silver to 0.500 fineness. The silver was, in fact, confined to shillings minted in considerable quantity in London and, to a lesser extent, in Bristol and Canterbury. Most of these shillings bore a date-in Roman numerals but, perversely, some of the later shillings minted at Durham House omitted the date. These undated shillings had a new motto on the reverse INIMICOS EIVS INDVAM CONFVSIONE (*As for his enemies I shall clothe them with shame* – Psalm 132, 18).

The 22 carat or 'crown' gold coins were introduced in October 1549. While the fineness was raised, the weight of the sovereign was substantially reduced, from 192 to 169.41 grains, and the subsidiary denominations – half-sovereign, crown and half-crown – were scaled down accordingly. The obverse of the sovereign continued to show the full-length portrait of the enthroned king, but the portrait was now more lifelike than before. A bare-headed profile of Edward appeared on the lesser denominations at first, but it was soon followed by the more conventional crowned bust. The coats of arms featured on the reverse of these coins were completely restyled, showing lion and dragon supporters on the sovereign, and oval shields with elaborate scrollwork on the smaller coins. As well as the TIMOR motto, previously introduced by the Durham House shilling, two new slogans graced the gold coins: SCVTVM FIDEI PROTEGET EVM (*The shield of faith shall protect him*) and LVCERNA PEDIBVS MEIS VERBVM EST (*Thy word is a lantern unto my feet* – Psalm 119, 105). This rash of inscriptions derived from the Old Testament reflect the reforming zeal of the religious establishment at the time. Of this series, only the half-sovereign bore a date. The extremely rare half-sovereigns of Durham House were even dated MDXLVIII – the year before they were authorised.

Two busts of Edward VI on Second Coinage gold half-sovereigns. (*Peter Clayton*)

Third coinage, 1550–53

During the last three years of Edward's brief reign there was another period of dual coinage which produced a multiplicity of coin types, values, weights and fineness. It is a period which continues to tantalise and bewilder the numismatic scholar; its effect on the general public of the early 1550s can be imagined. The merchant classes were confronted with 'fine' (23 carat) sovereigns tariffed at 30 shillings and 'crown' (22 carat) sovereigns worth 20 shillings; angels and half-angels in 'fine' gold, worth 10 shillings and 5 shillings; half-sovereigns, crowns and half-crowns in 'crown' gold, also tariffed at 10 shillings and so on; and an astonishing variety of silver coins which included the sterling (0.925 fine) penny of 8 grains and a base (3 oz) penny of 12 grains, with corresponding multiples and sub-divisions.

The angel and half-angel were deliberately revived as a means of distinguishing 'fine' from 'crown' gold and these coins retained their medieval designs. The new 'crown' sovereigns, however, introduced fresh obverse designs, showing a half-length portrait of Edward, crowned, armoured, and holding a sword in one hand and the orb of state in the other. The crowned shield on the reverse of the sovereign had supporters as before, but the more austere crowned shield on the reverse of the smaller gold coins was devoid of scrollwork and was flanked by the royal monogram. The 'fine' sovereign, and a curious double sovereign struck from the same dies, are extremely rare, while the half-angel is unique, but the other gold coins are more common, pointing to a substantial output of gold at the Tower under the direction of Sir John Yorke, whose initial was used as a mintmark.

Third Coinage gold sovereign with half-length portrait. (*Peter Clayton*)

Only shillings, pennies, halfpence and a handful of farthings were struck in base silver. All were produced in London, except for a plentiful supply of pennies minted at York and distinguished by a mullet mintmark. Only the shilling bore the crowned profile of the king, while a double rose (penny), single rose (halfpenny) and portcullis (farthing) graced the lower denominations.

The advent of the fine silver coinage of 1551 coincided with the appointment of Derick Anthony as chief engraver at the Tower. His salary of £30 per annum was 50 per cent higher than his predecessor, but this was merely in line with inflation. During Edward's short reign the price of goods more than doubled but wages and salaries only increased by half. Of the six denominations, four were entirely new, and all the designs marked a radical departure from previous types. Only the exceedingly rare penny, with its enthroned sovereign obverse, harked back to an earlier period. Only the two largest coins bore a date − rendered in Arabic instead of Roman numerals, for the first time – but the middle denominations now included notation of their value.

The most remarkable aspect of this coinage was the silver crown, England's first essay in the taler-sized coins which had circulated in Europe for several decades. These coins derived their name (later corrupted to dollar) from Joachimstal (Jachymov) in Bohemia where the Counts of Schlick mined large deposits of silver and coined it into large pieces from 1518 onwards. Even before that date, however, there were isolated examples of large-diameter silver coins, such as the guldiners, guldengroschen and snaphaans minted in Hungary, Switzerland and the Netherlands from the late fifteenth century onwards. The silver crown of Edward VI was seen as a dramatic pledge of currency reform. It seems to have been closely modelled on the handsome guldengroschen of the Tirol (1486), with its ornate equestrian portrait of the ruler, and the date in the field below the horse's belly. By contrast, the reverse, with its plain shield and forked cross, was stark in its simplicity, and its conservatism was heightened by the retention of the POSUI motto which had made its debut on the coins of Edward III. Only one type of crown was issued, but the half-crown is known with three different obverses, a walking horse with a plumed crest, a galloping horse and a large walking horse, the latter two without the plumes.

First silver crown, size of a taler (later corrupted to dollar). (*Christie's*)

For the shilling a new facing bust of the king was chosen, the portrait showing a youth of maturity beyond his years. The portrait was flanked by a rose and Roman numerals signifying the value in pence. Similar obverses were used for the sixpence and threepence, two entirely new denominations, and their values (VI and III respectively) were also inscribed in the field in order to inspire confidence and avoid the disputes which had been all too common in transactions involving the various debased issues. The reverses of all the fine silver coins were uniform in featuring the cross superimposed on a plain shield. With the exception of some sixpences and threepences inscribed CIVITAS EBORACI (*York*) on the reverse all of the fine silver coins were struck at the Tower.

(a)

(b)

(a) Silver sixpence Tony Davies and **(b)** threepence (*Royal Mint*) – two entirely new denominations.

Most of the credit for the fine coinage of 1551–53 must go to the Duke of Northumberland who had supplanted the Duke of Somerset in October 1549 and had his arch rival executed in 1552 on a trumped-up charge of treason. Northumberland was ambitious, ruthless and violent. The failing health of the king drove Northumberland into taking a wild gamble to secure the throne against Edward's half-sister Mary, a devout Catholic. He married his son Guilford Dudley to Lady Jane Grey, the eldest granddaughter of Henry VIII's younger sister Mary, and then browbeat the ailing king into vesting the crown in Lady Jane and her heirs male. Three days after Edward's death on 6 July 1553 Lady Jane Grey was proclaimed queen in London.

CHAPTER FOUR

Mary (1553–1558)

The Duke of Northumberland made one fatal mistake. He failed to arrest the Lady Mary, Edward's elder half-sister and his senior by 21 years. The daughter of Henry's first marriage to Katherine of Aragon, she had actually been named by him in his will as successor should Edward die, and although she made no secret of her staunch devotion to the old religion, Mary was regarded by many people as the natural successor. She escaped from London to East Anglia and rapidly gathered an army. Northumberland rode out to intercept her, but defection dogged his steps, and even in London Mary was proclaimed queen behind his back by some of his fellow-conspirators. In a matter of days Mary herself rode triumphantly into the capital amid scenes of genuine public rejoicing. Northumberland was totally discredited and soon found himself in the Tower, along with his unfortunate son and the hapless Lady Jane, the 'Nine Days Queen', who soon paid the supreme penalty on the scaffold. Mary's half-sister Elizabeth, daughter of Anne Boleyn, was sent to the Tower at this time and the Protestants were robbed of a figurehead round whom they might have rallied. Mary was now free to restore Catholicism, repealing or annulling the religious reforms of her father and brother, recalling or freeing Catholic priests and prelates and punishing those who had advanced the cause of the Reformation.

Mary set her seal on the restoration of Catholicism within the year by marrying her cousin Philip, the Habsburg prince of Spain, king of Naples and son of the emperor Charles V, at Winchester in July 1554. This marriage, and Mary's desire that her husband should reign equally with her as king-consort, roused fierce resistance and a series of rebellions broke out all over England in the spring of that year. This merely stiffened Mary's resolve to rescind all anti-papal legislation. Cardinal Pole was admitted as papal legate and the rooting out of heresy proceeded with a ruthlessness and vengefulness that earned Mary her sanguinary epithet. Although most of the 300 Protestants burned at the stake hailed from the Home Counties, revulsion to Mary was widespread. The Spanish connection did nothing to endear her to her subjects. It proved to be a one-sided arrangement. England's expanding overseas trade was still denied access to the Spanish Main or even the colonies of Spain's ally Portugal. While Philip induced Mary to declare war on France he refused to back her in her campaign against the Scots who had deposed her cousin and co-religionist, Mary. In the French campaign the Spaniards were victorious at St Quentin (1557) and Gravelines (1558) but England lost one of its last remaining footholds on the mainland and Mary herself asserted that Calais would forever be engraved on her heart.

Mary was 37 when she came to the throne, and past the normal age for child-bearing at the time of her marriage. She was deluded into thinking herself pregnant, when in fact it proved to be cervical cancer. She died on 17 November 1558, broken-hearted at the loss of Calais, the desertion of her husband and her failure to capture the hearts and minds of her people.

First coinage, 1553–54

Within eight weeks of her accession Mary had issued a proclamation condemning the parlous state of the coinage and expressing her wish to restore it to its pristine quality. She kept her promise by abandoning 'crown' gold and restricting her sovereigns, and lesser denominations to 'fine' gold of 23 carat $3\frac{1}{2}$ grain fineness. Four coins were minted – the sovereign of 30 shillings, the ryal of 15 shillings, the angel of 10 shillings and the half-angel of 5 shillings. The old weights (240 grains) were restored and stylistically the designs marked a return to the late medievalism of Henry VII. Only the sovereign and ryal bore dates, and these were rendered in Roman numerals. Mintmarks, in the form of a pomegranate or a half-rose, appeared after the first word of the legend. Conservatism permeated the details of the designs, especially the ryal with its portrait of the queen amidship. Derick Anthony

Gold sovereign of Mary I with allusion to restoration of Roman Catholicism. (*Christie's*)

and his deputy, John Lawrence, were responsible for all the coin dies of this reign. The reverses marked a return to the shield superimposed on a most elaborate rose, reminiscent of the first sovereigns of Henry VII. The motto was in Latin, more or less abbreviated and signifying *This is the Lord's doing and it is marvellous in our eyes* (Psalm 118, 23), an allusion to the restoration of Catholicism and, perhaps, Mary's succession itself in face of Northumberland's opposition.

Mary turned her back on the new denominations which had accompanied the reforms of her late brother. The groat and its sub-divisions were restored to favour. The only concession to the recent past was the use of a left-facing profile of the queen and the retention of the plain shield and forked cross on the reverse. Both groats and half-groats had shortened versions of the obverse legend found on the gold coins, while the penny was inscribed M D G (Maria Dei Gratia = *Mary, by the Grace of God*) and the motto in Latin *a rose without a thorn*. The reverse legend, used on all the silver coins except some pennies (which were merely inscribed CIVITAS LONDON), signified in Latin *Truth is the daughter of Time* – an ominous reference to the fact that, given time, Mary would undo all the anti-Catholic and anti-papal measures of her predecessors.

Second coinage, 1554–58

Probably the only tangible asset which the Spanish bridegroom brought to England at the time of his marriage was the 'twenty carts of bullion drawn by ninety-nine horses and two wagons of foreign coin', followed within a few months by a team of Spanish technicians equipped with the latest coining tools. About this time also there was a short-lived experiment at the Tower using a water-mill for rolling metal strip and cutting coin blanks. This was intended to produce coins of an even thickness and diameter but such innovations then, and for very many years thereafter, were strenuously opposed by the mint officials and their workmen. The first coinage of Mary, though stylistically florid, tended to be poorly executed, explained partly by the haste with which the coin were produced and partly, it is thought, by the temporary diversion of workmen to the new-fangled milling experiments. The new coinage, issued in the names of Mary and Philip as co-rulers, was technically far superior and, in the use of lettering and dates, far more up to date in concept.

Little in the way of gold was minted. The angels with the names of Philip and Mary on the obverse and their initials flanking the mast on the reverse, are much scarcer than their counterparts of 1553, while the corresponding half-angel is one of the major rarities of English coinage. On the other hand, the silver coinage was struck in great abundance, putting to good use the vast amount of bullion and foreign coin which Philip brought with him. The shillings and sixpences showed facing profiles of Philip and Mary on the obverse, with a crown over their heads. On the reverse an ornate crowned shield showed the elaborate quarterings of the Habsburgs in addition to the usual English heraldic devices. The date and Roman numerals signifying the value were regarded as optional extras, sometimes shown above or below the bust (date) or flanking the crown on the reverse (value).

Silver shilling of Philip and Mary with tactless inscription soon dropped. (*Christie's*)

The first edition of the shillings and sixpences bore the tactless inscription PHILIP Z MARIA D G R ANG FR NEAP PR HISP (*Philip and Mary, by the Grace of God, king and queen of England, France and Naples, prince and princess of Spain*). Later in 1554 the foreign titles were discreetly dropped. The traditional reverse legend was pluralised POSVIMVS DEVM ADVITOREM NOSTRVM, (*We have made God our Helper*). On the smaller coins – groat, half-groat and penny – a crowned bust of Mary alone appeared on the obverse and the forked cross on the plain shield on the reverse. The Latin motto was abbreviated according to the size of the coin. On the diminutive penny the obverse reduced the names and titles to P Z M D G but added, for good measure ROSA SINE SPINE [*sic*]. A curious hangover from the previous reign was the base (3 oz.) penny which bore the P Z M D G legend on the obverse but was otherwise identical with the pennies of 1550–53. The unique mintmark on this coin, an H and half-rose, is thought to refer to Henry VIII who had instigated base coinage.

CHAPTER FIVE

Elizabeth (1558–1603)

Reginald Pole, papal legate and archbishop of Canterbury, survived his queen by a few hours only. With their deaths collapsed the counter-reformation in England. Mary's real achievement was the return to economic if not financial stability, but this was overlooked in the widespread hatred of her religious policies. The death of Bloody Mary brought to the throne her half-sister, Elizabeth, the only surviving child of Henry VIII and Anne Boleyn. As an infant she had been given precedence over her elder half-sister but this doubtful privilege was abruptly withdrawn when Anne was beheaded. Henry had his marriage declared invalid and Elizabeth illegitimate. Though never subsequently legitimised her place in the succession after her half-brother and half-sister was secured by Act of Parliament shortly before her father's death. Elizabeth was reared a Protestant and was, therefore, a victim of her sister's paranoia, whenever insurrection threatened. She spent a brief period in the Tower at the beginning of Mary's reign but thereafter spent the ensuing years quietly at Hatfield.

Elizabeth came to the throne amid universal rejoicing, her popularity secured by the swift reversal of her sister's religious policies. She recognised that Mary's economic policies were sound and tried to continue them. In pursuance of her policy of curbing government expenditure and streamlining the antiquated system of taxation, Mary had commissioned the publication of a new Book of Rates (1558), and Elizabeth profited enormously from the great increase in revenue that resulted. Elizabeth lacked the positive support of Spain when she came to the throne, and later had to try and improve the coinage in the face of active opposition from that quarter. She did not benefit from the enormous influx of gold and silver which Spain imported from Mexico and Peru; England's continuing adverse trade balance in the early years of her reign saw to that. Systematic raids on Spanish shipping did not take place until 1567 and the English economy in the first decade of her reign had to rely on exports of wool to the Low Countries as the principal source of foreign earnings. Although the Elizabethan coinage eventually enjoyed a good reputation for its quantity, quality and stability, these features were acquired only after a long and sometimes painful process of economic overhaul.

An immediate problem was the vast quantity of base shillings of Edward VI which were still in circulation. Under Mary they had been devalued and circulated as ninepence or sixpence, depending on their fineness. This action had been taken on the advice of Sir Thomas Gresham, a prosperous City merchant who acted as financial adviser to the Crown until his death in 1579. Gresham's Law, which he is said to have formulated in 1558, states that 'bad money drives out good', i.e. an underweight or debased coinage in circulation will drive out the good coins which will be hoarded. In 1559 Elizabeth, on the advice of William Cecil, her chief minister, had these base shillings countermarked with a portcullis and re-circulated at 4 pence-halfpenny, while the baser shillings of the third period (1550–53) were countermarked with a greyhound and then passed current at 2 pence-farthing. This was a temporary expedient as these base shillings were rapidly phased out and demonetised in 1561, which explains their comparative scarcity.

Base silver shilling of Edward VI countermarked with greyhound and revalued at 2 pence-farthing. (*Peter Clayton*)

First coinage, 1558–61

The confusing array of coins in the first three years of this reign reflect the transitional nature of English currency at this time. To minimise the upheaval consequent on the change from a Catholic to a Protestant regime, Elizabeth tried at first to be conciliatory to Spain while, at the same time, avoiding direct conflict with France over Scotland whose nominal ruler, Mary Queen of Scots, was regarded by Catholics as the legitimate claimant to the English throne. As part of her conciliatory policy Elizabeth continued the type of coinage adopted by Mary, and in this respect she had the valuable support of Sir Edmund Peckham, the Master of the Mint, and Derick Anthony, who was to serve as chief engraver until 1599.

Elizabeth raised the fineness of silver by a pennyweight, bringing it almost up to the sterling fineness of 0.925. In gold, however, she returned to the dual system of 'fine' and 'crown' gold, using the latter mainly for overseas trade. There were four denominations in the old standard: the sovereign of 30 shillings, its half or ryal, the angel of 10 shillings and the half-angel. No examples of the ryal have ever come to light, although its existence is known from the Pyx records, and it was revived between 1583 and 1592. The sovereign followed the pattern of Elizabeth's predecessors and showed the queen on the throne. The reverse showed Elizabeth's coat of arms surmounting a five-petalled rose with a curiously abbreviated Latin motto signifying *This is the work of the Lord and it is marvellous in our eyes.* This quotation from Psalm 118 had been introduced by the Catholic Mary but Elizabeth saw no harm in appropriating it for her own coinage.

Fine gold sovereign of 30 shillings. (*Peter Clayton*)

The angel and half-angel differed little from their predecessors, though the bold Roman script imparted a more modern appearance than the outmoded Lombardic lettering previously used. The reverse showed an E and rose flanking the cross on the reverse.

There were four 'crown' denominations, though no example of the pound of 20 shillings has been found, despite its record in the trials of the Pyx.

Gold half-pound. (*Christie's*)

The three issued denominations have a certain uniformity about them, with a rather beaky profile of Elizabeth, and a reverse design showing the crowned arms, flanked by the monogram ER. The motto on the reverse – *The shield of faith shall protect her* – was a revival of that found on gold coins of Edward VI. In the earliest issues the inner circle on the reverse was a thin wire line but in the coins from 1560 onwards this was replaced by a more substantial beaded circle. The coins of this series comprised the half-pound, crown and half-crown.

In November 1560 Thomas Stanley succeeded Peckham as mint-master and the following month Thomas Fleetwood was appointed under-treasurer or master of a separate mint. To distinguish them Stanley's building was known as the Nether Mint and Fleetwood's was called the Upper Houses. The latter was established for the purpose of melting down base shillings and producing good coins of sterling silver. At this time the fineness was restored to the original 11 oz. 2 dwt and coins in this quality were struck by Fleetwood with a martlet mintmark, whereas coins in the lower standard of 11 oz. 1 dwt were struck in the Nether Mint and identified by their lis or cross-crosslet mintmarks. The earliest silver coins comprised the shilling of 96 grains, with corresponding sub-divisions of groat, half-groat and penny. In the crowned profile, arms were surmounted by a cross and POSVI motto; these coins adhered to the pattern of their predecessors. No dates were included, but the sequence of mintmarks enables them to be classified chronologically with some degree of accuracy.

Fine silver shilling by Thomas Fleetwood. (*Royal Mint*)

In 1560 a former employee of the mint in Paris, known as the Moulin des Etuves, sought refuge from his creditors and obtained employment in London. Eloi Mestrell was a Huguenot by religion and escaped from Paris at a time when religious differences were escalating into open civil war. He began working at the Tower Mint at a time when another experiment with the rolling mill and other mechanical equipment was being contemplated. Mestrell was given temporary accommodation in the Upper Houses and by the end of 1561 was producing beautiful silver coins of a uniform thickness, perfectly rounded and elegantly lettered, using a screw-press operated by horsepower. New dies engraved by Derick Anthony were used in this experiment and for the first time laid emphasis on the lettering. Hitherto the inscriptions were neglected since this was the part of the die which tended to be poorly struck by the hammermen anyway.

Mestrell's shillings, groats and half-groats were undated, like their hammered contemporaries, but the sixpences and threepences bore the date in Arabic numerals above the coat of arms on the reverse. Mestrell had his own mintmark, a six-pointed star which appeared on coins produced up to about 1566. The earlier coins had a small bust of the queen in a plain dress, but later issues had a tall, narrow bust in a plain dress (1561–62), a similar bust with ornamented dress (1562) or a large, broad bust with a very elaborate dress (1562–64).

Silver shilling of the Huguenot refugee Eloi Mestrell, produced by a rolling mill. (*Christie's*)

Middle period coinage, 1561–82

The coinage reform of 1561 was greatly assisted by a substantial drop in the price of silver on the world markets as a result of the vast imports by Spain from South and Central America. This made it uneconomic for people to melt down the base shillings for their metal content and also removed the incentive for speculators to hoard the new coins. It has been estimated that the Crown made a profit of £50,000 on the recoinage operation in the Upper Houses. A further benefit of the influx of cheap silver at that crucial moment was that it cushioned the effects of what was a drastic deflationary policy. At any rate there was no marked fall in the prices of commodities and rents remained steady. Nevertheless the ruthless cut in the value of the base testoons hit the lower classes and small savings were halved overnight. It is now considered that this policy contributed in no small measure to the poverty and unemployment which were recurrent problems for much of Elizabeth's reign and resulted in much social legislation from 1563 onwards, the forerunners of the modern Welfare State.

While the recoinage of 1561–62 was under way the country was in a state of financial ferment. One of the great unsolved mysteries of this period concerns the activities of an economic Fifth Column which sought to undermine government policy, and perhaps even Elizabeth's own position, by putting about rumours of impending devaluation. To scotch this canard Elizabeth issued a proclamation in January 1562 stating quite firmly that she had no intention of reducing values. That there was a well-organised body inimical to her at this time is proved by the existence of certain documents dated 4 March 1562, purporting to be a royal proclamation calling down the value of the 1561 coinage by one-third. No printed version of such a proclamation has ever come to light, but for many years scholars regarded these drafts as genuine, until a royal proclamation of 13 March – nine days after the supposed devaluation – came to light, setting out the dire penalties for spreading false rumours of devaluation.

This must have had the desired effect since the rumours were scotched and as the new coinage became more plentiful the country gradually recovered from its economic jitters. Gold coins continued to appear in the two standards of fine and crown alloys, but the most significant feature of the new coinage was the silver, now struck in 0.925 or sterling silver. There was a slight reduction, to 0.921 fine silver, in 1578 but the old sterling standard was restored five years later at the beginning of the third period of Elizabethan coinage.

The gold coins of this period are straightforward, three denominations valued at 10, 5 and $2\frac{1}{2}$ shillings being struck in each fineness. Those in 23 ct $3\frac{1}{2}$ gr. gold were the angel, half- and quarter-angel retaining the designs of the first period, while those in 22 ct gold were the half-pound, crown and half-crown, again using the queen's profile obverse and crowned coat of arms of the first coinage. A few pounds in crown gold were also minted but are exceptionally rare. Two of them are in the coin cabinet of the Ashmolean Museum and bear the rose mintmark of 1565. It was once thought that they were patterns but from their condition it is now considered that they must have actually been in circulation. The gold coins bore no dates but their sequence can be determined by the mintmarks. In addition there were several die variants. Production of 'fine' gold coins lapsed after 1560 and was not revived until 1567, but angels and their sub-divisions were minted from then until the end of the century. There was a very slight reduction in the fineness (by one-tenth of a carat) between 1578 and 1582. The 'crown' gold coins first appeared in this period in 1565 and continued until about the end of

22 carat gold half-pound. (*Peter Clayton*)

1571, when the dual standard was abolished for the time being.

The most significant feature of the reformed silver coinage of 1561 was the disappearance of the shilling and groat, due to the unpopularity of the former and the public's distrust of a coin which had been so much adulterated in Edward's reign. Of the lesser denominations which had appeared in the first period, the half-groat is known with the pheon mintmark of 1561–65 and was in regular production again from late 1566 until 1571. The penny made a belated appearance in 1565 and was produced continuously thereafter.

Emphasis was switched from thirds and sixths of the shilling to a more natural sub-division – half, quarter, eighth and sixteenth – and this gave rise to the sixpence, threepence, threehalfpence and three farthings respectively. The last two denominations reflected a change in the Elizabethan economy at the lower end of the scale. It must be borne in mind that such minute sums as a farthing or a halfpenny would buy an appreciable amount of goods or services and consequently there was a very real need for coins of these values. For practical purposes there had not been a silver farthing in circulation for many years and even the halfpenny had been reduced in size to the point where minting was scarcely practicable. Until such times as the idea of a token coinage in base metal was accepted the problem of these small amounts could only be solved by striking threehalfpence and three-farthings. These could be given in change for a half-groat and a penny respectively, the difference then representing a halfpenny's or farthing's worth of goods.

(a) (b)

(c)

Lower value silver coins of **(a)** threepence (*Peter Clayton*); **(b)** threehalfpence (*Royal Mint*); **(c)** three farthings (*Peter Clayton*), representing one-quarter, one-eighth and one-sixteenth of a shilling.

To avoid any confusion between these new denominations and the existing ones, which they closely resembled in size, the new coins from the sixpence downwards were identified by a rose on the obverse, immediately behind the queen's profile. This is alluded to in Shakespeare's *King John*:

. . . my face so thin
That in mine ear I durst not stick a rose
Lest men should say, 'Look, where threefarthings goes!'

The play, incidentally, was written in 1596 or 1597 – some fourteen years after the last of the threefarthings were minted. It would seem to imply that this much despised coin was still in circulation since Shakespeare delighted in such familiar or highly topical allusions, calculated to raise a chuckle in the audience.

The other distinguishing feature of the new denominations was the inclusion of the date in Arabic numerals, above the coat of arms on the reverse. A few sixpences are known without the dated reverse, while some sixpences (1561) and threepences (1568) have been recorded without the rose on the obverse.

During the 1560s Eloi Mestrell continued to produce milled coins in crown gold and sterling silver. To the shillings, sixpences and groats struck in 1561 he added the threepence, half-groat and threefarthings, but the bulk of his output was in sixpences and threepences, and these denominations exist in a variety of forms, the details of the queen's bust becoming progressively more elaborate. All of Mestrell's coins bore his six-pointed star as well as dates up to 1566, though his production peaked in 1561–62. After the recoinage was completed his services were no longer so valuable. Inevitably his employment had caused great anxiety and discontent among the hammermen who saw their own position threatened. Significantly, the quality of the hammered coins improved during this period as the craftsmen using traditional methods strove to demonstrate how age-old techniques were every bit as efficient as the new-fangled machines. Mestrell maintained a precarious position at the Mint in spite of the open hostility of the workforce, but he fell victim to the reorganisation of the Mint which took place in 1572. The posts of treasurer and under-treasurer, created by Henry VIII, were abolished and the former posts of warden and master-worker were restored. Sir Richard Martin, who was appointed warden, was a mint-master of the old school and lost no time in reporting to the Privy Council that 'neither the said engine nor any workmanship to be wrought thereby will be to the Queen's Majesty's profit'.

No dated coins by Mestrell have been recorded for 1565 or 1569, though

Milled silver sixpence by Mestrell. (*Peter Clayton*)

it seems likely that during these years he struck a few gold coins and silver shillings. The milled coins in 'crown' gold consist of half-pounds, crowns and half-crowns. The last milled coins produced by Mestrell were sixpences. A new design was introduced in 1567 using a small bust, but more decorative than the small bust of 1561. Later milled sixpences were surprisingly ungainly, with clumsy irregular lettering (1570–71).

Though dismissed in 1572 Mestrell continued to persevere with milled coinage. In 1574–75 Derick Anthony cut some handsome dies for sixpences and threepences which Mestrell struck by the milled process. This experiment, however, met with the disfavour of John Lonison, the master-worker, and Mestrell was not reinstated. Three years later he was convicted of counterfeiting, and hanged at Norwich – a very sad end for England's pioneer of mechanically produced coinage.

Third period coinage, 1583–1603

The coinage in the last twenty years of Elizabeth's long reign reflects the social and economic changes which were taking place. Since the advent of the Tudor dynasty in 1485 the population had doubled, to around 4 million. In the same period prices had trebled and unemployment was unacceptably high. A solution to the latter problem was sought in emigration, and this led to attempts to colonise North America, the settlement of Virginia being founded in 1585. Though this was a disaster, it did not deter the merchant companies of London from attempting the commercial penetration of the globe. The Eastland Company supplanted the Hanseatic League in the Baltic trade, while the Levant Company ousted the Venetians from the eastern Mediterranean and the Muscovy Company established trade links with Russia. Between 1570 and 1600 there was a dramatic expansion of English industry which fed the export drives of the merchant companies. It was this, rather than emigration, that solved the unemployment problem and brought economic stability and a new level of prosperity which makes the first Elizabethan era seem such a golden age. Prices continued to rise, but wages rose even faster and this was reflected in the great abundance of good coinage, particularly silver of fairly large denominations, available in the closing years of the reign.

Spain continued to block the English merchants from the lucrative American trade, though illicit trading in slaves and bullion continued to some extent. In 1568 the sporadic plundering of Spanish vessels by English privateers entered a new phase when a ship laden with silver from the mines of Mexico was captured. For some time Elizabeth continued officially to disavow such acts, but the rebellion of the Dutch Protestants in the Spanish Netherlands brought England and Spain into open conflict from 1572 onwards, and culminated in the Armada invasion attempt of 1588. Hostility between England and Spain continued to the end of the century and English seamen harried Spanish treasure ships unmercifully. No estimate of the bullion captured by privateers between 1569 and 1600 has ever been made, but its effect on the economy and the coinage must have been considerable.

In 1582 the awkward threefarthings and threehalfpence were phased out and replaced by the half-groat (after an absence of eleven years) and the halfpenny which had not been minted since the time of Edward VI. It was struck continuously from then until the end of the reign. The new half-groat can easily be distinguished from the threehalfpence by two pellets in the field behind the queen's bust, in place of the rose, but it differed from earlier half-groats in adopting the *rose without a thorn* motto which had appeared on the threehalfpence. Like its predecessors, it was undated, and we must rely on the sequence of mintmarks for approximate dating. The tiny halfpenny continued the portcullis motif of the earlier coins, while the reverse, with its cross and groups of three pellets, was the last vestige of medievalism in English coinage.

Silver halfpenny, lowest denomination struck in silver during this reign. (*Peter Clayton*)

At the same time the design of the sixpence was modified, abbreviating the queen's name to ELIZAB and spacing the lettering more evenly. The shilling, out of circulation since 1561, made a come-back and also showed the queen's name in this curiously abbreviated form. Henceforward the shilling tended to replace the sixpence as the most popular denomination. The only coin to remain unchanged was the penny. The coins continued to be struck in sterling silver, but in 1601 there was a slight reduction in weight, the penny dropping from 8 to 7.75 grains, with a corresponding reduction in the higher denominations. At this time England came into line with the Continent by reviving the silver crown and half-crown.

The large area of the crown encouraged the engraver to emulate the florid talers and gulden of the Continent. Elizabeth was portrayed in a richly

Large hammered silver half-crown. (*Christie's*)

jewelled head-dress, topped by the crown and set off by the exaggeratedly high ruff and extravagantly quilted shoulder of her gown. The splendid effect was marred, however, by including the orb and sceptre and this gives the obverse a rather cramped appearance. A similar obverse was used for the half-crown and both coins had a reverse showing the coat of arms in an elaborate frame. Considering that these large coins were hammered they exhibit a surprising degree of excellence in the striking, the lettering round the circumference being particularly fine.

The shilling associated with this series was a most attractive coin, with a neat profile of the queen, her hair flowing free, contained within the obverse by a beaded circle. The shield on the reverse was highly decorative but the *patonce* or leafy excrescences at the ends of the cross divided the legend awkwardly and the word MEVM had to be oddly abbreviated to MEV. The sixpence was the only coin of this series to bear a proper date on the reverse, and it had the usual sequence of mintmarks for good measure. The last three mintmarks corresponded with the last digits of the date: zero (April 1600–May 1601), numeral 1 (July 1601–May 1602) and 2 (May 1602–June 1603). It must be borne in mind that, under the Old Style or Julian calendar, the year ended on 24 March and not 31 December, so that technically the first three months of our modern year belonged to the preceding year for all legal purposes, including the trial of the Pyx which determined the mintmarks used.

Silver shilling, one of Elizabeth's most attractive coins. (*Peter Clayton*)

The gold coins of this period continued to be struck in the dual standard. The angel lasted until the end of the reign, struck in 23 ct 3½ gr. gold, but those with mintmarks 1 and 2 were slightly reduced in weight, from 1/72 of a pound to 1/73. Half- and quarter-angels were minted regularly until 1600 but were withdrawn when the weight of the angel was reduced. Two new denominations were included. The indenture of 1577 had authorised the sovereign of 30 shillings and the ryal or noble of 15 shillings, but these coins did not materialise until 1583. The design of the sovereign was similar to that of 1558–61 but the top of the throne did not extend beyond the tressure – the denticulated decoration round the field. Also the portcullis at the queen's foot was narrower and the mintmark appeared to the left of the queen's head instead of to the right as previously. The reverse differed only in minor respects.

The ryal had not been minted for thirty years and it is interesting to compare the treatment of the obverse on the coins struck by Mary and Elizabeth respectively. Whereas the Marian ryal conformed to the medieval tradition the Elizabethan obverse showed the queen in elaborate court dress instead of breastplate and armed only with the orb and sceptre. The ship was transformed from a medieval galley into a sixteenth-century galleon, with much greater emphasis on realism and less on stylisation. Curiously enough, the antique Lombardic script was retained for the inscriptions.

(a)

(b)

Gold ryals of (a) Elizabeth (*Peter Clayton*) and (b) Mary. (*Royal Mint*)

The sovereign was produced from 1583 until 1595, but the ryal ceased production in 1592, the year in which there was a switch yet again to 'crown' gold. The gold pound, half-pound and crown were then minted down to the end of the reign, and the gold half-crown only in 1592–95. The gold pound differed considerably from the rare pounds of 1565. The bust was now greatly enlarged and the dress made much more elaborate, while the crown almost touched the outer rim and divided the legend. Furthermore the legend itself was contained in a beaded circle, following the pattern of the half-pound, crown and half-crown of 1560 onwards. The coat of arms on the reverse was likewise enlarged so that the crown broke the legend, and a beaded circle

Gold sovereign of 30 shillings. (*Peter Clayton*)

was also added. The smaller 'crown' gold coins also had more elaborate profiles. Like the angel, the 'crown' gold coins suffered a slight reduction in weight in 1601. Henceforward 33½ gold pounds were minted from each pound weight of gold, and the lesser denominations were correspondingly reduced. The devaluation of the gold and silver currency at the beginning of the seventeenth century, despite the seeming abundance of precious metals in Britain and Europe, was symptomatic of a grave financial crisis. Crown revenues had not kept pace with inflation and the rise in the price of commodites, while there were increasing demands on the government. Since the 1570s England had been embroiled in a prolonged rebellion in Ireland which tied down an enormous garrison at vast expense. Financial and other assistance to the Scottish Protestants, to the French Huguenots and especially to the Dutch in their struggles against Spain took a heavy toll on the national reserves and it is no exaggeration to say that Elizabeth died in debt. If this seems paradoxical it should be noted that Spain, seemingly the wealthiest country in Europe at the time, was heavily in debt, the annual treasure fleets

Silver trade dollar for Far East trade, intended to rival the Spanish 'pieces of eight'. (*Peter Clayton*)

mortgaged to pay off the interest on vast loans from abroad. When the treasure fleets ceased to bale out the Spanish economy the country rapidly went bankrupt and was no longer a world power.

As the mercantile power of Spain declined, that of England continued to rise. In 1599 the Levant Company took the decision 'to set forth a voyage this present year to the East Indies and other Islands and Countries thereabouts, and there to make trade'. On the last day of 1600 Elizabeth issued a charter to these merchant venturers and thus launched the career of the Honourable East India Company. The royal charter was anticipated by the striking of large silver pieces, modelled on the Spanish dollar, for use in the East Indies. The obverse bore the queen's name and titles and featured the crowned shield flanked by the royal monogram, while the reverse depicted a crowned portcullis and the Latin motto found on the contemporary crowns. The portcullis dollar was the first of the British trade dollars to rival the Spanish pieces of eight, and ancestor of the trade coins which continued until the 1830s.

CHAPTER SIX

James I (1603–1625)

James Stuart, King of Scots, was a man of mature years when he ascended the throne of England on the death of Elizabeth, on 24 March 1603. The only son of Elizabeth's arch-rival, Mary Stuart, and Henry Lord Darnley, James was also the great-grandson of Margaret Tudor (sister of Henry VIII) who had married James IV of Scotland in 1503. A century was to elapse between that auspicious marriage, contrived as an act of diplomacy by Henry VII, and eventual peace between the two countries. In the interim came the disastrous defeat of the Scots at Flodden (1513), the 'rough wooing' of the infant Mary – as the campaign of 1543–48 is ironically known – and finally, the imprisonment and execution of Mary Queen of Scots in 1587. If these events left any scar on James he never showed it. Proclaimed King of Scots on the abdication of his mother (1567) when he was only a few months old, he was already a seasoned ruler, aged 21, when his mother was beheaded. He took pains to give no offence to his English cousin, and though posterity has often accused him of baseness in not lifting a finger to help his mother, there is little that James could have done at the time to avert her fate.

He played a waiting game which paid off when he received the summons to London in the spring of 1603. In fact the effusive reception when he arrived in London in April flattered him immensely and blinded him to the reality of the situation that, faced with possible civil war, a Scottish king was the lesser of two evils. James's solitary boyhood, reared by a succession of guardians and educated by the finest scholars of the day, gave him an intellectual breadth unequalled in a British sovereign since the time of Alfred the Great, but this was marred by his pedantic outlook. His garrulous behaviour, slovenly manner and strong Scottish accent did little to enhance his appearance, and explains his nickname of the 'wisest fool in Christendom'.

On arrival in London James created Robert Cecil Earl of Salisbury and shrewdly retained him as his chief minister. Outwardly, therefore, the old regime continued, and there were few changes in government under the new monarch. Elizabeth died in debt but James never at any time appreciated the need for economy. To him and the army of hangers-on that followed him south, England seemed immensely rich by comparison with poor Scotland. That the Jacobean period was, indeed, a time of economic prosperity was not due to James but rather to the merchants who took the initiative and expanded trade with Europe, the Levant, the Far East and even the New World.

First coinage, 1603−4

Within a week or two of his arrival in London, James issued orders to Sir Richard Martin, Warden of the Mint, to produce coins bearing his effigy. The dies for these coins were cut by Charles Anthony, who had succeeded his father Derick as chief engraver in 1599. Thus, both in design and execution, the coins of James I followed patterns established under his predecessor. To be sure, the change of ruler and the circumstances attending his accession brought about subtle differences in the coins. The coat of arms which, in varying forms, appeared on the reverse of all the coins of the first period (except the diminutive halfpenny) was now modified to include the Lion Rampant of Scotland and the Harp of Ireland in the second and third quarters respectively. The royal title was augmented by the inclusion of sco (Scotia) between the ANG (Anglia) and FRAN (Francia) of the Elizabethan issues.

Relatively few gold coins were struck in this period, and all of them in 22 carat 'crown' gold. For the first time, the term 'sovereign' was widely used to denote the pound coin and appropriately the obverse of this handsome piece portrayed the king crowned and carrying the orb and sceptre of sovereignty. The king was shown in a richly ornamented suit of armour and from an examination of the detail one can imagine the costly filigree work found on the breastplates and mailed gauntlets of the early seventeenth

Gold sovereign of James I, a term now widely used to denote the pound coin. (*Coin Monthly*)

Gold half-sovereign with unflattering profile. (*Royal Mint*)

century. The monogram IR (Iacobus Rex) appeared on the reverse, flanking
the coat of arms, while the Latin legend was a verse from the sixty-eighth
Psalm – 'Let God arise and let His enemies be scattered'. In contrast with
the splendid three-quarter length portrait of the sovereign, the crowned busts
on the half-sovereign, crown and half-crown did nothing to enhance the
unprepossessing appearance of the king. The profile on the half-sovereign,
in particular, made him look like a greybeard in his dotage, and not the man
of 37 in the prime of life. The half-sovereign bore the same Latin motto on
the reverse, but the smaller gold coins were inscribed TVEATVR VNITA DEVS –
May God protect the united. This was a reference to the two kingdoms, so
long divided but seemingly united at last. At this stage, however, the union
was little more than a pious hope, and more than a century was to elapse
before political union was fully achieved.

A more practical move towards the union of the countries was given
expression on some of the silver coins. When James came to the English
throne the currency of Scotland was tariffed at one-twelfth of its English
counterpart and thus a Scottish shilling was equivalent to an English penny.
As a first step towards unifying the currencies, James revived the system of
denoting the denominations of certain silver coins in Roman numerals. Thus
the English shilling bore the numerals XII in the field on the obverse, and
passed current as '12 shillings Scots' north of the border. Similarly, the
sixpence, half-groat and penny were respectively marked VI, II and I. At the
same time this device made the handling of money clearer – at least to those
of the general public who could read Roman numerals.

By 1603 the silver crown and half-crown had become widespread in
England and these denominations formed part of James's first coinage. He
revived the magnificent equestrian obverse which had appeared on the crowns
of Edward VI. Whereas the young Edward was depicted at full gallop James
was content with a much more sedate picture, the richly caparisoned horse
shown in a statuesque pose. A similar obverse appeared on the half-crown,
but the shilling and smaller denominations down to the penny showed a
crowned profile facing right. Only the sixpence bore a date on the reverse,
continuing the Elizabethan tradition. The tiny halfpenny continued the
portcullis obverse and cross and pellet reverse – almost a monetary fossil, but
now of so little account that it hardly seemed worth designing new motifs.

Silver half-crown, with revival of the equestrian obverse. (*Peter Clayton*)

A hangover from the previous reign was the inclusion of the ROSA SINE SPINA motto on the half-groat and penny.

Second coinage, 1604–19

The first coins of James I may be regarded as transitional, and were in production barely sixteen months. During this period the king and his advisers were planning a more permanent series which went into production in October 1604. In that month came the announcement that the united kingdoms of England and Scotland would now be known as Great Britain. Though parliament refused to ratify this union the name gradually took effect, and much of the credit for publicising it must go to the coins which were circulated from November 1604 onwards.

In place of the ANG and SCO of the first issue there now appeared MAG. BRIT. (Magnae Britanniae = *of Great Britain*). A hint of the imminent economic crisis was contained in the decision of 1604 to reduce the weight of the gold coins from the sovereign of 172 grains to 155 grains. This move was precipitated by the continued influx of Spanish-American silver in vast quantities, so that the value of silver in relation to gold was reduced.

At the beginning of the reign James's ministers made a strenuous efforts to reduce government spending. The peace with Spain in 1604 led to an immediate reduction in the amount of money expended on the army and navy, but this was balanced by James's decision to abolish the fines on religious recusants – both Catholic and Puritan – who did not conform to the practices and observances of the Established Church. This apparent liberalism did not last long; the lucrative revenue from fines on religious nonconformity proved too tempting and by the end of 1604 they were being imposed more rigorously than before. What amounted to a penal tax on Catholicism was one of the prime factors behind the conspiracy known as the Gunpowder Plot, discovered in November 1605.

During the first years of the reign prices continued to rise steadily. Wages rose at more or less the same pace, and the dramatic expansion of overseas trade brought a measure of prosperity to the country not experienced before. The uncontrolled influx of Spanish silver obligingly supplied the demand for money. Output of silver coinage at the Mint reached its peak between 1605 and 1609. Significantly, for the first time in history, the common people became accustomed to seeing and handling silver coins in some quantity, though many might go their entire life without ever seeing, let alone possessing, a gold piece. By 1610 the Crown was in debt to the tune of half a million pounds. The Earl of Salisbury, who had become Lord Treasurer in 1608, attempted to put the royal finances on a sounder footing. James's relations with parliament were bedevilled by his own highly mystic interpretation of the Divine Right of Kings, whereas parliament, conscious of its growing power with the rise of the middle classes, was inclined to question this. Early clashes between king and parliament were over various feudal dues, such as purveyance, wardship and the marriage of minors, which parliament wished to suppress (or take over) in exchange for a fixed income voted by its members. Salisbury masterminded the negotiations of this deal, known as the Great Contract. Though this would have put Stuart finances on a sounder footing it would have curbed some of the royal prerogatives and it is not surprising that the negotiations collapsed. James turned harshly on Salisbury, who never recovered from the shock of his king's ingratitude, and died in 1612.

James dissolved parliament in 1611 and henceforward tried to govern through his courtiers – a situation in which graft and corruption flourished all too readily. From the purely monetary viewpoint, the year 1611 was noteworthy for the breakdown in bimetallism, as gold continued to soar in value and silver to decline. All gold coins then in circulation were revalued by 10 per cent, resulting in inconvenient values of 5 shillings 6 pence and 2 shillings 9 pence for the gold crown and half-crown respectively.

The series of coins introduced at the end of 1604 consisted of five gold and seven silver coins. The gold coins in particular reflect the king's desire for the unification of his kingdoms. The twenty-shilling piece, hitherto

Gold unite, worth 20 shillings, reflecting the king's desire to unite his kingdoms of Scotland and England. (*Christie's*)

known as a sovereign, acquired the new name of unit or unite, from the inscription on the reverse FACIAM EOS IN GENTEM VNAM − *I shall make them into one nation* (Ezekiel 37, 22). The half-unite or double crown and the so-called Britain crown had an even more flowery inscription: HENRICVS ROSAS REGNA IACOBVS − literally *Henry the roses, James the kingdoms*, an allusion to Henry VII who had united the Roses of Lancaster and York, whereas James had united the kingdoms. The half-crown bore the legend TVEATVR VNITA DEVS which had appeared on the crown and half-crown of the first period.

An entirely new denomination was the Thistle crown worth 4 shillings, with its distinctive crowned rose and crowned thistle on obverse and reverse respectively. This coin was introduced as part of the scheme to unify the currencies of the two countries, since pieces tariffed at 48 shillings Scots were commonly used north of the border. The royal monogram IR flanked the heraldic flowers on both sides, but examples are quite plentiful with the monogram on one side alone.

Gold Thistle crown worth 4 shillings, introduced as part of scheme to unify the currencies of England and Scotland. (*Peter Clayton*)

In the silver coins the motifs of the first period were used in the crown, half-crown, shilling and sixpence, but with a new legend on the reverse. This was a quotation from Matthew 19, 6: QUAE DEVS CONIVNXIT NEMO SEPARET − *What God hath joined together let no man put asunder*. The smaller silver coins followed the pattern of the Thistle crown, with a rose on the obverse and a thistle on the reverse. On the half-groat the flowers were crowned; a smaller crown was adopted for the obverse in 1607 and coins with this variant are comparatively uncommon. On the penny the flowers were uncrowned. Both half-groat and penny had legends on obverse and reverse, incorporating the ROSA and TVEATVR mottoes respectively. An extremely rare variant of the penny, struck in 1611, has the TVEATVR motto on both sides. The halfpenny now came into line with the rest of the series and featured the rose and thistle motifs without crowns, and devoid of inscriptions as before.

Aesthetically the coins of this period were an improvement over the initial series, with some attempt at variation in the portraiture and also in the decorative treatment of the armorial reverses. At this time the engraving of dies seems to have been in the hands of Charles Anthony, with John Dycker and John Rutlinger as his assistants. The impressive profile of the king on the unite and double crown suggests the hand of John Acheson, James's Edinburgh goldsmith who had been responsible for some of the fine large gold pieces of Scotland, but the appointment of Scottish engravers at the Tower Mint was not definitely approved until the final year of the reign. As before, the sixpence was the only coin to bear a date, the others being put in chronological order by the sequence of mintmarks, ranging from the lis (1604–5) to the mullet (1611–12).

A limited quantity of coins in 23½ carat 'fine' gold was revived in 1606. These coins were struck mainly as presentation pieces, but also served to uphold the earlier English tradition for using gold of the finest quality, at a time when 22 carat gold was becoming universally regarded as the standard. The 'fine' gold series comprised four denominations, and both stylistically and epigrammatically they represent the last stage in the transition from medieval to modern in English coin design. The rose-ryal of 30 shillings followed earlier tradition by depicting a full-length portrait of the king on the throne, but by omitting the tressure found on Elizabethan coins the principal motif stood out more prominently. Both obverse and reverse had lengthier inscriptions than heretofore and this necessitated greater care with the lettering, though there was still an occasional hint of the medieval Lombardic style.

So-called spur-ryal, a gold coin worth 15 shillings. Name derives from a rose from which radiate stylised sun rays resembling a spur-rowel. (*Peter Clayton*)

The spur-ryal of 15 shillings derives its name from the dominant element on the reverse, a rose from which radiated stylised sunrays which to the unobservant resembled a spur-rowel. The mixture of crowns, lis and lions was much the same as before, but for the obverse there was a significant updating of the monarch in ship motif. This now depicted a ship which was obviously seventeenth century in design, right down to the twin tiers of gunports. The angel (10 shillings) adhered closely to the design used in Elizabethan times but the cross on the superstructure was now abandoned in favour of a plain mast-head and top-castle. All three coins bore the usual Latin verse from Psalm 118. The half-angel was not issued until 1612, by which time the revaluation of gold gave it a nominal value of 5 shillings 6 pence. Very few of these coins were produced, and then only sporadically from 1612 until 1619, so fine examples are exceptionally rare.

The economic crisis and revaluation of 1612

In 1612 England seemed to be a reasonably prosperous country, but an economic crisis was threatening. Since James had dispensed with parliament the Crown derived most of its revenue from the percentages levied on courtiers and companies who operated the various monopolies that governed the production and distribution of almost every commodity except bread. Over 700 monopolies existed, ostensibly to maintain industrial standards and protect trade, but often having the opposite effect. The elimination of competition tended to lower standards and expose the system to all manner of graft and corruption. Nevertheless this was a time of tremendous industrial expansion. Between 1540 and 1640 coal production rose from 200,000 tons to $1\frac{1}{2}$ million tons a year – three times as much as the rest of Europe put together. In the same period production of iron increased five-fold and many new industries, such as brick making, glass blowing and sugar refining, had been developed.

In 1612 the wages of both skilled artisans and unskilled labourers were virtually the same as they had been twenty years earlier. This wage freeze was operated through the Justices of the Peace in each county and borough, and as they were recruited from the ranks of the landowners and employers they had a vested interest in keeping wages low. At the same time, however, the retail price index of foodstuffs and other necessities of life had risen by 60 per cent over the same period. After 1612 wages began to rise and by the time of James's death had increased some 15 per cent, whereas food prices remained fairly stable.

External factors, however, played a major part also. The vast amount of silver pumped into the English economy in 1605–9 upset the fine balance between gold and silver three years later and it became necessary to revalue all the gold coins by 10 per cent. This drastic step was forced on the king by the insidious practice of clipping the gold coins and the subsequent disappearance of good gold coins from circulation. As an interim measure gold coins were demonetised if they were found to be more than two grains light, but this merely aggravated the situation since it reduced yet further the amount of gold coinage in circulation.

During the latter part of the period of the second coinage a new portrait of the king was adopted. Known to collectors as the fifth bust, it is distinguished from earlier profiles by having plainer armour and the king's hair is longer. It was introduced in 1613 and is found on the 'crown' gold coins – the unite, double crown and half-crown – which continued until 1619. The revaluation of gold obviously had the desired effect since the 22 carat coins of the fifth bust are more plentiful than their predecessors.

There were no appreciable differences in the silver coins from 1612 until 1619, except that there were far fewer of them in circulation than before the coinage reform in 1609. The cost of producing silver coins, relative to their actual value, rose considerably, and in certain years (as the Mint records show) only a token issue of silver coins was produced. The handsome silver crowns, so plentiful in 1604–7, were conspicuous by their absence, while the half-crown was struck only in 1615–16. A few sixpences were minted in 1613–15, but only shillings and pennies were struck more or less continuously throughout this period.

Third coinage, 1619–25

Attempts to resolve the problem of the value ratio of gold to silver came to a head in 1619. The weights and values of the silver coins remained unaltered, but there were radical changes in the weight of both 'fine' and 'crown' gold coins. The gold of the second coinage was not automatically called in, but the inconvenient values of these coins following their 10 per cent revaluation in 1612 ensured that they would be rapidly superseded by the new series. The production of this coinage was entrusted to Lord Knyvet, who had just succeeded Sir Richard Martin as Warden of the Mint. From Mint records still extant it appears that the work of cutting the dies for the gold coins was entrusted to William Holles or Halle. The coins differed from their predecessors in many important respects.

The ratio of gold to silver was now fixed at 1 : 14. Silver coins remained at the former rate of 7.66 grains to the penny of 0.925 fineness, but the gold coins were drastically reduced in weight. The rose-ryal, which had been re-tariffed at 33 shillings, was reduced to 30 shillings once more, and dropped in weight from 213.3 grains to 196.5 grains. It continued to be struck in $23\frac{1}{2}$ carat 'fine' gold, as were its sub-divisions, the spur-ryal and angel. The unite reverted to its former value of 20 shillings but adopted a new name in recognition of the distinctive portrait of the king on the obverse. The laureated profile of James, who liked to think of himself as 'the Augustus of the North', was in the best tradition of Roman Imperial coinage, and showed him with a laurel crown and toga – in sharp contrast to the crown and armour of previous issues. The pound piece became known as the laurel

Gold unite now called a laurel because of laureate profile of James I as 'the Augustus of the North', in best tradition of Roman Imperial coinage. (*Peter Clayton*)

and its sub-divisions the half- and quarter-laurel of 10 shillings and 5 shillings respectively. In fact the laurel merely followed an example in royal portraiture which had been established in France in the 1560s and continued by the Netherlands in the seventeenth century. Compared with previous portraiture the laureated profile was ungainly and coarse and this has given rise to doubts as to whether a competent craftsman such as Holles could really have been responsible. One theory is that the work was carried out by his subordinates, John Gilbert or Edward Green; but the Mint records do not show that these men were employed until 1624, about five years after the laurel was adopted. Dissatisfaction with the portraiture is evident in the relatively large number of busts used. The clumsy large bust of 1619–20 was superseded by a neater profile, used for both the laurel and half-laurel. The quarter-laurel was released later than the other denominations and did not use the large bust. Five busts altogether were used for the laurel, the last being even cruder than the first, but it is exceedingly rare being confined to only a handful of coins with the trefoil mintmark. The second and third busts were never employed for the half-laurel, but examples with the fourth are known with the spur-rowel mintmark indicating that this change was introduced at the end of 1619 or early in 1620. This remained constant on all half-laurels with the second or fourth busts.

Following the precedent of James's earlier silver coins, the laurel and its sub-divisions were marked with their value in shillings in Roman numerals: xx, x or v, the numerals appearing in the field behind the king's head. The reverse of these coins featured the crowned arms, the emblems of Scotland and Ireland being quartered with those of England. The motto on the reverse of the laurel was the same as the earlier unite, while the half- and quarter-laurel used the political slogan of James's own invention, hitherto inscribed on the double crown of the second coinage.

Innovation also extended to the coins struck in 'fine' gold. Like the laurels, they had their values clearly stated in Roman numerals: xxx, xv and x. The designs were considerably modified or completely altered. Thus an updated version of the king enthroned appeared on the obverse of the rose-ryal. The throne itself was of an entirely new design, and the king's robes were much more sumptuous, with a high ruff collar and the chain and badge of the Order of the Garter. The reverse featured the royal arms, but the previous rose motif was now omitted and an inner 'beaded band was decorated with tiny roses, fleur de lis and lions. The value xxx appeared immediately above the shield on the reverse.

The reverse of the spur-ryal remained the same, but the obverse was completely new. Here the Scottish influence can be seen strongly, the dominant motif being a crowned lion rampant holding the coat of arms between its paws, and having an upraised sceptre in its right paw. The value consisting of two Roman numerals was denoted by a capital letter on either side of the lion. The traditional motif of the Archangel Michael slaying the dragon remained unchanged on the angel, but the reverse was extensively modified. The coat of arms superimposed on the ship was now omitted and

Obverse of the Third Coinage gold spur-ryal showing strong Scottish influence. (*Peter Clayton*)

the armorial bearings applied to the ship's mainsail. A greater degree of naturalism was also injected into the styling of the ship's hull and super-structure. All three 'fine' gold coins bore some variation on the traditional A DNO FACTVM legend used on previous issues.

The silver coins of this period followed the pattern of their predecessors but there seems to have been a marked deterioration in design and die cutting. This is particularly noticeable in the crowns, where the lettering is clumsier, larger and less regular than in the crowns of 1604–7. The earliest striking of the 1619 crowns showed the Irish harp on the reverse with a scrolled frame; later crowns all had a bird-headed harp. The half-crown was similar to previous issues, but all examples showed the bird-headed harp. A new portrait of the king, known as the sixth bust, appeared on the shilling and sixpence and differed from earlier versions primarily in the more luxuriant growth of the king's hair.

James I silver shilling with sixth bust. (*Tony Davies*)

The mining of silver in Wales, which had been prosecuted in a desultory fashion since Roman times, assumed major importance during this period. Under Sir Hugh Middleton, who obtained the lease in 1621, the production of silver rose to a new peak. The metal was shipped to the Tower Mint and coins – crowns, half-crowns and shillings – minted from it can be identified by the inclusion of the Prince of Wales's three plumes as a crest to the shield on the reverse. Coins with the plumed shield are worth a small premium over the more conventional designs.

Third Coinage half-crown with plumes over shield to denote use of Welsh silver. (*Peter Clayton*)

Both silver and gold coins of the third period were struck in abundance and are still relatively plentiful. This belies the grim situation in England at the time of their currency. The recovery of 1619 was but a prelude to a depression of catastrophic dimensions. Exports were savagely hit by the Thirty Years' War in Europe, and famine and widespread poverty struck at home as a result of three very poor harvests in a row (1621–23). This calamity was crowned by an outbreak of bubonic plague in London which killed almost 36,000 of its inhabitants in 1625. In an atmosphere of economic chaos there were outbreaks of rioting, while parliament showed its discontent by impeaching Lionel Cranfield, Earl of Middlesex, the business tycoon who had actually come close to balancing the king's budget. These were ominous portents of things to come, as the senile James slipped into a final coma on 27 March 1625. Prince Charles was already firmly in control and it was he who reaped the whirlwind.

Base-metal farthings

During James's reign the enclosure of land was undertaken on a large scale. The peasantry who had held land in common since time immemorial tended to become landless and either gravitated to the new towns and cities which developed rapidly in the early seventeenth century, or remained as wage labourers on the land. Though they thus became poorer in real terms, this very large class of people paradoxically helped to stimulate the internal demand for food and manufactured goods, since they now had to purchase the things they could no longer produce for themselves. This created a tremendous demand for currency in very low denominations and aggravated the problem which was already becoming serious in the closing years of the sixteenth century.

The silver penny, threefarthings and halfpenny struck under Elizabeth and James I were physically too small to be practical, and yet there was a very real need for these denominations and even smaller values. Patterns for a base-metal subsidiary coinage (pence, halfpence and farthings) were produced in 1601, but Elizabeth's government baulked at the idea of abandoning silver, even at this lowly level, and traders were allowed to take the law into their own hands by issuing farthings in lead and other base metals. This practice arose in the 1590s and though Elizabeth at first made every effort to suppress it the traders continued unabated. By 1612 there were as many as 3,000 different tokens circulating in London alone.

Ever jealous of the royal prerogative, James decided that if he could not suppress this practice he might as well take it over. Consequently he granted a monopoly in 1613 to Lord Harington to strike copper farthings in the king's name. Harington began producing farthings at premises in the appropriately named Tokenhouse Yard in London but died shortly after receiving the patent. His widow continued the operation until 1615 when she sold the patent to the Duke of Lennox, on whose death in 1624 it passed to his widow, the Duchess of Richmond. These farthings were tariffed at 6 grains of copper and it is thought that the much smaller pieces of similar design were half-farthings, the latter being much scarcer. The obverse featured the crown and crossed sceptres with an abbreviated Latin legend signifying *James, by the Grace of God, of Great Britain*, while the reverse depicted a crowned harp and the Latin legend *King of France and Ireland*. Occasionally an initial letter or mintmark was incorporated but the majority of these coins were unmarked.

The Lennox farthings are more plentiful than their Harington counterparts, as they were struck over a much longer period. They followed the same designs but the crowns were larger and, on the reverse, extend to the beaded rim. An elusive variant is oval-shaped, with the inscription beginning at bottom left instead of top right. These farthings were struck about 1624 and it is thought that they were intended mainly for circulation in Ireland.

Harington copper farthing, extensively forged, from which derives the phrase 'not worth a brass farthing'. (*Peter Clayton*)

The copper farthings were never made legal tender, were sold with a 10 per cent premium in the pound and similarly redeemed. They had a very mixed reception from the public and circulation was uneven; some areas had a surfeit of them while others saw relatively few. They varied considerably in size, weight and quality of striking and, not surprisingly, were extensively forged – a factor which stiffened consumer resistance. The phrase 'not worth a brass farthing' dates from this episode. In 1616 a redemption centre was established in London, but in other parts of the country people often experienced great difficulty in exchanging them. The entire project had that half-baked quality which marked so many of the fiscal and economic measures of the Stuarts. It would have been much better had production of base-metal farthings been undertaken by the Royal Mint, but, despite his experience of base-metal coinage in Scotland, James would not agree to a regal issue. This attitude was adopted by his successors and even when they did half-heartedly agree to base-metal farthings and halfpence they seldom provided sufficient quantities to meet demand. Numismatically, of course, we are the richer for the immense scope of three centuries of tradesmen's tokens, but at the time this must have been a grievous problem for the long-suffering public to bear.

CHAPTER SEVEN

Charles I (1625–1649)

Political and economic crises dominated the seventeen years of Charles's effective reign. There was a slight recovery of the economy between 1625 and 1631 but then a series of bad harvests led to renewed depression. The economy picked up slightly in 1633 but this was followed by stagnation and from 1638 onwards the political situation had a deleterious effect on trade and the economy in general. It is hardly surprising, therefore, that the numismatic history of this reign is rich and varied. Quite apart from the political and economic situation, this was a period of considerable undercurrents at Tower Hill, petty squabbles and major disputes between the various officials of the Mint, the engravers and technicians, and these upheavals have also left their mark on the coinage.

Tower Mint coinage, 1625–42

Charles was at first content that the Mint should continue with the dies of his late father and the plague of 1625–26 delayed the introduction of coins bearing the effigy of the new king anyway. The staff of the Mint were decimated by the epidemic, to such an extent that the French *quart d'écu* coins brought by Henrietta Maria as her dowry could not be recoined into English money and were put into circulation without countermarking.

Charles contemplated a debasement of the coinage to alleviate his financial troubles, in 1626 and 1640. In 1626 some gold and silver coins were struck on blanks lighter by some 7 per cent, but these lightweight coins were hastily recalled. When the matter was raised in 1640 it never progressed as far as actual striking of lighter coins. A few shillings have survived from the experimental reduction in August 1626 and weigh 81.6 grains instead of almost 93 grains, and may be recognised by their long cross mintmark.

When Sir Robert Harley was appointed Master of the Mint in November

1640 he was ordered to continue striking 'crown' gold and sterling silver at the previous weights. The only concession to hard times was a very slight reduction in the weight of the 'fine' gold angel, from 65.72 grains to 64.71 grains, and at this time production of rose-ryals and spur-ryals was discontinued. The angels were permitted mainly because they were required as touch-pieces for scrofula and the majority of extant examples, like their predecessors, have been pierced for suspension round the wearer' neck. The earliest angels were struck without a mark of value, but from late 1626 onwards they had a Roman numeral x in the field on the obverse.

The gold coins which actually circulated were undated as before, but the sequence of mintmarks, from the lis (1625) to the triangle in a circle (1641–43), permits accurate dating. There were three denominations in 'crown' gold – the unite, double crown and crown. The first issue of these coins, in 1625–26, was made from dies prepared by Edward Green and John Gilbert who had already established a measure of notoriety from their inept handling of James's laurel coinage. The first gold coins of this reign bear a clumsy portrait that is almost a parody, with an inordinately large ruff out of all proportion to the tiny head. An elusive variant of the unite obverse has a flat single-arched crown on the king's head, whereas the normal version has a high double-arched crown. Similar clumsy profiles appear on the earliest double crowns and crowns. Charles is probably best remembered nowadays as the great art connoisseur who laid the foundations of the magnificent royal collections, and we may be sure that his aesthetic sensibilities were offended by these coins. Shortly after his accession he appointed the Keeper of the Royal Pictures, the Dutchman Abraham Vanderort, to design new dies and supervise the production of the coinage. Vanderort had a reputation as a wax portraitist and medallist and the designs he subsequently produced had too high a relief to be practical for coinage.

Nevertheless, the Vanderort designs do have commendable features, with a more sensitive modelling of the king's face and beard. In the hands of incompetents like Green and Gilbert, however, the designs were mishandled and the results were seldom satisfactory. The effigy on the unites in particular tends to have a disjointed appearance, with the head, ruff and bust in three

Charles I first bust gold unite. (*Peter Clayton*)

separate elements – not a good omen for the king whose head was later parted from the rest of him! The second bust appeared on unites struck early in 1626 with the calvary cross mintmark. An extremely rare variant has the mintmark below the bust instead of at the top of the coin. A third bust was modelled and used from 1630 to 1632, similar to the preceding type but with the draped scarf on the king's armour pulled back. Improved busts, along the same lines, were used for the crown and double crown during the same periods. All three coins originally had a square-topped shield on the reverse, but an oval shield flanked by the royal monogram was introduced simultaneously with the third bust in 1630. In 1632 a fourth bust was adopted for all three coins and depicted the king with a small lace collar instead of the elaborate ruff, and the ribbon of the Order of the Garter. The last versions of the gold coins struck before the outbreak of the Civil War showed variations mainly in the collar.

James I had been the first monarch to break with the strictly biblical mottoes found on his coins. This trend was continued by Charles I and greater use was made of slogans of a quasi-political, rather than a religious nature. The reverse of the angel was inscribed AMOR POPVLI PRAESIDIVM REGIS (*The love of the people is the king's protection*) – one of the great numismatic ironies of all time. The reverse of the unite bore the appropriate legend FLORENT CONCORDIA REGNA (*Kingdoms flourish through harmony*). Only the crowns and double crowns continued the devotional element with CVLTORES SVI DEVS PROTEGIT (*God protects those who worship Him*).

Charles I gold angel with legend that was to have a grim irony: *The love of the people is the king's protection.* (*Peter Clayton*)

The silver coins were struck in ample quantities in all denominations and underwent considerable changes during their currency. The values were the same as the previous reign and comprised the crown, half-crown, shilling, sixpence, half-groat, penny and halfpenny. These coins vary in complexity. The diminutive halfpenny, devoid of inscription or mintmark, retained its rose obverse and reverse throughout the entire period without any alteration. All of the other coins, however, underwent numerous changes, some subtle, others of considerable magnitude. Both the crown and half-crown depicted the king on horseback on the obverse. There are four major and four minor types of the crown obverse alone, varying in the size of the horse, the presence or absence of decoration on or around the horse, and the position of the

Silver crown of Welsh silver, denoted by plumes on reverse. (*Peter Clayton*)

sword held by the king. The half-crown is even more complex, with four major and nine minor types, again mainly the styling of the horse and rider. The shields on the reverse of these coins also underwent many changes, an oval garnished shield replacing the original square-topped variety in 1632. A round garnished shield was also used for some of the later half-crowns.

The shilling was even more complicated, reflecting the relatively greater output of this denomination. Apart from the lightweight variety of 1626 there were four major types with at least a dozen sub-types. The king was progressively portrayed with a ruff and a lace collar of various sizes. The amount of armour revealed beneath his scarf, the shape of the crown and the styling of the king's beard were other variable features. The shape and elaboration of the shield on the reverse also varied considerably, further variants including the CR monogram above or flanking the shield and the use of the Prince of Wales's plumes to denote Welsh silver.

There were four major types of the sixpence but fewer sub-types. This denomination was the only one to include a date as well as a mintmark. The major variants include the large and small Roman numerals on the obverse, the inclusion of the Welsh plumes, differences in the portraits following the same pattern as the shillings, and alterations to the shape of the shield on the reverse. A few sixpences of 1630−32, with the plume or rose mintmarks, may be found without a date, and thereafter this feature was omitted, since the shape of the shield was altered and no longer provided space at the top for a date.

Crowned rose-type silver half-groat. (*Peter Clayton*)

The half-groat and penny continued the style of the previous reign until 1630 when the rose motif and the ROSA SINE SPINA motto were abandoned. Thereafter both coins substituted a bust of the king on the obverse, at first in ruff and mantle but latterly in a lace collar of various styles. Variations of both coins consist of the presence or absence of inner circles on the reverse, the position or omission of the monogram and the shape of the shield.

The legends on the silver coins are of great interest, in view of the political situation of this period. Charles was a firm believer in absolute monarchy and held that he exercised his rights over his subjects by direct descent from God. The so-called Divine Right of Kings found expression on the reverse inscription of the larger denominations: CHRISTO AVSPICE REGNO (*I rule under the auspices of Christ*). The half-groats and pennies from 1630 onwards bore the legend IVSTITIA THRONVM FIRMAT (*Justice strengthens the throne*). Since the dissolution of parliament in 1629 Charles had flouted the laws of the land with increasing frequency, making a mockery of the motto on those very denominations which would have been handled most often by the great bulk of the populace.

Silver shilling with legend expressing doctrine of Divine Right of Kings – 'I rule under the auspices of Christ'. (*Tony Davies*)

The copper farthings instituted under James I were continued under Charles. The Duchess of Richmond struck farthings until 1634 when she sold her lease to Lord Maltravers. Both patentees struck farthings on round or oval flans, the latter probably circulating as half-farthings. The first of the Richmond farthings had the die clumsily altered and CARO (Carolus = *Charles*) superimposed on the original IACO (Iacobus = *James*) inscription, and as a rule traces of the original inscription can be discerned. Later fresh dies were procured with the CARO inscription, but there was a variant with the mis-spelling CARA. Considerable variation may be found in the crowned harp of the reverse, eagle-headed, beaded and scroll-fronted by turns. Subtle variations in the crowns include the circlet with five or seven jewels. The Richmond oval coins follow similar patterns, their chief differences being the inclusion of a mintmark on either or both sides.

The Maltravers round farthings differ mainly from the Richmond coins in having an inner beaded circle separating the inscriptions from the central motifs. They may be found with the mintmark on the obverse alone, or on

Maltravers copper farthing. (*Peter Clayton*)

both sides and one curious variant which is not uncommon has different mintmarks on both sides. Only one type of Maltravers oval is known and this has the king's Latin name rendered in full. In 1636 the Irish harp was replaced by the English rose. The so-called rose farthings continued the Maltravers tradition of an inner circle and this gives rise to the major variants, with the crossed sceptres wholly within, or partially breaking the circle. The country name was originally abbreviated as BRIT but a late variant dropped the T. The last of the Maltravers rose farthings had single-arched crowns and a single rose, and finally the obverse was redesigned to show the crossed sceptres squashed below the crown. Forgery was a recurring problem and, as a security device, a brass plug was inserted in the centre of the copper.

The work of Nicholas Briot

A native of Lorraine, born in 1579, Nicholas Briot was something of a child prodigy, excelling both as a designer and a die cutter. At an early age he worked at the Hôtel de Monnaie in Paris, improving the technical and aesthetic qualities of the French coins in the early seventeenth century and reviving interest in machine production which had languished since Mestrell's hasty departure in 1560. He devised a technique for rolling and cutting blanks which resulted in coins of a more perfectly round shape then had hitherto been feasible. His improvements in coin production came into effect about 1616 but he suffered first apathy and later outright hostility from his colleagues. He got into debt and it is said that he fled the country to avoid his creditors, but it seems more probable that he was disillusioned by the intransigent attitude of his superiors, and decided to try his luck in England.

When he arrived in London in the autumn of 1625 his reputation as a designer and mint-master was well established, and he had no difficulty in securing from Charles I an appointment at the Mint. His exact status appears to have been left rather vague; at first he was subordinate to Vanderort but was given a free hand in the design and engraving of the Great Seal of England in 1626 and had virtual control over the selection and engraving of the king's portrait on both coins and medals. Significantly he was paid the princely salary of £250 per annum – much more than Messrs Gilbert and Green, whose resentment of this foreign interloper can well be imagined.

Their own unseemly brawling came to a head in 1628, however, when their conduct was the subject of a special inquiry by the Council. Subsequently Gilbert left the Mint and entered the world of commerce, eventually becoming a leading figure in the City of London.

Meanwhile Briot installed a rolling mill and improved the blanking press. He probably also deserves credit for instigating the process of applying a grained edge to coins. Blondeau at the Paris Mint took the credit for this invention but he was a pupil of Briot who probably worked on some rudimentary graining machine prior to 1625. At any rate, he continued these experiments at the Tower Mint and used a knurling machine to apply edge marking to his coins. Between 1628 and 1631 he designed a number of portraits of the king and produced some handsome patterns, including a series of unites with crowned or uncrowned busts of Charles. He also produced a pattern for a five-unite coin, only one example of which has survived and bears the rose mintmark of 1631–32. Charles seems to have held this piece in the highest esteem and he took it with him to the scaffold in 1649. Before the headsman performed his duty, Charles handed the piece to Bishop Juxon who attended him at his execution, and from this incident it derived its nickname of the Juxon Medal. It now reposes in the collection of the Department of Coins and Medals at the British Museum.

In addition, Briot produced patterns of gold and silver coins in low relief. Patterns dated 1630 bore a Latin inscription AVSPICIIS REX MAGNE TVIS (*By your goodwill the king becomes great*) – a singularly ironic slogan! A pattern for the half-crown had the motto (O REX DA FACILES CVRSUM ATQVE AVDACIBVS COEPTIS) (*Oh king, take the easy road and give assent to rash undertakings*). Presumably this was a *cri de coeur* from Briot at the commencement of his work on milled coinage and the rash or bold undertakings referred to were his coinage experiments. However, it could also be interpreted as a plea to the king to take a bolder, more decisive line with parliament which, in 1628, was about to be sent into limbo for eleven years. These and other patterns were studied by a royal commission in 1631, as a result of which Briot was authorised to strike coins for general circulation, using the machine processes. He was employed in this capacity for an initial period of twelve months (1631–32),

Briot pattern half-crown of 1628. (*Coin Monthly*)

but at the end of that period the Mint reverted to the earlier hammered process. Nevertheless Briot was appointed engraver general with an increase in salary to £300 per annum.

Briot was responsible for the improved busts of the king which graced the coins issued in 1630–31, before he began work on the milled coinage the following year. The milled gold, struck in 22 carat fineness, comprised the unite, crown and double crown, with a crowned profile facing left (obverse) and a crowned shield (reverse), and the usual legends. An initial B appeared as a mintmark on the reverse, and the values were expressed in shillings by Roman numerals in the field to the right of the king's profile. Briot also struck a few angels in 'fine' gold, similar to the hammered angels but slightly smaller and much neater in appearance, with the B mintmark on the reverse.

Silver crown of Briot's first milled coinage, 1631–32. (*Peter Clayton*)

There were six denominations in the first silver milled coinage, with mintmarks of a flower and B (obverse) and B alone (reverse). Here again, these coins echoed the hammered coins which Briot had designed, but the lettering is outstanding and the detail in the profiles and armorial bearings is much finer. Some time in 1631 Briot was also in Edinburgh, superintending the resumption of copper coinage at the Scottish Mint. He installed machinery there and produced Scotland's first milled coins – not without the usual hostility and controversy, and considerable opposition from Thomas Acheson, Master of the Edinburgh Mint. When Acheson died in 1635 Briot was appointed his successor, though he continued to hold his position as engraver general at the Tower. This plurality of office caused a major outcry, but the matter was resolved fairly amicably when Briot's daughter married Sir John Falconer who succeeded his father-in-law as Master of the Edinburgh Mint in 1638.

Briot then returned to London where he was employed for a further period of twelve months at the Tower Mint. During this period he produced half-crowns, shillings and sixpences by mechanised processes. These coins have the anchor mintmark (used on the hammered coins from May 1638 to July 1639), together with the initial B (half-crown and shilling) or a mullet mintmark (sixpence). The half-crown was similar to that struck during the earlier experiment, but new busts were adopted for the smaller denominations, differing primarily in the falling lace collar which was now plain with a broad border. On the reverse the forked cross no longer extended to the rim, but stopped short at the inner circle.

Silver sixpence of Briot's second milled coinage, 1638–39. (*Peter Clayton*)

Briot produced other patterns at the Tower, briefly in 1634, and again in 1638–39. They include a threepence with the curious Latin slogan signifying *the safety of the republic is the supreme law*; in this era before the Civil War, the term 'republic' was loosely applied to the state or the government and did not acquire its narrower definition of a non-monarchical regime until a decade later. A half-groat showing a sceptre and trident, symbolising land and sea power, was inscribed *One rules over both*. Another half-groat had a radiate rose and the inscription FLOREBIT IN AEVVM (*He will flourish for eternity*). Other Briot patterns, in silver or copper, included six-farthing and five-farthing pieces, pence, halfpence and farthings. The halfpenny was unusual, for its time, in having the value expressed in English, of a sort: A HALF PENI.

Pattern by Briot for a five-farthing piece. (*Coin Monthly*)

Briot also produced coins in 1638–39 by the more traditional hammered process, comprising half-crowns and shillings with the mintmarks of an anchor or a triangle over an anchor. Though struck by hand, they are a vast improvement over the ordinary hammered coins of this period, with much neater and more regular lettering. The Briot hammered half-crowns also have a ground line beneath the horse's hooves, absent in the ordinary hammered coins, with a square-topped instead of a round-topped shield on the reverse. The shilling closely resembled its milled counterpart in the portrait of the king, but the reverse has a square-topped shield over a short cross fleury similar to that found on the ordinary hammered shillings. Here again, the quality of the lettering and the detail in both the bust and the armorial bearings sets this coin apart from its ordinary counterpart. Briot's hammered coins are decidedly elusive and are usually worth about twice as much as his milled versions.

Considerable mystery shrouds the later career of Briot. Ostensibly he remained in the employment of the Tower Mint, though Green was appointed chief engraver there in 1642 following the outbreak of the Civil War. In fact, however, it would appear that King Charles summoned Briot to York in the summer of 1642 to establish minting operations at the Royalist headquarters. His coining equipment was seized by Parliamentary forces at Scarborough on the way. Thomas Rawlins was employed by the king as his chief engraver, but the influence of Briot remained strong and can be discerned in some of the beautiful pieces produced at York and Oxford in the earlier part of the war. After the battle of Marston Moor in 1644 Briot followed the Royalists to Oxford where he died in 1646. At the Restoration in 1660 his widow petitioned Charles II for a small pension and this was subsequently granted.

The provincial coinage of the Civil War, 1642–48

After eleven years of arbitrary rule, and the imposition of taxes without the assent of parliament, Charles was forced to give in and summon parliament. Matters had been brought to a head by Charles's unwise attempt to force episcopalianism on the Scots who thereupon invaded the northern counties with a highly disciplined, well-trained army. National morale sank to its lowest ebb in 1639 and finally the taxpayers went on strike. Even the City of London refused to help the king financially any longer. Although peace was negotiated with the Scots, Charles could only secure a loan from the City on condition that parliament was recalled. The so-called Long Parliament of 1641 wasted no time in ruthlessly bringing Charles's ministers to book for their wrongdoings in the past decade. The Earl of Strafford was the main scapegoat and went to the block in May 1641. Archbishop Laud was also impeached but not executed until January 1645 and episcopacy abolished the following year. Other ministers of the Crown fled abroad rather than risk the wrath of a vengeful parliament drawn largely from the mercantile, professional and small landowning classes.

The Irish rose in revolt in November 1641 and massacred thousands of English settlers. In the power struggle that ensued between king and parliament over the reconquest of Ireland parliament drew up the Grand Remonstrance indicting royal policies; Charles retaliated by trying to arrest five members who were regarded as the ring-leaders of the Opposition. Charles and his guards arrived too late; the birds had flown and the abortive arrest was turned into a mammoth demonstration of anti-Royalist feeling, Charles lost face by this episode and decided to quit London. From March 1642 onwards the country was virtually in a state of civil war though hostilities did not break out until October. In the interim both sides sparred verbally. Parliament's Nineteen Propositions (2 June) claimed the whole sovereignty and government to themselves, while Charles replied with his Declaration at Wellington, Shropshire in September affirming his willingness to uphold the Protestant religion, the laws of England and the liberty of parliament – a manifesto which was reduced to a three line slogan inscribed cynically on many of the coins struck in various parts of England under Royalist control over the ensuing years.

The king's standard was formally raised at Nottingham on 22 August – regarded as the opening day of the Civil War. Broadly speaking, the Royalists controlled the northern and western districts while the Parliamentary forces controlled London and the south-east, parts of the Midlands and the important provincial towns such as Bristol and Gloucester. Throughout the war the Tower Mint continued to strike coins in the king's name, perpetuating designs which had been in use before the outbreak of hostilities. On the Royalist side coins were produced in a number of provincial mints whose competence depended on the quality of both labour and machinery available at the time.

The Aberystwyth Mint

Silver-mining in Wales and the Lake District had been nationalised (in modern parlance) under the Tudors, but by the 1630s was becoming unprofitable. It was then that Sir Thomas Bushell of Lundy, a West Country financier and entrepreneur, stepped in and offered to take over mining operations on a lease from the Crown. In 1631 he began overhauling the principal mines in the Aberystwyth district but was not content merely with the extraction and refinement of the metal; citing the medieval provincial mints as a precedent, he urged that the silver should be coined on the spot. Charles I agreed and in 1637 Bushell was appointed Warden and Master of the Aberystwyth Mint which was to operate as a branch of the Royal Mint in London. Dies were cut in London and supplied to Bushell's mint at Aberystwyth Castle, all but the three smallest denominations being marked on obverse and reverse with the plumes device. This mintmark varied considerably in size and minor details. Bushell also applied his own personal device, an open book. The coins were undated but struck from 1638 until 1642, and comprised half-crowns, shillings (six varieties), half-groats (three types) and pennies, with variations in the inner circles and the rendering of the king's name in full or an abbreviated form. Groats, threepences and

Silver shilling struck at Aberystwyth. (*Peter Clayton*)

halfpence were added to the range at a subsequent date. Three quite distinct busts were used for the groat, differing in the collar as usual, and in the presence or absence of armour at the shoulder. The five main types of the threepence can easily be distinguished by their obverse legend, Hibernia (*Ireland*) being variously abbreviated to HIB, HI or H, and in the use of colons instead of full stops. Only one type of halfpenny was struck, with a rose obverse and a plume reverse.

Considerable mystery surrounds the later history of minting at Aberystwyth. Coining ceased abruptly on the day following the Declaration at Wellington and it seems likely that Bushell was ordered on or about that date to transfer the mint to the Royalist headquarters at Shrewsbury. Coins of the Aberystwyth type, with a mintmark of a crown instead of an open book, exist in all seven denominations. At one time it was thought that they were struck at Aberystwyth from January to March 1646, but a later theory attributed them to Combe Martin from October 1647 to May 1648. During that period Bushell is known to have been in north Devon, but the current view is that the coins were struck at a temporary mint in Furnace, Cardiganshire. Students are still divided as to the date of minting, some placing it as early as 1645 and others narrowing it to 1647–84. The so-called Aberystwyth-Furnace coins are comparatively scarce, both the shilling and sixpence being exceedingly rare.

Shrewsbury Mint

Bushell began minting coins at Shrewsbury in October 1642 but when the Court was transferred to Oxford the following December, Bushell and his staff moved too. The Shrewsbury Mint was, therefore, operational for nine or ten weeks at most and its output was confined to the larger denominations. Unique examples are known of gold unite and triple unite, allegedly struck at Abersytwyth and Shrewsbury respectively. The unite differed from its Tower contemporary in the plume mintmark on the reverse, while the triple unite echoes the sentiments of the king's Wellington Declaration and differs from the subsequent, and much better known, gold coins of this size minted at Oxford in its obverse mintmark.

Otherwise Bushell's entire production at Shrewsbury consisted of silver. Considering the ephemeral nature of this mint, its output was truly phenomenal. The need for larger denominations, and the extreme scarcity of gold, led to the minting of very large and clumsy silver pieces in denominations of crown, half-pound and pound. This established a precedent for high-value coins in metals other than gold and it is not too fanciful to suppose that the idea of the silver pound came from Prince Rupert of Bohemia and the Rhine, the king's nephew and cavalry commander, who must have been familiar with the handsome multiple talers used in Germany at that time.

Aesthetically, however, there is little to be said in favour of the Shrewsbury pound, the equestrian portrait being little more than a parody of the

Silver pound-piece struck at Shrewsbury. (*Peter Clayton*)

Briot crowns struck at the Tower. Late in October the Royalists commanded by Prince Rupert met the Parliamentary forces at Edge Hill in the Midlands. Technically the battle was a draw, but as the Parliamentarians withdrew towards London the Royalists claimed it a victory and were thus enabled to occupy Banbury and Oxford. The later Shrewsbury pounds took note of this victory by depicting the king's horse trampling on a trophy of arms. A rare variant shows a cannon among the pile of arms at the horse's hooves. Around the edge on the reverse these coins bore the Latin motto *Let God arise and His enemies be scattered*, a phrase used by James I but now invested with a new meaning. Across the centre, in two lines, was RELIG. PROT LEG. ANG. LIBER. PAR. – a much-abbreviated form of the Latin for the three principles of the Wellington Declaration. The date appeared below, with Roman numerals of value and three sets of plumes above.

The half-pound, crown and half-crown followed the same basic patterns, with numerous variations in the styling of the equestrian portrait and subtle differences in the plumes on the reverse. Normally the half-crown bore no mark of value but a few are known with Arabic numerals 2 and 6 flanking the plume – the first instance of a value denoted on any English coin in this manner. Both half-crowns and shillings are known with Aberystwyth obverse dies showing the open book mintmark. The reverse die used for the Shrewsbury shillings bore a modified form of the Declaration, while the obverse showed the king as before. Apart from minor inconsistencies explained by the primitive methods of die engraving, the Shrewsbury coins exhibit considerable variation in the styling of the plumes, lacking the horizontal fillet of the Aberystwyth type and varying enormously in thickness.

Oxford Mint

After the victory at Edge Hill the king moved his headquarters to Oxford and in December 1642 Bushell set up the Royalist mint there. Possession of the university city gave Charles a bonus – the college plate which not only boosted his supply of silver but enabled him to strike gold coins in some quantity. Bushell began minting coins in late December or early January 1643. The earliest coins were, in fact, dated 1642 and bore a plume mintmark that differed from the Shrewsbury mark in having a band and scrolled ribbon instead of a coronet. Later coins were inscribed OX or OXON. There was also a marked improvement in the coins as time passed, doubtless due to help from Briot, but mostly as a result of the appointment in July 1643 of Thomas Rawlins as chief engraver.

The unite and triple unite showed the king holding a sword in one hand and an olive branch in the other – a hint of the alternatives offered to his Parliamentary opponents. The reverses of the gold coins bore the Declaration, in two or three lines, in straight or wavy lines and sometimes on a continuous scroll. There were many variants in the obverses.

Gold triple-unite struck at Oxford in 1644. (*Peter Clayton*)

The silver coinage of Oxford was exceedingly diverse and comprised pound, half-pound, crown, half-crown, shilling, sixpence, groat, threepence, half-groat and penny. The larger denominations (down to the half-crown) showed the king on horseback, while various busts graced the lower values. The Declaration usually appeared in two lines on the larger coins, and in three lines on the values from shilling to half-groat. Even some of the pennies bore a minuscule version of the Declaration, though most retained the plume motif, with many variants. There was an incredible range of obverse and reverse dies at Oxford. Rawlins produced a brilliant pattern crown showing the king riding over a panorama of Oxford – the only English coin ever to feature identifiable scenery after the manner of the German civic talers. Through all the vicissitudes of the first Civil War Oxford remained the Royalist capital, and did not surrender to Cromwell until 24 June 1646.

Rawlins pattern silver crown of Oxford. (*Peter Clayton*)

York Mint

Originally Charles had intended to establish York as his capital, since it was an important stronghold in an area of widespread Royalist sympathies. Briot received secret instructions to go there in the autumn of 1642 and establish a mint there. Despite a considerable setback, when the minting machinery coming by sea was captured by Parliamentary privateers off Scarborough, the York Mint functioned tolerably well. It produced silver coins in some quantity and many of them were well struck, though others were of indifferent

Silver threepence struck at York. (*Peter Clayton*)

quality. They may be recognised by their mintmark of a lion passant gardant, while some of the later half-crowns and shillings bore the abbreviated Latin name EBOR. By and large, the York coinage followed the pattern of the Tower issues. There was a wide range of obverses for the half-crown, with the usual variety of equestrian portraits. The shields on the reverse may be oval, square-topped, garnished or flattened, decorated with lion's skin or flowers, and a similar diversity may be found in the shillings. Of the smaller coins, only sixpences and threepences were minted. Two major varieties exist of the sixpence, with and without the CR monogram flanking the shield.

In the early summer of 1644 Prince Rupert campaigned in the north with considerable success, but on 2 July at Marston Moor he suffered one of the major defeats of the war. As a result, the Royalist strongholds in the north fell into Parliamentary hands, and with the surrender of York the minting of Royalist coins there ceased.

Chester Mint

Chester was one of the few Royalist towns to hold out after the debacle of Marston Moor. Half-crowns were struck using plate commandeered by the military authorities. The dies were of quite a high quality and it has been surmised that they were supplied from Oxford and not engraved locally. Nevertheless they incorporate the three gerbs or wheatsheaves from the civic arms as a mintmark, and some of the earlier coins have the abbreviation CHST beneath the horse's hooves. The reverses show a variety of shields – oval, crowned or square-topped, while one type has the Declaration. A few three-pences were also struck, with the king's bust (obverse) and square-topped shield (reverse) and a mintmark of a horizontal wheatsheaf.

Silver half-crown struck at Chester. (*Peter Clayton*)

Truro Mint

Cornwall, under Sir Ralph Hopton, was one of the first counties to declare for the king and a Royalist mint was established at Truro by Sir Richard

Vyvyan, at first using a trunkful of gold and silver plate collected by Lord Robartes. From time to time other consignments of plate contributed by the Cornish nobility were coined at Truro which used a rose mintmark. Very few of the gold unites and silver pounds of Truro have survived. The latter were struck from crown dies using blanks of double thickness. A curious feature of the obverse was that the king was turned in the saddle to face outwards. The same dies on flans of normal thickness were used to strike crowns, but there is a reverse variant with twelve scrolls surrounding the shield. Some of the Truro crowns and half-crowns have a curiously bloated horse on the obverse.

Silver half-crown struck at Truro. (*Tony Davies*)

The half-crowns are a particularly interesting group, due to the wide variety of obverse and reverse dies used. Nevertheless, the bulk of the Truro coins consisted of shillings, with small or large effigies combined with oblong, round or oval shields.

In 1643 Hopton's army invaded Devon, and virtually annihilated the Parliamentary forces on 16 May at Stratton after an indecisive encounter on Dartmoor in April. This left the whole of the West Country in Royalist hands, and an army led by Lord Hertford and Prince Maurice (brother of Prince Rupert) advanced southwest from Oxford and joined up with the Cornishmen. Exeter was captured and Bath besieged. Vyvyan transferred his mint to Exeter in September 1643 though his commission to do so was not dated until January 1644. There are numerous types of half-crown which may have been struck at either Truro or Exeter in this period. All have the rose mintmark, but subtle differences in both obverse and reverse dies.

Exeter Mint

The silver struck at Exeter continued the rose mintmark, though a few coins dated 1645 bear a castle mintmark. Every denomination from the crown to the penny was struck there, an interesting feature being the inclusion of the date on the reverse. As at Truro, the greatest variations occur in the

Silver shilling struck at Exeter. (*Tony Davies*)

crowns and half-crowns which display the usual range of interpretations of the equestrian portrait, from the sensitive engraving of Briot to the grotesqueries perpetrated by local engravers. Both half-crown and shilling may be found with a shield or Declaration reverse. The half-groat is known with either a shield or a large rose on the reverse, but only one type each of the sixpence, threepence and penny was produced. It seems likely that the Briot obverse and Declaration reverses were sent from Oxford to augment the dies cut locally. The last of the Exeter coins were dated 1645, though minting probably continued until April 1646 when the city fell to the Parliamentarians. Latterly the only Royalist army of any size remaining in the field had been Hopton's but even his appeal to the local patriotism of the Cornish levies failed to stem the onslaught of Cromwell's New Model Army.

Bristol Mint

Hopton followed up his victory at Stratton by hammering General Waller's army at Lansdowne and capturing Bath in July 1643. At Roundway Down on 13 July Waller's remnants were caught in a pincer movement by Hopton and Prince Maurice. The Royalists now advanced on Bristol, the second city in England, which fell after a brief siege on 26 July. Bushell was sent thither to establish a mint as soon as possible and capitalise on the capture of such an important city. The Bristol coins can be identified by the abbreviation BR or the very distinctive Bristol version of the three plumes which Bushell had previously used at Aberystwyth and Shrewsbury. A few gold coins were struck, but only two or three examples of the unite have survived, while the half-unite is unique.

The coins follow closely the pattern of the Oxford coinage, with elegant equestrian figures on the higher values and good profiles on the smaller coins, but one major difference lies in the position of the Latin motto on the reverse which begins at the top and not on the left, as on the Oxford coins. The coins consisted of a wide variety of half-crowns and shillings, a much more restricted range of sixpences, groats and threepences, and a relatively few half-groats and pennies, only one type each being recorded of the latter. All but the two lowest values bore a date on the reverse, from 1643 to 1645.

Silver threepence struck at Bristol, 1644. (*Peter Clayton*)

Though the coins usually follow the Shrewsbury and Oxford pattern there are some unusual variants which include the 1643 half-crown with acorn and pellet mintmark and a curiously flattened crown on the king's head, the crudely sculpted effigies on some of the shillings and the threepence combining an Aberystwyth obverse (with open book mintmark) and a Declaration reverse of 1644.

In the summer of 1645 the Parliamentary forces under Fairfax advanced on Goring's Royalist army in the West Country. The latter were defeated at Bridgwater in July, and Somerset and Dorset gradually fell to the New Model Army. After the fall of Sherborne Castle Bristol itself was besieged in late August and surrendered on 11 September.

Lundy, Appledore and Barnstaple

The minting of coins at Bristol came to a halt when the siege began, and Bushell was able to evacuate his equipment intact. Current thinking now favours Lundy as the most probable site of Bushell's minting activity in the latter part of 1645 and 1646 since he had been governor of that island for a number of years, and it offered far more security than any mainland base. Coins of the Bristol types but with A or B mintmarks belong to this period. The initials have tentatively been assigned to Appledore and Barnstaple or Bideford respectively. Several denominations may be found with a plumelet mintmark. Bushell continued to mint coins for the Royalist cause until mid-1646 when Oxford capitulated and Charles took refuge with the Scots, thus bringing the First Civil War to a close.

Silver sixpence of 1646 probably minted on Lundy. (*Peter Clayton*)

Weymouth

The victories of Hopton in the autumn of 1643 placed Weymouth in Royalist hands in September and it remained one of the king's strongholds until June 1644 when it fell to the Roundhead Earl of Essex. During that period coins were probably minted in or near Weymouth though there has not so far been any documentary evidence for this. The coins themselves, however, are proof enough that minting was carried on there. Stylistically they resemble the Tower issues of the period but are often crude to the point of parody. The coins which have positively been assigned to Weymouth consist of half-crowns, of which a considerable number were struck. With various combinations of obverse and reverse dies there are no fewer than fourteen major types, many of them featuring a w mintmark on the obverse. Additionally numerous privy-marks (helmet, castle, lions, rose, star or lis) were used.

The rendering of the equestrian portrait varied considerably, from the fine Briot type to the coarse local versions which show Charles alternately tall and thin or squat and very fat! The shields on the reverse were more competent but ran the full gamut of types, with or without monogram. One variant has the novel addition of two lion's paws at the sides, and there is also a scarce type with the Declaration reverse.

Lesser denominations, comprising mostly shillings, but including some sixpences, groats, threepences and half-groats, were probably struck at Weymouth though none bears the w mintmark. The reverses bear the assortment of privy-marks associated with the Weymouth half-crowns. The shillings were produced in large numbers, using three obverse and eight reverse dies which varied enormously in elegance and technical quality. The smaller coins were confined to one major type apiece, but the plethora of privy-marks gives them considerable scope for study.

An extremely rare unite has been attributed to Weymouth. The obverse has the standard motif, showing the king with sword and olive branch, but no mintmark is included in the legend. Attribution to Weymouth rests on the style of the reverse shield, which has lion's paws on either side – a Weymouth idiosyncrasy. A unite of similar style but incorporating a lis mintmark is attributed to Sandsfoot Castle.

Silver shilling probably struck at Weymouth. (*Peter Clayton*)

Sandsfoot Castle

Barely a mile along the Dorset cliffs from Weymouth stands this castle which was a Royalist fortress during the First Civil War. Half-crowns of the Weymouth type, with the letters SA beneath the horse, have been attributed to this place, the theory being that they were minted here before production was transferred to the nearby town. This would explain why only a few coins have the SA mark while others show traces of these letters partially erased. The privy-marks (helmet, rose and lis) are also found on these coins and are derived from elements in the Weymouth coat of arms. These SA coins are of considerable rarity.

Siege coinage

The battle of Marston Moor was the turning point of the war, yet, within three weeks of their victory, the Parliamentary forces were in disarray and dissension had broken out in their ranks. Parliament did not press home its advantage and consolidate its victory by mopping up the isolated pockets of resistance that remained. Although the war was effectively won in July 1644 sporadic fighting continued for a further two years and it was not until after the execution of Charles I in January 1649 that the Civil War came to an end. During the five years after Marston Moor the Royalists were virtually on the defensive, waging a kind of guerrilla warfare or tying down huge Parliamentary forces in a series of great sieges. The small, compact, walled towns which were still a common feature of England in the mid-seventeenth century made siege warfare possible. The very poor state of roads, which made communications uncertain at the best of times, paradoxically helped the besieged Royalists to break the blockade and replenish their stores of food and ammunition. Makeshift coinage was produced by the Royalists in six of their besieged strongholds between 1644 and 1649. All of these crude pieces are of considerable interest and rarity.

Within weeks of Marston Moor the town and castle of Scarborough were besieged, but the Royalists managed to hold out until June 1645 when their armies were completely routed at Naseby. Even after the town capitulated the castle continued to hold out for some time. In 1648 the castle again declared for the king and was besieged for three months. During the siege of 1644–45 coins were produced by order of the garrison commander Sir Hugh Cholmley and consisted of crude pieces of silver plate, hammered flat and stamped with a castle device and the value below. The denominations were surprisingly varied, due to the haphazard method of cutting, so that pieces had to be stamped with their value according to weight. The values so far recorded are: 4 pence, 6 pence, 7 pence, 9 pence, 10 pence, 11 pence, 1 shilling 1 penny, 1 shilling 2 pence, 1 shilling 3 pence, 1 shilling 6 pence, 1 shilling 9 pence, 2 shillings, 2 shillings 2 pence, 2 shillings 4 pence, 2 shillings 6 pence, 2 shillings 10 pence, 3 shillings, 3 shillings 4 pence, 5

Siege piece cut from silver plate at Scarborough; value 2 shillings 6 pence. (*Peter Clayton*)

shillings, and 5 shillings 8 pence. Values were expressed by punching letters s or D, with Roman numerals below. These coins were uniface, but examples are known with the name in full and the date, with OBS (Obsidium = *siege*) engraved on the reverse, possibly at a much later date.

Carlisle was besieged from October 1644 until July 1645 when the morale of the garrison collapsed with the news of the disaster at Naseby. The conduct of the defence of Carlisle by Sir Thomas Glemham was spirited and efficient, but in the end nothing could withstand the onslaught of the Scots, who had become the allies of the Parliamentarians after the latter had agreed to accept a Presbyterian form of church government in England as well as in Scotland. Glemham only surrendered to David Leslie after his hard-pressed troops were reduced by famine and disease. In the latter part of the siege, when supplies of coin were running low, Glemham authorised the production of coins in denominations of 1 shilling and 3 shillings. Considering the primitive conditions, these coins were well struck on both sides of a reasonably circular flan. The obverse showed a large crown surmounting the royal cypher and the value, while the reverses were inscribed OBS CARL (Obsidium Carleoli = *Siege of Carlisle*) and the date, two variants for each value being recorded.

Silver shilling siege-piece from Carlisle. (*Peter Clayton*)

Newark Castle at the junction of the Rivers Trent and Devon endured three sieges during the war. The raising of the first siege on 21 March 1644 by Prince Rupert was his most impressive feat of arms and though he had a further thirty years of military service ahead of him he never surpassed it. It was also the last major victory for the Royalists and unwittingly hastened their downfall, since it directly precipitated the showdown at Marston Moor. Subsequently Newark was under siege in the winter of 1644 and spring of 1645, and again from 4 November 1645 until 6 May 1646 when it surrendered to General Leslie. He later changed sides, fought for Charles II at Dunbar and Worcester and was imprisoned by Cromwell. At the Restoration in 1660 he was raised to the peerage and rather tactlessly took the title of Lord Newark.

During the summer of 1645 diamond-shaped coins were issued at Newark under the authority of Sir Richard Willis. The obverse showed a large crown flanked by the royal monogram, with the value in Roman numerals below, and the reverse was inscribed OBS/NEWARK with the date beneath. There was one type of half-crown, three types of shilling and one type of sixpence. The variants consist of the name NEWARK or NEWARKE, the shape of the crown and the date, both half-crown and shilling being struck in 1645 and 1646, while the sixpence appeared only in the latter year.

Silver half-crown piece struck at Newark, 1645. (*Peter Clayton*)

The half-crowns struck at Worcester in the early summer of 1646 conformed to the standard Royalist type, with equestrian portrait obverse and armorial reverse, but are classed as siege coins since they were produced in Hartlebury Castle when it was beleaguered by Parliamentary forces. In the guerrilla period it had been the headquarters of a flying column of Royalist cavalry and it was to extirpate this group that the Roundheads laid siege between March and May 1646. The half-crowns minted there have a mintmark of HC on the reverse and a pear mintmark on the obverse – an allusion to the fruit-growing for which Worcester is famous.

The First Civil War technically ended with Charles's surrender to the Scots on 5 May 1646. Thereafter the king was used as a pawn by the three emergent factions – the Scottish Covenanters, the Parliamentarians and their military wing, the New Model Army led by Oliver Cromwell. Gradually the Scots and the Presbyterian element among the Parliamentarians combined with the Royalist remnant and declared for the king. The first act in the Second Civil War was the mutiny of Colonel Poyer and his troops at Pembroke Castle in February 1648. Kent rose in the king's name and the navy defected *en masse* to the Royalists. Pontefract was captured by the Royalists, Scarborough declared for the king and Colchester became the centre of a Royalist rising in Essex. After Fairfax quelled the Kentish rebellion he began the siege of Colchester which posed a threat to London. The town's garrison was commanded by Sir Charles Lucas, an experienced and popular soldier. After the decisive defeat of the Royalists at Preston on 17 July, however, Royalist resistance crumbled. Colchester, reduced to starvation, surrendered on 28 August, Sir Charles Lucas being executed by firing squad on the spot. Numismatically this siege is remembered by a unique ten-shilling gold piece weighing 66 grains and featuring a view of the castle gateway.

Pontefract was an important Royalist stronghold and endured siege on four occasions. It fell into Royalist hands in June 1648 after a surprise coup. The New Model Army reacted swiftly and by the beginning of July General Lambert made an attempt to recapture it. His forces were repulsed and Pontefract then settled down to a wearisome siege. The battle of Preston had, in fact, been fought between the Roundheads and a Scottish army advancing on Pontefract to raise the siege. Despite the setback at Preston, however, the Royalists continued to hold Pontefract long after resistance had vanished elsewhere. A handful of two-shilling pieces and a quantity of shillings were produced in the usual manner by cutting pieces of plate and striking them with dies having a circular beaded border though all of the two-shilling pieces and many of the shillings were cut in a diamond or lozenge shape. The usual obverse showed the crowned CR monogram with the appropriate Latin motto DVM SPIRO SPERO (*While I breathe, I hope*). The reverse showed a triple-turreted castle surrounded by OBS, the value in Roman numerals, the mintmark PC and the date 1648.

After Charles was beheaded at Whitehall on 30 January 1649, Pontefract continued to hold out, and even struck a few shillings in the name of the late king's youthful successor, the reverse legend reading CAROLVS SECVNDVS.

Silver two-shilling siege-piece from Pontefract. (*Peter Clayton*)

The last act of defiance by the Pontefract garrison was the striking of a shilling early in 1649 in which the obverse was modified. In place of the hopeful motto was the inscription CAROL II D G MAG BR ET H REX (*Charles II, King of Great Britain and Ireland*) while the centre showed a crown above a Latin text HANC DEVS DEDIT (*God gave him this*). The reverse had a new inscription round the castle gateway POST MORTEM PATRIS PRO FILIO (*on behalf of the son, after the death of his father*). A few gold unites were also struck at Pontefract from the same dies, either the original DUM SPIRO SPERO type or the POST MORTEM version; both are very rare. At the end of March 1649 Pontefract was forced to capitulate to Lambert and the castle was then demolished. The castle which had witnessed the brutal murder of Richard II 250 years earlier was the last place in England to proclaim the Divine Right of Kings — one of the great ironies of history.

CHAPTER EIGHT

The Commonwealth (1649–1660)

While the Royalists were forced to establish various temporary mints all over the country in the areas under their control, parliament never lost control of the metropolis and coining continued at Tower Hill as though the Civil War had never existed. All the coins struck at the Tower from 1642 until 1649 followed the pre-war patterns. Such was the innate conservatism of the English that parliament did not dare to alter the coinage and though the struggle was often bitter it continued to acknowledge – numismatically at least – the kingship of Charles. Even after the king's surrender at Southwell in 1646 and his subsequent confinement, his position as head of state was never in doubt. Until such times as he was removed, by abdication or death, he was still the king, and there was never any thought that the coins used by parliament should do other than acknowledge this.

Such are the exigencies of war that the money supply actually increased enormously in this period. Of the £8¾ million worth of coin estimated to have been struck at the Royal Mint between 1629 and 1649 the bulk belonged to the last seven years. Such vast quantities meant a considerable sacrifice in quality. David Ramage fled to the Royalist camp taking with him coining tools and dies. Briot and Rawlins overtly aided the king and the latter was actually appointed chief engraver in June 1643. Sir John Coniers continued in office as Lieutenant of the Tower and under him Edward Green held the appointment of chief engraver. He was ably assisted by Edward Wade and Thomas Simon and these men became joint chief engravers on Green's death in 1645. Wade himself died three years later, leaving Thomas Simon to become chief engraver to the Commonwealth that emerged after the king's execution.

From 1642 to 1648 the Tower Mint produced unites, crowns and double crowns in 22 carat gold in considerable quantity, following previous patterns with mintmarks instead of dates. Various busts of the king graced the obverses, while the coat of arms surmounted by a crown appeared on the

Gold double crown struck by the Commonwealth at the Tower Mint. (*Peter Clayton*)

reverse. A fair amount of crowns, a considerable quantity of half-crowns, shillings and sixpences, some half-groats and relatively few pennies were also struck. Inflation diminished the need for the smaller coins. Wages fell slightly during the war, while food prices rose steeply. The upheavals of war over much of the countryside were coupled with a succession of bad harvests. In the latter part of the war, when wages had begun to climb again, their real value was actually at its lowest point since the Depression of 1611 and far below their worth in terms of wages in Elizabethan times.

A wide range of die types was used for the silver coins, starting with some pre-war types but gradually descending in quality to virtually crude parodies of Briot's sensitive portraiture. Only one type of penny was used, similar to the pre-war pattern but with a bust that showed the king as a much older man.

Commonwealth coinage, 1649–60

Apart from the right-wing factions which defected to the Royalists in the Second Civil War, there were various centre and left-wing groups within the broad framework of the Parliamentary side, ranging from the moderates led by Cromwell to the Levellers (radical democrats) and Diggers (communists). The left-wing groups merely took to their logical conclusion the aims for which the war was ostensibly fought, but in demanding universal suffrage, the abolition of the monarchy, the peerage, the great corporations, tithes and the Established Church, they were bound to upset the upper and middle class leaders of the Parliamentary side who saw the Civil War merely as a struggle for power with the king. Soon after Charles was executed the Levellers rose in rebellion, but this was savagely crushed by Cromwell and Fairfax at Burford in May. On their way back to London the Victors of Burford paused in Oxford long enough to receive honorary degrees – the mark of gratitude from the intensely conservative university and one-time Royalist stronghold.

Politically the change from a monarchy to a commonwealth was effected by the occupation of London in the winter of 1648 by the army, the purge of parliament by Colonel Pride, the trial and execution of the king on a charge of treason to the Commonwealth of England, and the abolition of the monarchy and the House of Lords. The remnant of parliament, known as the Rump, continued to sit until April 1653 when it was expelled by Cromwell. Technically England was a republic from January 1649 until April 1653 when Cromwell established the Protectorate with himself as Lord Protector. The main achievement of the Rump had been the sale of ecclesiastical lands and the estates of some 700 Royalists, yielding over £7 million which was used to finance the conquest of Scotland and Ireland, the construction of Blake's navy and the conduct of the first Anglo-Dutch War. Bad harvests continued until 1651 but the increased money supply from the sale of forfeited estates led to a quite startling recovery and prosperity. Excellent harvests in 1653–54 resulted in a general raising of the standard of living and explain the general acquiescence of the people when Cromwell substituted his own brand of monarchy in 1653.

Under Thomas Simon there was a marked improvement in the quality of the coinage. The gold consisted of unites, double crowns and crowns, while the silver comprised crowns, half-crowns, shillings, sixpences, half-groats, pennies and even halfpence. Despite the economic and political upheavals of the recent conflict, the Commonwealth managed to keep the weight and fineness of its coins on the same level as before, but there the resemblance ended.

The design of the coins reflected the wave of puritanism that now swept the country. Portraiture, smacking of the cult of personality, was decidedly out. In its place came armorial devices, but without any of the garnishing and fancy touches which characterised previous coins. The obverse showed a simple shield bearing the cross of St George, while the reverse of all gold and silver coins down to the sixpence showed twin shields emblazoned with the cross of St George (England) and the harp (Ireland). The curious linking of shields inspired the derisory nickname of 'breeches' coinage. A contemporary couplet about the coins made a pointed reference to the Rump Parliament:

A silver pair of breeches wrought,
Such as you see upon an old Rump Goat.

Commonwealth silver shilling of 1651, part of the so-called 'breeches' coinage. (*Peter Clayton*)

The inscriptions were rendered entirely in English, Latin being regarded as a mark of popery – an attitude which must have grieved John Milton, Cromwell's Latin secretary and one of the ablest scholars of his time. The obverse was inscribed THE COMMONWEALTH OF ENGLAND, with a mintmark at the top, while the reverse on coins down to the sixpence had the date at the top and the pious invocation GOD WITH US. On the smaller coins the English and Irish shields were shown on opposite sides. All except the halfpenny had the notation of value expressed in Roman numerals. Only two mintmarks were used and could have had only vestigial importance, since they spanned a comparatively long period, and dates were also used. These marks were a sun (1649–57) and an anchor (1658–60). No dates or mintmarks appeared on the three smallest coins, whose types remained constant throughout the Commonwealth period. There was no appreciable variation in the dies of the larger coins either.

In 1651 there was a curious contest between Pierre Blondeau, Briot's former pupil at the Paris Mint, and David Ramage, quondam defector to the Royalists, over the production of pattern coins using new French machinery and the discarded equipment from the 1631–39 experiments respectively. The milled patterns were distinguished by lengthy edge inscriptions. Ramage's patterns were the most diverse, including gold and copper pieces as well as silver.

The Protectorate (1653–59) and Republic (1659–60)

Between April 1653 and January 1655 Cromwell gradually extended his arbitrary rule, eventually dissolving parliament and governing through a system of eleven military districts, each administered by a major general. During this period of renewed autocracy Thomas Simon prepared dies for a new coinage, restoring all the features associated with the monarchy – portraiture, royal symbols and Latin inscriptions, with more than a hint of that very Divine Right which Charles had claimed.

There were two gold coins, a fifty-shilling piece of which very few specimens are extant, and a broad or twenty-shilling piece. Both bore a left-facing profile of the Lord Protector 'warts and all', truncated at the neck and with the victor's laurels on his brow. The reverse had a plain shield quartered with the arms of England and Ireland, surmounted by the Scottish lion. The shield was topped by a crown, traditional emblem of monarchy, flanked by the date. The legend on the obverse was OLIVAR D. G. RP ANG SCO ET HIB &C PRO (*Oliver, by the Grace of God, Protector of the Republic of England, Scotland and Ireland et cetera*), while the reverse had the motto PAX QVAERITVR BELLO (*Peace is sought by war*). The fifty-shilling coin also had an edge inscription, a somewhat contracted Latin tag which translates as *A protection to the letters* (on the face of the coin), *the letters* (on the edge) *are a crown and a safeguard to the coinage*. The broad had a grained edge. Brooke records that pattern broads were struck in silver as well as gold, and that there was also a half-broad.

Gold pattern broad or twenty-shilling piece showing the Lord Protector, 'warts and all'. (*Peter Clayton*)

The silver coins consisted of crown, half-crown, shilling and sixpence. They had the same Latin legends as the gold pieces, but the Lord Protector was portrayed as a full bust draped with toga in the Roman fashion, while the shield on the reverse was scrolled and garnished. Both crown and half-crown had edge inscriptions, while the other coins had grained edges. The gold coins and the half-crown were dated 1656 while all of the silver coins were dated 1658. It is thought that the bullion from which these patterns was struck came from a consignment captured from the Spanish treasure fleet in 1656, following a brilliant naval campaign by Admiral Blake which gave Britain one of its first overseas colonies, Jamaica. Some £2,000 worth of gold and silver was given to Blondeau to coin using the milled process in new premises in Drury House. Blondeau was promised new equipment but nothing came of it, as Cromwell died on 3 September 1658, the anniversary of his decisive victories at Dunbar and Worcester.

On his deathbed Oliver nominated his son Richard as his successor. The attempt to establish a Cromwellian dynasty failed because Richard had neither the ability nor the will to govern, and agreed amicably to his dismissal by the Long Parliament, reconvened in May 1659. The army now resumed control and restored a republican government without much enthusiasm. Negotiations were opened with Charles Stuart, living in Breda, Holland, and on 25 May 1660 Charles II returned to England after a decade in exile.

Copper coinage

Under the Commonwealth no provision was made for a base-metal subsidiary coinage, so the gap left by the Richmond and Maltravers farthings had to be filled by countless merchants and tradesmen who issued their own tokens. Pennies, halfpence and farthings, in circular, octagonal, square, diamond or heart shapes, were produced in great abundance. A few pattern copper farthings were produced officially, including one portraying Cromwell and inscribed in English CHARITIE AND CHANGE. David Ramage seems to have been mainly employed at this time in the production of patterns for low-denomination copper coins, whose inscriptions echoed the twin reasons for their issue – as alms or poor relief and as small change. Nothing came of these experiments during the Commonwealth, though undoubtedly they laid the foundations for the subsidiary coinage under the later Stuarts. Among these interesting patterns are the coppers inscribed THE COMMONS PETICION – THE POORES RELEFE and the pewter pieces with the legend ENGLANDS FARDIN FOR NECESSARY CHANGE.

CHAPTER NINE

Charles II (1660–1685)

The Restoration and its aftermath was a period of tremendous social upheaval. The rich got richer and the poor became poorer. For the first time England was truly polarised into the class system which has only begun to break down within living memory. It was a period of considerable paradox: the creation of vast estates as many ancient families, lesser gentry, freeholders and the yeomanry were liquidated; many new industries were developed, with factories replacing the former cottage occupations; but 50,000 demobilised soldiers gave rise to the first unemployment crisis; powerful oligarchies at one extreme obtained a near monopoly in many areas while, at the other extreme, attempts by the workers at 'combination' gave rise to trade unions in their embryonic form.

The wages boom under the Commonwealth gave way to a slump in 1661–62. Average wages dropped slightly at a time when food prices went through the roof and this decline in the real value of money continued until about 1674. The landless labourers who now swelled the population of the cities, however, still had a better living standard than their predecessors under James I. Bad harvests in 1660 and 1661 account for the sharp rise in the price of foodstuffs but thereafter there was a gradual recovery which was only partially offset by the Great Plague of 1665.

Hammered coinage, 1660–62

At the time of the Restoration there was an abundant gold and silver coinage in circulation, comprising the coins of the Commonwealth as well as many older and badly worn coins of the pre-1649 period. On 27 June Charles ordered the resumption of coinage following the patterns of his father. At first, it seemed as if Charles II was turning the clock back and eschewing the use of machinery. In August orders were given for the removal of the

Blondeau and Briot machines from the Tower Mint, but this decision was reversed in May 1661 when it was decreed that henceforward all coins should be machine-made. The new milled coinage did not appear until 1662 and for the time being the traditional hammered process was used.

In September 1661 Charles ordered the demonetisation of all Commonwealth coins from 30 November, though an extension until mid-January was given for the payment of taxes. To the government's credit, the called-in Commonwealth coins were redeemed at full face value, no matter how worn or clipped they might be. This policy was later extended to the older hammered coins which were gradually demonetised after the introduction of the new milled coins.

Main responsibility for the interim hammered coinage fell on Thomas Simon, but he was engaged on the engraving of the Great Seal and six months elapsed before the coin dies were ready. The first of the new coins did not appear until February 1661. There were three 22 carat gold coins – the unite, double crown and crown – using the old Latin slogan translated as *through harmony may the kingdoms flourish* and the elaborately garnished shield which was such an outstanding feature of the pre-war coinage. The obverses broke new ground with a left-facing profile of the king wearing laurel leaves instead of a crown. Great attention was paid by Simon to the detail of the king's luxuriant tresses and the elaborate lace collar. The king's name and titles were rendered in Latin and the coins were undated, but had a crown mintmark on the obverse. Initially they were struck without any indication of value but later Roman numerals were added.

Charles II gold unite. (*Peter Clayton*)

The silver coinage was likewise undated. In the first issue the coins had neither a mark of value nor inner circles on obverse and reverse; in the second issue (mid-1661) Roman numerals denoting pence appeared on the obverse behind the king's head; and in the third issue (late 1661 onwards) beaded circles were added to both sides, separating the inscriptions from the field. Stylistically the silver followed the pattern of its pre-war counterparts, with a crowned bust on the obverse and the arms and fourchee cross on the reverse. Another echo of pre-war times was the motto *I reign under the auspices of Christ*

Silver twopence showing value (in roman numerals) to right of king's bust. (*Peter Clayton*)

which Charles I had used to bolster his claim to rule by Divine Right. The first and second issues comprised half-crown, shilling, sixpence, twopence (as the half-groat was now known) and penny. There were few major varieties, the most important being the penny without mintmark (first issue) and the twopence and penny with legend beginning at bottom left instead of top right (second issue).

The quality of the hammered coins did not live up to the superlative craftsmanship of the engraver, and points to a great deal of haste in production. Doubtless the coiners were trying to prove to the last that their age-old methods of striking were every bit as fast as the new machinery then being installed, but they were fighting a losing battle.

Milled coinage

Thomas Simon was sent to France on 8 November 1661 to secure the services of Blondeau to whom the princely sum of £1,000 was paid for his machinery. In February 1662, while this was being installed at the Tower Mint, a competition was held between Simon and a Dutch artist, John Roettier, to determine who should have the honour of designing the dies for the milled coins. As a result, Roettier was given the task and Simon's employment virtually ceased thereafter. Not to be outdone, however, he produced a crown based on Roettier's accepted design, and added minuscule lettering round

Thomas Simon's Petition crown of 1663. (*Peter Clayton*)

the edge: 'Thomas Simon most humbly prays your Majesty to compare this his tryall piece with the Dutch and if more truly drawn & embossed more gracefully order'd and more accurately engraved to relieve him.' The elegance and beauty of Simon's Petition crown cannot be denied but it was to no avail. Simon retired in 1663 and two years later fell victim to the last of the great epidemics which periodically scourged the city of London. The Great Plague claimed the lives of 69,000 Londoners and severely disrupted the work of the Mint for upwards of a year.

The milled coinage was not introduced until 1663. On 9 March Samuel Pepys wrote in his Diary: 'There dined with us today Mr Slingsby of the Mint, who showed us all the new pieces both gold and silver, that are made for the King by Blondeau's way; and compared them with those made for Oliver. The pictures of the latter made by Symons, and of the King by one Rotyer, a German I think, that dined with us also.' The Diary contains an entry on 19 May giving a long description of the various coining processes: the casting and rolling of the strips, the blanking, annealing and edge marking of the flans and the striking of the coins using screw presses operated by horsepower. Pepys also mentioned that 'they now coyne between 16 and 24,000 pounds a week' giving some idea of the Mint's output at that time. Mr Slingsby, referred to above, was the Master of the Mint. The 'Rotyer, a German I think' was, of course John Roettier. It is alleged that Philip Roettier lent money to Charles II when he was living in Holland in somewhat reduced circumstances, and that the king then promised to give employment to Philip's sons when he was restored to his throne. Charles kept his word and later employed not only John but also his brothers Joseph and Philip who worked as assistant engravers at the Tower Mint in the 1670s. John came to London in 1662 and was chief engraver from 1670 to 1698.

The new milled coinage eventually consisted of twelve denominations, four in gold and eight in silver, as well as sporadic issues of halfpence and farthings in base metal in the latter part of the reign. The milled gold coins included the same denominations as the hammered series but at slightly reduced weights. This was balanced, however, by the use of edge lettering or graining which prevented clipping and gave the new coins greater reliability than ever before. First of the gold coins to appear was the twenty-shilling piece, now known for the first time as a guinea on account of the fact that it was minted from metal imported from the Guinea Coast by the Royal African Company. Guineas were strucked annually until 1684 and used four different effigies of the king in that period, with a reverse showing four shields bearing the heraldic insignia of England, Scotland, Ireland and France, each surmounted by a crown. In the interstices of the shields were two crossed sceptres, with a rose superimposed in the centre. The digits of the date flanked the crown at the top while the Latin legend, continued from the king's name on the obverse, continued to proclaim him as king of Great Britain, France and Ireland, an ironic claim, as will be apparent from the background to the silver coins.

The two-guinea piece was introduced in 1664 but was only struck spas-

Gold five-guinea piece, 1668. (*Peter Clayton*)

modically until 1671 and annually from 1675 to 1684, a different bust being used in each period. The magnificent five-guinea piece, similar to the crown in size but struck in 22 carat gold, made its debut in 1668. The first bust, with pointed truncation, was used until 1678 and the second, with rounded truncation, from 1678 until 1684. The last of the gold coins, the half-guinea, appeared in 1669, using the pointed truncation bust until 1672 and the rounded bust from then onwards. Mintmarks showing an elephant or latterly an elephant and castle, were used on many of these coins to denote the source of the bullion and add considerably to the interest of this series.

The milled silver coins were likewise introduced over a period of years. First to appear was the crown, in 1662, followed by the half-crown and shilling (1663) and then the smaller coins. Of these, the penny, twopence, threepence and groat were originally issued undated but from 1670 onwards a date appeared on the reverse.

In 1662 Charles finalised negotiations (which had probably been initiated while he was still in exile) for the sale of Dunkirk to France. This was the last remnant of the English dominions on the French mainland dating back beyond the Hundred Years' War to a time when William the Conqueror was Duke of Normandy. The sale of Dunkirk, a seaport which had become strategically untenable by the seventeenth century, raised emotive issues in England and led to the downfall of Clarendon, the minister who was unlucky enough to be associated with the deal. Charles probably got the best of the bargain, since Louis XIV paid out one and a half million *écus* in silver. Under the terms of a secret treaty between Charles and Louis, the latter also paid out a subsidy to Charles for the remaining years of his reign, and this was subsequently converted into English coin. The silver coins which originated in this rather discreditable manner bore no mintmark. Others, coined from the silver of the West Country and Wales, bore the traditional mint-marks of a rose and three plumes respectively, while some coins from silver imported by the Royal African Company bore an elephant (1666) or an elephant and castle (1681).

The largest of the silver coins was the crown, on whose edge Blondeau applied a Latin inscription DECVS ET TVTAMEN (*An ornament and a safeguard*)

Silver crown, 1662, first bust. (*Peter Clayton*)

which neatly summed up the dual function of edge lettering, enhancing the appearance of the coin but also effectively preventing clipping. Subsequently the date 1662 was incorporated in this inscription. The laureated profile used in the early versions of these coins showed too prominent a chin, but this was modified in the second bust (1664–71). The original reverse had Irish and Scottish shields at 9 o'clock and 3 o'clock respectively, with quadripartite shields at top and bottom showing the French and English arms in alternate quarters. A new reverse was adopted in 1663, showing the English lions in the top shield and the French lilies in the bottom shield. The king's titles continued to refer to France – no longer justifiable after the sale of Dunkirk and, in view of the secret subsidy from Louis, incredibly tactless. Another feature of the crowns from 1663 onwards was the inclusion in the edge inscription of ANNO REGNI (*in the year of the reign*) followed by the date in Roman numerals. Later crowns had this date expressed in words.

The first of the half-crowns appeared in 1663, a different bust being used each year from then until 1666, though none was issued in 1665,when production of coins was severely curtailed by the Plague. That things were far from normal in succeeding years is shown by the use of overstruck dates on the 1664 die as late as 1669. Plentiful production of half-crowns was resumed in 1670. Four busts were used for the half-crown, the fourth or large bust being used for the coins of 1672–84. Only 1678 – the year of the Popish Plot when there was a marked recession – is a scarce date in the series of half-crowns, though there are some extremely rare variants in the later coins, mainly due to the inclusion of the Welsh plumes. A few half-crowns of 1681 have the elephant and castle mark.

Shillings were struck in considerable quantities in 1663, using at least two obverse dies. So many shillings were struck that year that no more were needed until 1666. A second and more flattering profile was adopted in 1666, but only a handful of shillings were struck from this die and it was not generally used until 1668. The second bust was used until 1683, but production fluctuated considerably and some dates are very scarce. As with the higher denominations, there were variants with the elephant, elephant

Silver shilling, 1663, first bust. (*Christie's*)

and castle, rose or plume mintmarks. A fourth bust, with much older
features, was employed for the majority of 1683 shillings and those dated
1684.

The sixpence was not introduced until 1674 and was quite straightforward. Only one bust was used, without mintmarks or die variants. Sixpences
were struck every year until 1684, those of 1678 and 1682 being overstrikes
on the previous dates. The larger denominations, down to the sixpence, had
the king's personal monogram, entwined c's, in the interstices of the shields
on the reverse. The four smallest coins, after an original undated issue with
a shield reverse, each had a distinctive reverse based on the theme of the
king's initial. The groat or fourpence had four c's entwined to form a cross,
the threepence had three c's interlocked in quasi-Celtic fashion, on the
twopence two c's overlapped facing each other, and on the penny a single
c appeared. In each case a crown surmounted the cypher and was flanked by
the digits of the date. The date twopence first appeared in 1668 and the other
three denominations followed in 1670. Their regular issue thereafter has
given rise to the myth that they were intended as Maundy money, and it
has become fashionable to collect them in year sets. Charles revived the Royal
Maundy ceremony but at first only silver pennies were distributed to the

Silver sixpence, introduced 1674. (*Royal Mint*)

Silver groat or fourpence, with four c's to make a cross. (*Peter Clayton*)

deserving poor. Conversely, all four denominations of the so-called Maundy series, were intended for general circulation.

Base-metal coinage

No attempt was made to curb the circulation of tradesmen's tokens until 1672 when a regal issue in base metal was struck. Copper halfpence and farthings were declared legal tender for payments under sixpence. Their obverse portrayed the king laureated and in Roman armour, with the Latin legend CAROLVS A CAROLO, signifying *Charles (II) in succession to Charles (I)*. The reverse of these coins showed the seated figure of Britannia, a revival of an allegory found on Roman coinage. It will be remembered that the Duchess of Richmond had acquired the patents for the copper coinage in 1624. By a curious coincidence the model for Britannia on the coppers of Charles II was another Duchess of Richmond. Frances Teresa Stewart (1648–1702) had been maid of honour to Catherine of Braganza, wife of Charles II. He became infatuated with her but in 1667 she eloped with the Duke of Richmond and Lennox and secretly married him. Later she returned to court and resumed her position as one of the king's mistresses. Copper halfpence were struck in 1672–73 and 1675, while the farthings appeared in 1672–75 and 1679.

1675 copper farthing, with Britannia – a revival from Roman coinage – modelled on the Duchess of Richmond. (*Peter Clayton*)

Tin farthings with a copper plug in the centre were struck in 1684–85. They had a similar obverse and reverse to the previous issue but had an inscribed edge in Latin – NVMMORVM FAMVLVS, signifying *servant of coins* (i.e. a subsidiary coinage). It was in this humble and inauspicious manner that the Britannia types, later gracing the bronze pennies and ending up on the decimal fifty pence, were born.

CHAPTER TEN

James II (1685–1688)

Charles died on 6 February 1685 without any legitimate offspring, and was succeeded by his brother James, Duke of York. James's childhood had been spent in the down-at-heel gentility of the exiled court in France but he had become a professional soldier and served with great distinction. At the Restoration he was appointed Lord High Admiral and Lord Warden of the Cinque Ports, effectively head of the navy which he professionalised and overhauled. Through his wife Anne Hyde, daughter of Lord Clarendon, he became a convert to Catholicism in 1671. After Anne's death that year her two daughters, Mary and Anne, were reared as Protestants. James remarried in 1673, his bride being the Catholic princess, Mary of Modena. Opposition to James then, and later as king, stemmed from his religious beliefs and indirectly from his desire to extend toleration to all sects, a situation which the Establishment, both ecclesiastical and secular, found intolerable. The Whig aristocracy intrigued with William of Orange, who had married James's elder daughter, and eventually invited him to seize the throne. William landed at Torbay in November 1688 and James fled to France the following month. The so-called Bloodless Revolution was then followed by four years of bloody campaigning in Scotland and Ireland (1689–93) as James tried to regain his throne.

The coinage of James II was struck in the same denominations and weights as the milled coins of Charles II, the dies being engraved by John Roettier. The five-guinea piece appeared in 1686 with a left-facing bust and a heraldic reverse following the previous pattern, but with four sceptres between the shields. Of the gold coins, only the guinea appeared in the first year of this reign. The first bust, with the ribbons behind the head turned downwards, was used in 1685 and early in 1686, but later coins had a bust with the ribbons upwards. Half-guineas were minted in 1686–88 with no appreciable difference in their dies. Two-guinea pieces did not appear until 1687. Those dated 1688 were, in fact, overstruck on coins dated 1687. All four gold coins

Gold five-guinea of 1687 with elephant and castle mintmark. (*Peter Clayton*)

may be found with or without the elephant and castle mintmark below the king's bust.

Of the silver coins, only the penny, threepence, shilling and half-crown were issued in 1685, the twopence, fourpence, sixpence and crown appearing in 1686. The penny broke new ground with an entirely different reverse and a distinctive treatment of the profile on the obverse. Taking the initial c motif of the previous issue as a precedent the new penny made very neat use of the fact that the initial of the king's name in Latin (IACOBVS) was the same as the Roman numeral for one. Thus the coin had a Roman numeral or initial I surmounted by a crown, while the twopence was inscribed II, the threepence III and the fourpence IIII – the last being a perfectly acceptable alternative to IV (as a glance at antique clock-faces will show). The obverse of the four smallest denominations depicted the king with short hair – a refreshing change from the full-bottomed wig featured on the larger coins. On his temples lay the laurel wreath in the style of the Roman emperors.

Completely redesigned James II silver penny. (*Coin Monthly*)

Considering the large number of shillings which were struck, it is surprising that this denomination should have contained so little variety. Only one bust was used for the obverse during the four years of production,

Silver groat or fourpence of James II. (*Royal Mint*)

and this followed the style of the gold coins. The reverse had a similar arrangement of heraldic shields and sceptres. Like the fourpence, the shillings of 1687 were overstruck on those of 1686. The sole variety of note is the shilling of 1685 with a plume mintmark in the centre of the reverse, only two examples having been recorded.

The remaining three silver coins exhibited major varieties. The crown and half-crown made use of both busts, distinguished by the ribbons. All of the 1686 crowns used the first bust, while those of 1687–88 used the second. By contrast, the half-crown made greater use of the first bust and coins dated 1685–87 were issued with this obverse. A few coins of 1687 and all of the 1688 half-crowns bore the second bust. The sixpence used the same effigy throughout, but two different reverses may be discerned, differing in the shape of the shields. The first type was used in 1686 and the early months of 1687, while the later type was used for the majority of 1687 coins and those dated 1688.

1684 tin farthing, with copper plug. (*Coin Monthly*)

James authorised halfpence and farthings in tin with a copper plug in the centre. Unfortunately the innate instability of tin means that the great majority of surviving examples are in poor condition. Like their predecessors these coins did not bear the usual royal titles but were merely inscribed IACOBVS SECVNDVS, with BRITANNIA as a caption to the seated allegory of Britain on the reverse. The date appeared in the exergue on the reverse, a precedent which was gradually extended to all subsidiary British coins in the ensuing centuries, until the advent of decimal coinage in 1968. Two busts were used, the first showing James in Roman armour and the second in a draped toga.

CHAPTER ELEVEN

William and Mary (1688–1694)

William of Orange, hereditary Stadholder of the Netherlands since the over-throw of the oligarchy in 1672, married Princess Mary, elder daughter of the Duke of York and Anne Hyde, in 1677, a diplomatic marriage which aimed at healing the breach between countries which had recently been at war. Thereafter England was aligned with Holland against the rising might of France and the ambitions of Louis XIV. It was the failure of the Whigs to convert James II to this anti-French alliance, as much as fears of the restoration of Catholicism that triggered off the Revolution in 1688. A convention parliament was summoned on 22 January 1689, James was formally declared to have vacated the throne by his flight, and on 13 February William and Mary were proclaimed joint sovereigns. The rest of the year was taken up in settling various constitutional matters. Henceforward England was a constitutional monarchy, the first of its kind in the world. William regarded the English throne mainly as a bargaining factor in his continuing struggle with Louis XIV and was absent campaigning in Europe for much of the time. The routine business of governing the country devolved on Mary and the worry and responsibility of government undoubt-edly hastened her untimely death from smallpox at the age of thirty-two. Thereafter William reigned alone until his death in 1702.

The first gold coins of this reign appeared in 1689 and were struck from new dies engraved by James and Norbert Roettier. Conjoined profiles of William and Mary appeared on the obverse with the Latin legend GVLIELMVS ET MARIA DEI GRATIA. The reverse featured a shield with quarterings for the arms of England (first and fourth), Scotland (second) and Ireland (third), surmounted as an inescutcheon by the rampant lion of the House of Orange. A crown above the shield was flanked by the digits of the date. The reverse legend read MAG. BRI. FR. ET HIB. REX ET REGINA (*King and Queen of Great Britain, France and Ireland*), thus adding piquancy to William's lifelong feud with Louis XIV, but curiously omitting any reference to the Netherlands of which he was the legitimate ruler.

Gold five-guinea piece of William and Mary. (*Peter Clayton*)

The coinage of this reign was severely affected by the sharp rise in the price of silver in Europe. English silver was coined at a face value less than it would fetch abroad, and consequently began to drain overseas. This, in turn, led to a sharp rise in the value of English gold so that the guinea reached a point at which it was worth 30 shillings – an increase of 50 per cent by the end of the joint reign. This economic instability was brought about by the decrease in imports of bullion from America as the Spanish mines were gradually worked out, together with the much higher level of prosperity in Europe and a far larger population, factors which had enormously boosted the money supply.

At the beginning of the reign the guinea was tariffed at 21 shillings 6 pence. No appreciable difference may be discerned in the dies used for this coin which was minted annually from 1689 until 1694. Half-guineas were struck from 1689 onwards. The small flan posed problems for the engraver and the conjoined profiles were badly proportioned and unflattering in the original version. A new die was engraved and used from 1690 and remained in use until 1694, though relatively few half-guineas were minted. The higher denominations did not appear until 1691. The five-guinea piece was minted each year from then until 1694, but relatively few two-guinea coins were struck. None was minted in 1692 at all, but a reasonable supply appeared in 1693–94. These gold coins may be found with or without the elephant or elephant and castle mintmarks.

By contrast with the gold, the silver of William and Mary was decidedly patchy. The only denominations which appeared in the course of each year of the joint reign were the penny, threepence and fourpence. Twopences were struck each year except 1690 and half-crowns in every year except 1694, but the remaining denominations appeared only intermittently. The chief reason was the disparity between the face and intrinsic value of the silver coinage. At this time 5 shillings 2 pence worth of coins were produced from an ounce of silver – but silver was worth 5 shillings $3\frac{1}{2}$ pence an ounce. Inevitably the overvalued English coins soon drained out of the country. Moreover, the wars which had a severe effect on the economy of Western Europe were aggravated by the sharp decline in the imports of bullion from Spanish

America and the failure of the central European mines to keep up with the demand.

The reverse of the penny followed the style of the preceding reign, with a crowned Roman numeral, but the twopence, threepence and fourpence abandoned Roman numerals in favour of Arabic figures. The crowned numerals thus laid down the pattern which has been followed by the silver Maundy money to this day, although at this time only the penny was used in this religious ceremony and the coins were struck for general circulation. The Latin inscriptions on the silver coins were similar to those on the gold coins. In the first version of the penny (1689) an attempt was made to contain the profiles within the inscription but this resulted in a hopeless distortion of the portraits and from 1690 onwards height was gained by breaking the inscription to allow the heads to touch the rim.

There were no variations in the twopence, but two major types exist for both the threepence and fourpence. In the first busts for both coins the laurel wreath on the king's head has no tie at the back, but the second bust incorporates this feature.

Of the higher denominations, only the half-crown was struck in appreciable quantities with any degree of continuity. The earliest version, struck in 1689, had profiles which exposed a fair amount of the ample proportions of Queen Mary and confined her husband to the left side of the obverse. This gave his head a rather elongated appearance, though not so bizarre as the rendering on the diminutive half-guinea. The first version of the reverse had a crowned shield depicting the three leopards (England), three lilies (France), lion rampant (Scotland) and harp (Ireland) in the quarters, with the lion of Orange superimposed. Late in 1689, however, a new shield was adopted in which the lilies and leopards were reduced to alternate quarterings in an escutcheon which was itself used for the first and fourth quarterings of the shield. Coins with the first bust and second shield were struck in 1689 and 1690. In 1691 a new obverse, giving William a more generous share of the field, was adopted. Sufficient of Mary's profile was depicted, however, to show that her proportions had become even more Junoesque in the interim.

Silver crown of 1691. (*Peter Clayton*)

The second bust was used with an entirely new reverse which, in fact, reverted to an earlier pattern in which four shields, with the leopards, lion, harp and lilies, were arranged in the form of a cross with the lion of Orange in a central cartouche. Each shield was crowned and the interstices bore the entwined MW monogram of the joint sovereigns and a digit of the date. Half-crowns of this type were minted in 1691–93. Crowns of this type were also struck, in a limited quantity confined to 1691–92. Shillings with similar designs were issued in 1692–93 and sixpences in 1693–94.

The base-metal subsidiary coinage continued the pattern of the preceding reign, both in the treatment of the motifs and in the composition of the alloy. Tin blanks were used, with small rectangular plugs of copper inserted in the middle as a security device. Both farthings and halfpence were produced in small quantities in 1689, with small draped busts of the rulers on the obverse and the now customary Britannia on the reverse. Even rarer are the farthings of 1690, with date overstruck on 1689. Large cuirassed busts were employed for a handful of farthings with the overstruck date, and also for a regular issue of farthings and halfpence in 1690–92.

Tin had been used as a measure to help the ailing Cornish tin industry, but it was a most unsatisfactory medium for coinage. Copper was reintroduced in 1694 after a lapse of twenty years. Cuirassed portraits of William and Mary appeared on the obverse, with Britannia on the reverse, and the date in the exergue. Both farthings and halfpence were struck in considerable quantities. In addition to the regular issues there were various patterns, some with an armorial reverse inscribed ENGLISH COPPER and others depicting an elephant on the obverse and the civic arms of London on the reverse, with the motto GOD PRESERVE LONDON. Subsidiary coins for use in Carolina and New England were struck in 1694 using the elephant obverse.

CHAPTER TWELVE

William III (1694–1702)

The death of Mary in 1694 forced William III to devote more of his attention to the running of his island kingdom. By this time, however, peace had been restored in Ireland and the Scottish Highlands subdued by the ruthless extirpation of the Macdonalds of Glencoe in 1692. In the first year of William's reign on his own the Bank of England was founded by William Paterson of Dumfries who also helped to found the Bank of Scotland the following year. The establishment of these two great national institutions put the financial affairs of both kingdoms on a sound footing.

Since the expulsion of James II parliament had gradually assumed direct control of fiscal and monetary policy and it was it, rather than the king, which decided on a major reform of the currency in 1695. Although milled coins had been in circulation for years, a considerable quantity of hammered coinage, much of it badly worn and clipped, continued to circulate and this had a tendency to drive the better milled coins out of circulation. The Act of 1695 which remedied this situation gave the public twelve months in which to surrender their old hammered coins in exchange for brand new milled pieces. This decision was regarded by the public as little more than a licence to give the old hammered coins a final clipping before turning them in and there is no doubt that speculators made an enormous profit on the deal.

This Act, more than anything else, established the integrity and probity of the British government in financial matters and laid the foundations for a reputation which has continued to this day. The deficit between the old hammered coins and the new milled coins amounted to £2.7 million which the government recouped by a house duty, the so-called window tax. The currency reforms of 1695–96 applied only to silver, and hammered gold continued to be current until 1733.

This enormous programme entailed a considerable amount of work spread over a year. In the interim those hammered coins which were still unclipped continued to circulate and to prevent unscrupulous individuals from clipping them they were officially pierced through the centre. The tremendous volume of new coins required was too much for the Tower Mint to handle, and branch mints were consequently set up at Bristol, Chester, Exeter, Norwich and York; coins struck there in 1696–97 also bore initial letters B,C,E,N or a lower-case y respectively. That the king had become a mere cypher in such matters is shown by the fact that the order for the new coinage dies was made by Charles Montagu, Chancellor of the Exchequer, on 18 November 1695 – more than a week before William made his speech to parliament and a fortnight before the enabling Act was passed.

There was an air of desperation – almost panic – in the manner in which the great recoinage was carried out. The large number of dies required have all the hallmarks of haste in their preparation. Letters were cut inverted or reversed, punctuation was omitted and even, in a few rare instances, the four shields of the reverse were arranged in the wrong order!

The crown alone seems to have been struck entirely in London. Three busts, differing mainly in the position of the hair, and three reverse dies, varying mainly in details of the Irish harp, were used. Only one example of the second bust and first harp has been recorded. The enormous range of half-crowns can be reduced to manageable proportions by dividing them into the major categories. The first of these had small shields, the second large shields and a harp of the first type, while the third had large shields and a restyled harp. Each of these major types may be found without a mintmark, or with the initial letters of the subsidiary mints beneath the bust, and all with the date 1696. Like the crown, examples of both the half-crown and the shilling with the second bust (hair across breast) are unique, while similar versions of the sixpence, dated 1696, are extremely rare, but more plentiful dated 1697. In 1698 a new reverse was adopted for the half-crown, the detail in the large shields being substantially modified, and struck in considerable quantities until 1701. In the latter year half-crowns from African and Welsh silver are known with the elephant and castle or plumes privy-marks respectively.

Silver crown of 1696. (*Peter Clayton*)

Apart from the crown, the shilling and sixpence were also struck in 1695, prior to the great recoinage, with a profile of the king on his own. Both coins, as the most popular denominations in circulation, were struck in vast quantities and inevitably yielded the greatest number of die variants. The shillings with the first bust were struck at the Tower in 1695–97 and at all five subsidiary mints in 1696–97, York using both capital and lower-case initial letters in both years. As well as the unique second bust, already mentioned, the third bust was introduced at Chester and York in 1696 and used generally at the Tower and all branch mints in 1697. A modified form of this bust was also used for shillings struck at the Tower in 1697–98, some of the later date having Welsh plumes in the angles between the shields on the reverse. The third bust was also used at Bristol and Chester in 1697. By 1698 the volume of shillings required had slackened off and production was thereafter confined to the Tower Mint. A new bust – generally known as the 'flaming hair' bust – was used in 1698–99, while a fifth, with a more restrained coiffeur, was used in 1699–1701. Coins struck from Welsh silver may be found with a plume below the king's bust (1700) or plumes in the angles on the reverse (1699 and 1701), while those struck in 1699 from silver mined in the west of England had roses in the angles.

Silver shilling, 1700, with fifth bust of William III. (*Peter Clayton*)

Not surprisingly, the enormous output of sixpences also resulted in a large number of variables, making for an immense series of collectable varieties. The three busts were combined with a range of armorial reverses differing in the size of the crowns and the details of the harp. Added to this was the complexity of the initial letters used by the branch mints in 1696–97 and the later privy-marks of plumes and roses, which followed the same pattern as the shillings. The smallest silver coins, by contrast, were fairly straight-forward. Apart from the unique fourpence of 1697 these coins were not struck until 1698 but all four were produced annually thereafter until 1701. Fourpences were also minted in large quantities in 1702 – the only coin struck in the last year of the reign. These coins continued the pattern previously established, with a crowned numeral of value on the reverse.

The upheavals of the silver coinage had little effect on the gold coins, apart from the use of a single profile, the dies for which were engraved by a young Dutchman, John Croker, who was probably also responsible for the crown and 'Maundy' dies. Two dies were used for the five-guinea obverse, the latter having finer detail in the hair. The first bust was used in 1699 and 1700 and the second in 1701. A similar bust was used for the two-guinea coin, which was only struck in 1701.

Guineas with the first bust were minted in 1695–97, but a new die with prominent lettering and a more striking profile was introduced in 1697 and used with a new reverse in which the harp was given a human head. This combination was used for most guineas dated between 1697 and 1701. A third reverse, with a scrolled harp, was used in 1701, while a third bust with much finer detail was also adopted late that year. Only one major obverse type was used for the half-guinea, but two reverses, differing in the style of the harp, were used in 1695–96 and 1697–1701 respectively. All of the gold series may be found with or without the elephant and castle mintmark.

Gold guinea of 1695 with first laureate bust of William III. (*Peter Clayton*)

Considerable quantities of copper farthings and halfpence were struck throughout this period, showing the king in Roman armour, with the usual Britannia reverse. The king's name was rendered as GVLIELMVS TERTIVS instead of III DEI GRA as on the precious metal coinage. There were three types of halfpenny, differing in details of the reverse. In the first type (1695–98) Britannia's right hand was raised and the date appeared in the exergue; in the second (1698–99) the date appeared at the end of the legend round the circumference; and in the third (1699–1701) Britannia's right hand rested on her knee. Most farthings conformed to the first type and were dated from 1695 to 1700. A second type, with the date at the end of the legend, was also used in 1698–99.

CHAPTER THIRTEEN

Anne (1702–1714)

The younger daughter of James II and Anne Hyde succeeded to the throne, on the death of her brother-in-law from pneumonia following a fall from his horse, on 8 March 1702. Most of her life had been spent in quiet obscurity with her husband, Prince George of Denmark, and her only really close friend was Sarah Churchill. On her accession Anne appointed her husband generalissimo and Lord High Admiral, while her favourite John Churchill got a dukedom and the captain-generalship of the army. Her reign was characterised by a prolonged power struggle between the Tories and Whigs. The Marlboroughs intrigued with the Whigs and when a Tory majority was secured in the parliament of 1711 the one-time favourites (with whom relations were now sour) were dismissed. The Tories worked to secure the succession of Prince James, the son of James II, whose birth in 1688 had been denounced by the Whigs as an imposture; the Whigs and the Duke of Marlborough favoured the claim of George Louis, Elector of Hanover, through his descent from Elizabeth of Bohemia, the 'winter Queen' and daughter of James I. Anne's sudden death on 1 August 1714, four years after the death of her only child to survive infancy, caught the Tories unawares and the Whigs engineered the succession of George Louis peacefully.

Anne's reign was marked by domestic tragedy and increasing isolation. Her health was grievously affected by the quarrels of her courtiers and the factiousness and jealousy which soured her friendships. She took no interest in the arts, yet this was to be regarded as a period of cultural renaissance in England. Her reign was marked by the prolonged struggle with Louis XIV, but Marlborough's brilliant victories in Europe and Rooke's exploits at sea brought Britain the status of a major world power. Internally, her reign was notable for the political unification of Great Britain. Two centuries after the romantic union of the Thistle and the Rose and a century after the union of the Crowns, England and Scotland were still very much apart, and their separateness tended to be exacerbated by political and economic factors, particularly Scottish support for the Jacobite cause and the exclusion of Scottish merchants from English trade. Anne saw that the survival of Britain could only be assured if the kingdoms were united, and though the way in which the Act of Union was forced on the Scottish parliament was highly questionable, the beneficial results were immediate. The Union of 1707 is of considerable importance numismatically, since it was the watershed between the two halves of Anne's reign.

Pre-Union coinage, 1702–7

All of the English coin dies in this period were cut by John Croker. A left-facing bust of the queen gives a good idea of her ample proportions at the time of her accession. Her prodigious appetite was well known and gave rise to a popular quatrain of the 1690s:

> King William thinks all
> Queen Mary talks all
> Prince George drinks all
> And Princess Anne eats all.

Of the gold coins only guineas and half-guineas were minted in 1702 and no further issues were regularly made until 1705 when guineas, half-guineas and five-guineas were struck. Both higher values appeared in 1706 but guineas alone were produced in the early part of 1701 before the Union. A very few guineas and half-guineas were issued in 1703 with the word VIGO beneath the queen's bust, and alluded to Admiral Rooke's capture of Spanish bullion at Vigo in 1702. The pre-Union gold coins had reverses showing the four crowned shields and crossed sceptres of the previous pattern. The shields showed the leopards, lion rampant, lilies and harp respectively, with the English rose at the centre.

In the silver series only shillings were struck in 1702, the reverse being similar to the gold, but without the sceptres and having the star of the

Shilling of 1703 struck from silver captured at Vigo. (*Peter Clayton*)

Garter in the centre. Shillings from Welsh silver had tiny plumes between the shields. A large part of the silver captured at Vigo was used for 1702 shillings and those with the name below the bust are as plentiful as the ordinary variety. All of the shilling; struck in 1703 bore this word, and in the same year crowns and sixpences, similarly marked, were also released. Half-crowns inscribed VIGO are also quite plentiful, but this denomination was also issued without the inscription and is comparatively elusive. The four smallest denominations – penny, twopence, threepence and fourpence – were also issued in 1703, with the crowned numeral reverse which was now standard. They alone were unaffected by the political changes of the Union and retained the same obverse and reverse designs until the end of the reign. No pennies were minted in 1704 or 1707 and no fourpences in 1707. None of the smaller coins was struck in 1711–12 and this, therefore, reduces the number of 'Maundy' sets to seven, with the dates 1703, 1705–6, 1708–10 and 1713.

Of the larger coins, only the shilling was struck in any quantity with reasonable regularity, owing to the chronic shortage of silver throughout the reign, apart from the Vigo windfall of 1702–3. None was struck in 1706, while in other years coins were often issued with plumes in all four angles or with plumes and roses in alternate angles to denote the source of the silver. Half-crowns with plumes in the angles were minted in some quantity in 1704 and 1705, and coins with roses and plumes were abundantly produced in 1706–7. No sixpences appeared in 1704, but a large amount appeared in 1705 and may be divided into four varieties, according to the reverse (with shields engraved by Croker or more crudely by Samuel Bull), with or without roses and plumes. Sixpences with roses and plumes appeared in 1707. Crowns with plumes in the angles were issued in 1705 and those with both roses and plumes appeared in 1706–7.

Post-Union coinage, 1707–14

The Treaty of Union was approved by the Scottish parliament in January 1707 and subsequently ratified at Westminster. It is curious, therefore, that the five-guinea should have anticipated the outcome by appearing with the revised shields but dated 1706. It is not known whether Croker or Bull engraved the new reverses but they differed in two important respects from the pre-Union type. The English rose at the centre on the gold coins was replaced by the star of the Garter, as on the silver, and the top and bottom shields were vertically halved and contained the heraldic elements of England and Scotland in each half. The Irish harp and French lilies appeared in the other shields as before. Much broader shields were used for the five-guineas of 1709.

Production of guineas and half-guineas with the new reverse began in the middle of 1707. Halves were minted each year thereafter down to 1714, but no major varieties occurred. Three busts were used for the guineas. The first

Third bust 1711 gold guinea of the post-Union coinage. (*Peter Clayton*)

was designed by Sir Godfrey Kneller and was the type used in the pre-Union coinage; it is known on guineas of 1707 and 1708, the latter being very rare. The second bust was designed and probably also engraved by Croker himself and barely a handful of 1707 guineas are known with this type, but it was used for most 1708 guineas and all of those dated 1709, with or without the elephant and castle privy-mark. A third bust, also designed by Croker, showed the queen with coarser features and a more prominent double chin. It was used for guineas struck in 1710—14. The last of the gold coins to appear was the two-guinea, which was not added to this series until 1709. No appreciable variants have been noted for the years in which it was struck, 1709, 1711 and 1713—14.

The Act of Union had a major repercussion on the silver coins. The Edinburgh Mint, which had a continuous history spanning four centuries, was gradually run down after 1707 and closed in 1709. In the interim crowns (1707—8), half-crowns (1707—9), shillings (1707—9) and sixpences (1707—8) were struck at Edinburgh for circulation throughout the United Kingdom, with the new type of reverse. Their origin was denoted by a mintmark beneath the bust. This usually consisted of a capital E, but all shillings and some sixpences also included a tiny star. In addition, distinctive profiles of the queen, engraved at Edinburgh, were used for shillings and sixpences, and are also noted with the variation in mintmarks.

1707 shilling struck from Vigo silver in Edinburgh — hence letter E. below bust. (*Peter Clayton*)

The post-Union silver struck at the Tower Mint is less complex. The second bust was used for crowns struck in 1707—8 but no further issue was made until 1713 when a third and coarser bust was used, with roses and plumes on the reverse. Ordinary half-crowns were produced in 1707–9 and 1713, while 'plumes' half-crowns appeared in 1708 and 'rose and plume' coins in 1710 and from 1712 to 1714. The greatest variety occurs in the shillings, due to their comparatively large output. A third bust designed by Croker and probably engraved by Bull was used for ordinary shillings minted annually from 1707 until 1711. 'Plume' shillings appeared in 1707–8, while 'rose and plume' shillings may be found with the second bust (1708), third bust (1708 or 1710) and fourth bust or older and coarser bust (1710, 1712 and 1714) or 1713 overstruck on 1712. The shillings of 1711 had the reverse without roses or plumes.

A similar pattern was followed by the sixpence, only one bust being used throughout. Coins minted in 1707–8 and 1711 had a plain reverse but some produced in the first period had plumes in the angles, while all of those struck in 1710 had both roses and plumes.

Queen Anne farthing, struck only in last year of her reign. (*Coin Monthly*)

No base-metal halfpence were minted at all and farthings were confined to the last year of the reign. Both obverse and reverse dies were cut by Croker and this humble coin is one of the more elegant examples of his work. The profile of the ageing queen is more sympathetic than the usually gross portraits found on the silver coins, and the figure of Britannia on the reverse is singularly graceful. Probably because Queen Anne farthings were only struck in 1714 and were always rather elusive, stories began to circulate much later on that they were of enormous value. The most extraordinary event concerning this coin occurred in Dublin in 1814 when a man was prosecuted for borrowing and detaining a Queen Anne farthing. Counsel for the prosecution related the old canard that only three examples had been struck and added that a reward of £500 had been offered for a lost specimen. The judge and jury swallowed this tale and the unfortunate defendant was sentenced to a year's imprisonment!

CHAPTER FOURTEEN

George I (1714–1727)

By the Act of Settlement (1701) succession to the English throne devolved on Sophia, dowager electress of Hanover and sister of Prince Rupert, the erstwhile cavalry commander in the Civil War, once the immediate Stuart line ceased. The death of Princess Anne's son William in 1700, and the deaths in 1702 of William of Orange and the Electress Sophia, left the way open to the latter's son George Louis, who had succeeded to the Hanoverian throne on the death of his father in 1698. George's connection with the English throne, through the female line, was very tenuous and it has been calculated that he had no fewer than fifty-seven cousins with a stronger claim. Many of them were automatically debarred because they were Catholics and, besides, Hanover was a useful ally of Holland and Britain in the struggles against France which temporarily abated with the Treaty of Utrecht in 1713. Even so, George's accession to the throne was not a foregone conclusion and many Tories favoured Prince James Francis Edward, the 'Old Pretender'. A consensus of government ministers, however, felt that a Stuart succession would lead to civil war and when Anne suddenly fell ill they acted with commendable speed to strengthen the Tower and Edinburgh Castle, seal the ports and prepare mayors and garrison commanders for the proclamation of King George the moment the queen expired. George's accession, on 1 August 1714, was therefore accomplished quite smoothly.

The Jacobite backlash, which resulted in widespread rebellion in 1715, paradoxically helped to stabilise the country. The uprising was easily crushed and opponents of the Hanoverian succession discredited. Thereafter the United Kingdom enjoyed comparative tranquillity, which the abortive Jacobite rebellion of 1719 barely disturbed. George took little interest in his new kingdom, using it to advance the interests of Hanover. He was content to leave the daily routine of government to his ministers and in this period the cabinet system advanced in power and prestige. That George attached more importance to his position as Prince Elector of Hanover than as King of Great Britain and Ireland is revealed by the inscription which appeared on the first coin of his reign, the guinea of 1714. The reverse, reciting his German titles in abbreviated form, included the letters PR (*Prince*). From 1715 onwards, however, this was dropped from the guinea and omitted in the legends of all the other coins.

Work on a new series of coins was put in hand almost immediately after the accession though only the guinea was ready before the end of the year. Relatively few of the 'Prince Elector' guineas were struck. All of the obverse dies for the new coinage were engraved by Croker, while most of the reverse dies were cut by the Swiss jeweller, Johan Rudolf Ochs. Croker's obverses followed the well-established tradition of a right-facing profile and the usual titles in an abbreviated Latin form. The reverse motif was the cruciform arrangement of shields surmounted by crowns, with the Garter star in the centre. The gold coins had sceptres in the angles while the silver coins had a variety of privy-marks. Round the circumference of the reverse was a recital of George's German titles in abbreviated form: BRVN. ET L. DVX S.R.I. A. TH. ET (PR.) EL. – *Duke of Brunswick and Luneberg, Arch Treasurer of the Holy Roman Empire and (Prince) Elector.*

Croker cut a new obverse die for the guineas minted in 1715. This type, known as the second head, differed from the first in the detail of the king's hair and the ribbon at the back. This head was regarded as unsatisfactory and a third bust was produced a few months later and used for the vast majority of guineas released in 1715. Guineas with this bust were issued early in 1716 but were rapidly superseded by a fourth bust which evidently met with satisfaction since it was used for all guineas until 1722 and a fair proportion of those minted in 1723. A few guineas of 1721–22 are known with the elephant and castle mark. In the latter year, when George was in his sixty-third year, a more mature profile was adopted for the guinea and showed the heavy jowls and thickening of the neck as well as the puffy eyes which were a Guelph family characteristic. This bust was used for most guineas of 1723 and all of those struck in 1724–27. George died in June 1727 but very few guineas had been minted prior to that, and consequently those bearing that date are quite elusive. Only those guineas struck in 1726 can be said to be fairly plentiful, and this was the only year in which they were also issued with the elephant and castle mintmark.

Half-guineas were minted each year from 1715, with the exception of

Fifth bust gold guinea. (*Peter Clayton*)

1716. Relatively few halves were issued, however, and those dated 1721 and 1723 are extremely rare, while those of 1715, 1720 and 1724 are scarce. The elephant and castle mark was only used in 1721 – a rarity with or without this mark. One bust sufficed for all half-guineas until 1725 when an older portrait was adopted. Halves of 1725 are quite plentiful, but those of 1726 and 1727 were issued in decreasing numbers. No five-guinea pieces were minted until 1716 and thereafter they appeared only intermittently, in 1717, 1720 and 1726. Two-guineas did not appear until 1717 and thenceforward only appeared in the same years as the five-guineas. In each case only one set of dies was employed, and none is recorded with the elephant and castle mark. Although gold was in short supply in this reign, silver was even scarcer, and it was during one of those periodic shortages that embarrassed the government that the issue of the tiny quarter-guinea was sanctioned. This coin was struck in 1718 in considerable quantities, at the expense of the guinea which was not released that year. The profile of the king on this coin was little short of parody, but it was less popular on account of its size and no further issues were made.

The tremendous growth in the economy in the early years of the eighteenth century and the increase in the money supply put a severe strain on the gold reserves, but an effort was made to issue guineas and half-guineas in reasonable quantities. Many of these coins drained abroad, partly because they were rather undervalued in Britain and partly because they were used to pay Hanoverian and mercenary troops in George's service. This is a pattern which became more accentuated as the century wore on. For the moment, however, it was the acute famine in silver which caused the greatest problems. To be sure, silver was still being imported into Europe in vast quantities, but Britain was cut off from normal supplies by her wars with France and Spain. Consequently the silver coinage of George I is sparse by comparison with the gold. Of the eight denominations, only the shilling was minted in any quantity. The obverse dies of the silver coins showed George in a Roman toga with laureated hair. Only the four largest coins (sixpence to crown) recited his titles in full, the smaller coins (penny to fourpence) restricting the inscription to GEORGIVS DEI GRA on the obverse and MAG. BRI. FR. ET HIB. REX on the reverse. The smaller coins retained the crowned

Silver half-crown of 1720 with roses and plumes in angles. (*Royal Mint*)

numerals, while the higher denominations featured the four shields surmounted by crowns. These coins often bore sets of initials in the angles to denote the source of the bullion.

The smaller coins were struck at intermittent intervals and it is only possible to make up two 'Maundy' sets – 1723 and 1727. The most prolific of the silver coins, the shilling, set the pattern for the other higher denominations. Two busts were used, differing in the ribbon at the back of the king's head. The first bust was used for shillings of 1715–23. The normal coins had roses and plumes alternately in the angles denoting the use of silver provided by the Company for Smelting Pit Coale and Sea Coale, but shillings of 1720–21 were issued without any privy-marks. The second bust was used with roses and plumes for shillings struck in 1723–27. Shillings minted from silver supplied by the Welsh Copper Company bore this company's initials beneath the bust and were issued in 1723–26.

Half-crowns were struck sporadically from 1715 to 1726, a single bust being used. Examples dated 1715 with void spaces between the shields are regarded as proofs, the normal issue having roses and plumes. Much smaller privy-marks were used for the coins dated 1726. Crowns were first minted in 1716, and again two years later with 1718 overstruck on 1716. A few crowns appeared in 1720, overstruck on 1718, and even fewer in 1726. No sixpences appeared until 1717 and then there was a three-year gap before they appeared again. Smaller roses and plumes were used on sixpences released in 1726.

Quite a large minting of the four larger coins was made in 1723 with the marks ss and c in alternate angles on the reverse, denoting bullion supplied by the ill-fated South Sea Company, which had been founded in 1711 with the intention of taking over some £9 million of the national debt in exchange for a monopoly of trade with South America. Despite its name it was primarily a financial corporation, intended as a Tory counter to the Whig-orientated Bank of England. It over-reached itself in 1719 when it formulated a scheme to take over all £51 million of the national debt. Shares in the company soared and triggered off a wave of speculation in which hundreds of companies were formed and issued shares for the most incredible

1723 silver half-crown with ssc South Sea Company in the angles. (*Christie's*)

purposes. The government passed the aptly-named Bubble Act in 1720 to check this irresponsible activity. When the South Sea Company sued four of these companies in a vain bid to demonstrate to the public how reputable it was, confidence sagged and share values dipped, then plummeted sharply and by the end of September the financial market had utterly collapsed. The bursting of the South Sea Bubble almost destroyed the Whig government but out of the chaos emerged Robert Walpole who became, in effect, the first prime minister in 1721 and continued in office until 1742. Part of the assets of the South Sea Company, used to pay off its debts, was the large quantity of silver which was used for the coins of 1723 and which serve, to this day, as a reminder of one of the most colourful episodes in English financial history.

Copper halfpence and farthings did not appear until 1717 and continued the tradition of portraying the king in the garb of a Roman emperor, while the reverse had Britannia with the date in the exergue. The halfpence of 1717–18 and the farthings of 1717 were struck on thick flans, hence their nickname of the 'Dump' issue. A second type of each coin, on broader and thinner flans, appeared in 1719 and continued until 1724. The farthings of this reign tend to be scarcer than the corresponding halfpence.

CHAPTER FIFTEEN

George II (1727–1760)

George Augustus, Earl of Cambridge (1706) and Prince of Wales (1714) was, like many of his successors, often at odds with his father. As king, he was virtually devoid of any ability to govern the country but had one saving grace: he recognised ability in others and knew when to give way to them. It was during his long reign of thirty-three years that Britain was truly transformed into a constitutional monarchy with the king as a mere figurehead and all real power in the hands of the prime minister and the cabinet. Paradoxically, he was the last British monarch to lead his troops personally into battle, at Dettingen in 1743. In personal appearance he was one of the best-looking of the Hanoverians, lacking the grossness which characterised his father, his brother the infamous Duke of Cumberland and his descendants George III and George IV. The earliest profiles, engraved by John Croker, show quite sensitive features and a firm jaw, but the prim little mouth that betrayed his inherently petty nature.

The only coins which appeared in the first year of his reign were the guinea and the shilling, the commonest gold and silver denominations. The first guineas of 1727 attempted to cram in the usual array of abbreviated titles on the reverse, using very tiny lettering which is scarcely legible. A new reverse was rapidly engraved with more prominent lettering which necessitated reducing the size of the shield. The first type of guinea is elusive, though both versions of the 1727 guinea are scarce anyway. Those minted in 1728 are even scarcer if anything, and this set the pattern for the gold coinage of this reign. Apart from some proofs in 1729 with a slimmer bust, no guineas were issued until 1730, and only in 1731 was anything like an abundant quantity produced, but fewer were produced in 1732. Guineas minted bullion supplied by the East India Company bore the letters E.I.C. below the truncation of the king's neck.

A new obverse die, with larger lettering, was introduced in 1732. Guineas of that date with this die are very rare but from then onwards it was used regularly until 1738. By that time George was in his fifty-fifth year so a less youthful portrait was required. The task of engraving new dies for the entire coinage was entrusted to Croker's assistant, John Sigismund Tanner, a native of Saxe-Gotha who had worked at the Royal Mint since 1728. This portrait is known as the intermediate head and was used until 1746. Guineas appeared fitfully from 1739 to 1741 and apart from a very few in 1743 none appeared again until 1745. The obverse die was then modified and the lettering enlarged. A new profile was adopted in 1747, when the king was sixty-four. This was engraved by Tanner and it shows how the king's features had coarsened in old age. Guineas were minted in reasonable quantities from 1747 until 1760, except for 1754 and 1757.

The half-guinea followed a similar pattern, with Croker's young head from 1728 until 1739, an intermediate head by Tanner in 1740 and 1745–46 (a specimen dated 1743 is believed to be unique), and Tanner's old head on coins from 1747 to 1760. Theoretically they were minted annually, but those dated 1730 and 1737 are extremely rare, while halves dated 1733 and 1735 have never been discovered, though they are believed to exist. Half-guineas with the E.I.C. mark were issued in 1729–30 in some quantity but those dated 1731, 1732 and 1739 are exceedingly rare. Like the guineas, no halves were minted in 1754 or 1757 and those dated 1749 are a major rarity. As the supply of gold improved towards the end of the reign the minting of half-guineas correspondingly rose and those of 1759–60 are particularly plentiful.

Gold two-guinea piece of 1739 with intermediate laureate head designed by John Tanner. (*Christie's*)

No five-guineas were minted until 1729 and thereafter only spasmodically, in 1731, 1735, 1738 and 1741. Paradoxically, the coins with the E.I.C. mark, issued in 1729, are more plentiful than those without. An older head by Tanner was adopted in 1746 and subsequently used in 1748 and 1753. The two-guinea was even more fleeting in its appearance. Intriguingly, the first of these appeared in 1734 with the date overstruck on 1733 – a year in which no two-guineas were actually issued. Two-guineas were struck regularly in 1735 and 1738–39. Tanner's intermediate head was used for coins in 1739–40, while the old head was used in 1748 and 1753. In 1733 the last of the hammered gold coins were demonetised. This was heralded by a commendable attempt to produce a sufficiency of guineas that year, though the other three denominations were neglected.

The production of silver coins in this reign was patchy. Reasonable quantities were produced in the first twelve years but thereafter they were minted sporadically. There was a silver famine in Britain in the mid-eighteenth century, despite the improved techniques of mining and refining in Latin America and Central Europe which meant a superabundance of the metal. Much of this silver was siphoned off, however, by the growing trade between Mexico and the Philippines along which route the Spanish dollars made their way eventually to China and Southeast Asia.

The Hanoverian connection did little for the British economy. British gold was exported to pay Hanoverian troops and Hessian mercenaries hired by George II in his interminable wars with France. The underlying cause of these wars, fought in Europe and North America, was economic, and it was in this sphere that they were largely waged. France and Spain sought to cut off Britain's silver supplies and the measure of their success is evident in the conspicuous lack of silver coinage from 1739 onwards, with one notable exception.

Between 1741 and 1744 Admiral George Anson made a round-world voyage, the chief object of which was to raid the Spanish ports on the Pacific seaboard of South America. In June 1743 he captured a Spanish treasure ship loaded with bullion from the silver mines of Peru, with an estimated value of £1¼ million. On his triumphant return to England Anson was raised to the peerage and the bullion was used to mint coins: the five-guinea (1746), the guinea and half-guinea (1745), crown (1746), half-crown (1745–46), shilling (1745–46) and sixpence (1745–46). These coins bore the word LIMA (the Peruvian capital) below the king's bust.

For the silver coins Croker engraved busts of the king in Roman dress armour, an unusual feature being the lion's mask decorating the shoulder piece. As on the gold coins, the king was shown in the full-bottomed wig

Five-guinea of 1746 struck from silver taken from captured Spanish treasure ship laden with bullion from mines of Peru, by Admiral George Anson. Hence word LIMA. (*Peter Clayton*)

fashionable in the early eighteenth century, a concession to the Roman idiom being the laurel crown. Larger lettering was adopted for the obverse in 1734 and shillings were struck in comparative abundance from then until 1739 and at two-yearly intervals thereafter, with Tanner's old bust from 1743 onwards, and privy-marks of roses and plumes, or roses alone to denote silver from the west of England mines. After the Lima shillings, production fell sharply and no shillings were issued from 1747 until 1750 when an attempt was made to strike a large supply. Relatively few were issued in 1751 and no more until 1758 when the largest quantity in one year were minted.

The sixpences followed a similar pattern, with Croker's young bust on coins from 1728 to 1741 and Tanner's old bust from 1743 until 1758. The presence or absence of the plumes, plumes and roses or roses privy-marks on the reverse add to the variety of these coins. The subsidiary silver coinage did not appear until 1729, the year in which they were used more or less exclusively for the royal Maundy ceremony. Even then, no attempt was made to produce sets each year and there were many years between 1730 and 1745 when none was minted at all, while from 1746 until 1759 only pennies were struck. It was not until 1760 that all four coins were produced again. Croker's young bust was used throughout this long period of more than 30 years.

Half-crowns did not appear until 1731; those with that date and a plain reverse are thought to have been proofs. The normal issue had roses and plumes on the reverse and an abundant quantity was produced in 1731–32, but fewer coins appeared in 1734–35 and very few in 1736, the latter with rose alone on the reverse. 'Roses' half-crowns were struck in some quantity in 1739 and 1741. Tanner's old bust was used for intermittent issues from 1743 onwards, but production tailed off in 1751. Crowns did not make their debut until 1732 and thereafter followed the pattern of the half-crowns, with the young bust (1732, 1734–36, 1739 and 1741) and the old head (1743, 1746 and 1750–51). The last issue, with no privy-marks, was produced from imported silver and, significantly, is the scarcest crown of this reign.

Considering the dearth of subsidiary silver coinage for general circulation it is surprising that no attempt was made to strike pennies in copper. Copper halfpence were produced in abundance from 1729 to 1754 and farthings from

Silver half-crown, young head of George II with roses on reverse. (*Royal Mint*)

Copper farthing of 1735. (*Peter Clayton*)

1730 to 1754, but no base-metal coins appeared after the latter date and thus triggered off the spate of trade tokens from the mid-eighteenth century onwards. As with the earlier issues, these coins featured the king in Roman dress (with the Roman hairstyle instead of the usual wig) on the obverse and the seated figure of Britannia on the reverse. The date appeared in the exergue beneath Britannia. Croker's young bust was used for the coins up to 1739 and Tanner's old bust thereafter. Halfpence from 1740 to 1745 (with the exception of 1741 when none was issued) showed the king's name as GEORGIUS, but thenceforward the form GEORGIVS was used. GEORGIUS farthings were released only in 1741 and 1744, while those inscribed GEORGIVS appeared in 1746, 1749–50 and 1754. The farthings were never as popular as the halfpence and several dates – 1732, 1734, 1741, 1744 and 1750 – are notably scarce.

CHAPTER SIXTEEN

George III (1760–1820)

The king who ascended the throne on 25 October 1760 was a very different person from his grandfather, George II. He was the first Hanoverian ruler to have been born in England, a fact he emphasised in his inaugural speech to parliament in 1761. George III had the longest reign of any English king up to that time, a dubious distinction. In the first two decades George controlled Treasury patronage and by shrewd manipulation of the elections secured absolute power, summoning and dismissing ministers almost at will. He was not without vigorous opposition, from John Wilkes onwards, but on the whole he governed firmly and wisely in those early years. The disastrous war with the American colonies (1776–83), however, resulted in a censure motion against the Crown in parliament (1780) and George considered abdicating on two occasions. On the latter occasion (1783) he set out a very detailed admission of failure and though he did not go through with his intention to abdicate this marks a very clear division in British constitutional history. Thereafter no monarch has had the same control over parliament. The middle period of this reign was dominated by the younger William Pitt, MP at 21 and prime minister at 24. He held this supreme office from 1784 until 1806 (with a gap in 1801–4), when he died at the early age of 46. He was the architect of national recovery and the economic miracle which transformed Britain, after the only war Britain ever lost, to become the most powerful country in Europe in the space of a single decade. Undoubtedly the stress created by the responsibilities of conducting the French Revolutionary and Napoleonic Wars, in which Britain was often alone against France and her satellites, brought Pitt to his early grave. Such was the firm foundation he had laid down that the government continued to prosecute the war successfully, though peace was not attained until 1815. Long before that, however, the insanity which had begun to manifest itself as early as 1765 had overtaken the king. The last years of his reign were, in fact, a regency under the Prince of Wales (1811). Madness, compounded by blindness, brought this reign to its tragic and pathetic close.

First period, 1760–86

During the first twenty-five years of this reign, official coinage reached its nadir. Gold coins alone were struck in any quantity – and even this is a relative term – while silver was virtually non-existent and copper disappeared after 1775. The only gold coins in general circulation were the guinea and its sub-divisions. Larger coins exist only as patterns dated 1768 (two-guinea), 1770 (five-guinea) and 1773 and 1777 (both denominations), and these are all exceedingly rare. The guinea alone was minted with any degree of regularity, four profiles being used. The first was designed by Tanner, but probably engraved by his assistant Richard Yeo, as Tanner's eyesight was failing. The first head was only used in 1761 and scrapped as unsatisfactory. A second profile was engraved by Yeo and used for guineas of 1763–64. This was larger and better proportioned than the first. A third, altering the tilt of the forehead and chin, was used for guineas from 1765 until 1773. A more mature bust was adopted in 1774 and used until 1786, with the exception of 1780. These guineas are fairly straightforward with no major variants. The reverse had a heraldic shield garnished in the prevailing rococo fashion, with quarters showing conjoint arms of England and Scotland, the tripartite arms of Brunswick, Luneberg and Hanover, and the lilies and harp of France and Ireland. The Latin titles had the usual string of abbreviations signifying the king's royal, ducal and electoral status.

Gold guinea of 1761, George III first head. (*Peter Clayton*)

Half-guineas parallel the development of the guinea, but were not so frequently or so abundantly minted. The first head was used in 1762–63, the second intermittently from 1764 to 1774, the third, a much coarser bust, for a very few halves in 1774 and a larger quantity in 1775, and the fourth, the mature profile, from 1775 until 1786 (again, with the exception of 1780 and 1782). The tiny quarter-guinea was only minted in 1762. Although it was struck in some quantity it was unpopular and never quite filled the gap left by the larger silver coins.

This reign began when the Seven Years' War (1756–63) was at its height and Britain was denied access to the rich supplies of Spanish-American silver. No large coins were produced in this period at all, and the only shillings were those struck in 1763 for the use of Hugh, Earl of Northumberland, to distribute to the populace when he was installed in Dublin as Viceroy of

1763 'Northumberland shilling' for distribution to populace of Dublin. (*Coin Monthly*)

Ireland that year. About £150 worth of silver was coined into these 'Northumberland' shillings which bore a youthful bust of the king by Yeo and a cruciform arrangement of shields on the reverse. No sixpences were minted either, and the four smallest denominations were only produced sporadically. The threepence alone appeared in 1762 and was produced in considerable quantities. Complete 'Maundy' sets are only possible for 1763, 1766, 1772, 1780, 1784 and 1786. The young bust of the king was retained throughout the entire period, with the usual crowned numeral reverses.

Subsidary copper coinage was produced during a very brief period only (1770–75), the king being portrayed in the Roman style, with the seated Britannia on the reverse. Halfpence were minted annually, but farthings only appeared in 1773–75 in sizeable quantities, and a few in 1771. The comparative trickle of copper coins in this period seems all the more surprising, given the virtual absence of silver. Unfortunately, the government never faced up to the problem, and felt that anything less than silver was somehow beneath its dignity. After 1775 the situation became well-nigh intolerable. The movement of population from the countryside to the new towns and cities, as the Industrial Revolution got under way, created an even greater need for coins of low face value, and the dearth of such money led to the evils of the truck system in which employers gave goods in exchange for labour. Tradesmen and innkeepers filled the gap with an enormous range of copper tokens which often served the dual purpose of advertisement and fiduciary coinage.

Second period, 1787–1816

An important trade treaty was negotiated with France in 1786, during one of those rare lulls in the almost continual warfare of the eighteenth century, and one result of this was a sudden influx of silver into Britain after years

123

of shortage. In the same year Pitt introduced the sinking fund and floated a £6 million loan from the public. He radically altered the tax system, shifting the balance to a wide range of indirect taxes of which the window tax was to become the most notorious. The economy took a turn for the better by the spring of 1787 and this encouraged an attempt to put the coinage back on a proper footing. The issue of silver coinage proved to be short-lived but there was a comparatively plentiful supply of gold, and this continued to be minted in considerable quantities almost to the end of the century, when the cost of conducting an expensive war took its toll.

The rococo ornament on the reverse of the gold coins gave way in 1787 to the much plainer and more functional spade format which was to give its name to the guineas of the ensuing period. Lewis Pingo, chief engraver of the Royal Mint, was responsible for the dies which incorporated a more mature profile of the king. The spade guinea was an immediate success though its familiarity to succeeding generations may be due mainly to the fact that it was parodied in the brass gambling counters of the nineteenth century, with their legend 'In memory of the good old days' in place of the king's titles. Spade guineas were struck each year from 1787 to 1799. Up to 1794 they were produced in reasonable quantity but as the war with revolutionary France began to strain the national resources the volume of gold coin decreased. In 1798 there was something like the pre-war output but few guineas were struck in 1799 and no more were produced for domestic consumption thereafter. The last of the guineas appeared in 1813 and were destined exclusively for Wellington's army in the Peninsula. A new profile of the king showed him with shorter hair and thick neck, while the coat of arms on the reverse was surrounded by the Garter. The so-called military guinea is the scarcest of the George III guineas.

1787 gold 'spade guinea' – often copied in brass for nineteenth century gaming counters. (*Peter Clayton*)

Half-guineas with the spade reverse were struck in 1787–1800 (except 1799). The Garter reverse was used in 1801–3 with an older portrait of the king. New dies, designed by Nathaniel Marchant and engraved by Pingo, were used for the halves of 1804–13 and portrayed the king with the short hair which had become fashionable after the outbreak of the French Revolution. The 'short hair' half-guineas are not so common as their predecessors, those dated 1805 being very rare. None was struck in 1812 while those dated

Gold third-guinea, tarriffed at 7 shillings, issued because of shortage of silver. Issued 1797–1804 and intermittently thereafter. (*Peter Clayton*)

1811 and 1813 are elusive. The chronic silver shortage inspired the issue of tiny third-guineas, tariffed at 7 shillings, which were minted in 1797–1804 and intermittently thereafter. This was the first coin designed by Nathaniel Marchant – not an auspicious start since the portrait of the king was nothing short of ludicrous. Wisely, however, no attempt was made to cram the usual coat of arms on to the reverse; the crown was the only motif and this gave the reverse an elegance which is oddly at variance with the crude profile on the obverse. Two reverse types were used, with the date at the foot (1797–1800) and in the field (1801–3), the latter also having a new inscription FIDEI DEFENSOR BRITANNIARUM REX (*Defender of the Faith, King of the Britains – i.e. the British Isles*). This title was adopted following the dissolution of the Irish parliament in 1801 and the creation of the United Kingdom. This style of reverse legend was later adopted by the Garter half-guinea and the military guinea of 1813. The change in legend and greater emphasis on the spiritual title set the pattern for most nineteenth-century coins. At long last the preposterous claim to the French throne was abandoned, doubtless because Britain was now championing the Bourbon *émigrés* against the revolutionary regime. The third-guinea adopted the short-hair profile in 1804. Thirds were struck in 1806, 1808–11 and 1813, the last dates being very elusive.

In 1787, when the market price of silver dropped substantially, some £87,000 worth was coined for general circulation, mainly in shillings and sixpences. Lewis Pingo is thought to have designed and engraved the dies for these coins, showing the king with full wig on the obverse but with a new reverse motif showing crowns in the angles of the shields instead of surmounting them as before. This permitted larger, more angular shields, but with the same layout of heraldic elements. Variants include the obverse

Silver shilling of 1787 with hearts in Hanoverian shield. (*Christie's*)

with or without a pellet over the king's head, and the reverses with no stops beside the date or with and without tiny hearts in the Hanoverian shield. The sixpence used only one obverse die, but the reverse may be found with or without hearts.

After this promising beginning the price of silver rose steeply and production of further coins became impossible. In 1798 several London bankers acquired a quantity of silver which they sent to the Mint for coining into shillings. About £30,000 worth of bullion was coined but before this consignment could be dispatched to the banks in question the Lords of the Committee in Council issued an order banning them and they were subsequently melted down. A very few escaped the melting pot and have survived under the name of the Dorrien and Magens shillings, from the Name of one of the banks involved, Messrs Dorrien, Magens, Mello, Martin and Harrison. Apparently Barclay's and Hoare's banks had also sent bullion to be coined, but this practice was stopped by an ordinance of 1798, giving as the reason the fear that such coins might have stimulated a demand from the general public for more, at a time when the government was powerless to effect this.

Significantly there were very few subsidiary silver coins in this period. They were not released with an older bust until 1792. The reverses showed the crowned numerals, but these figures were much thinner and rendered in cursive script, hence the nickname 'Wire Money' applied to this series. At the same time the size of the crown was greatly reduced and brought into the field, the date was moved from the top to the foot of the circle, and the lettering of the king's titles given more prominence and space. This elegant innovation was not repeated when the small silver coins next appeared in 1795. On that occasion more substantial numerals, surmounted by larger crowns, were employed, though the date remained at the foot. These coins were also issued in 1800, so Maundy sets can be made of both dates.

'Wire Money', so called from thin cursive script. (*Coin Monthly*)

During the period of token coppers the Birmingham partnership of Matthew Boulton and James Watt emerged as one of the most prolific producers, using steam-powered presses at their Soho Mint. Technically this mint was far ahead of its royal counterpart and, in Conrad Heinrich Küchler, it had a designer and engraver of considerable talents. Boulton and Watt specialised in all manner of copperware and had had some experience with the nascent American coinage, so they did not rest until they had secured a contract to strike copper coins for general circulation in Britain. Following

Copper 'cartwheel' penny, weighing 1 ounce, struck by Boulton and Watt in Birmingham on their new steam press. (*Coin Monthly*)

the recommendations of the Liverpool Committee in 1797 Boulton and Watt struck their famous cartwheel coins. The twopence weighed 2 oz. and the penny 1 oz.; unlike previous copper coins these pieces actually contained metal of their face value. This was a step backwards from the concept of fiduciary coinage inherent in the earlier subsidiary coppers, but such a compromise was probably the only way in which Boulton could have persuaded the government to take the radical step of substituting copper for silver.

The coins derive their nickname from the raised rim on which the inscriptions appeared incuse. These inscriptions followed the tradition of earlier coppers, and bore the shortened version of the king's title (obverse) BRITANNIA and the date (reverse). Again, the king was shown in Roman garb, a toga replacing the armour of the 1770s. Although Küchler is generally credited with designing these coins it is now known that the Coin Committee, which met in the spring of 1797 to consider designs, approved a reverse drawn by Nathaniel Dance whose drawing showed Britannia seated on a rock by the sea, with a man o' war on the horizon. In Dance's version the rock was engraved with the dates June 1st, June 23rd and February 14th – 'Three memorable Naval Victories obtained over Your Majesty's Enemies in the present War'. The dates refer, in fact, to Lord Howe's Glorious First of June (1794), Hotham's capture of three French ships (1795) and the defeat of the Spanish navy by Jervis off Cape St Vincent (1797). The Committee rejected this interesting idea and substituted an oval shield bearing the Union Jack. Britannia was shown cradling a trident in her left arm, while holding out the olive branch of peace with her right hand. The same design was used for both coins; similar halfpence and farthings, produced by the Soho Mint were never authorised and can only be regarded as patterns. The smaller coins were not issued until 1799 and then differed fundamentally from the cartwheels in having raised beaded rims with lettering in relief within the circumference. The twopence proved to be too heavy and clumsy for widespread acceptance and no further issues of this denomination were made. A new series of penny, halfpenny and farthing, with a short-haired bust of the king, was produced in 1806–7. The copper coinage from the Soho Mint

1799 copper halfpenny. (*Coin Monthly*)

amounted to £679,311 – a trifle by modern standards but, coming after the famine in regal subsidiary coinage, it must have seemed a welcome change and enabled the authorities to prohibit tokens.

While the government was making a valiant attempt to grapple with the problem of copper coinage, the lack of silver was increasingly exacerbated by the gradual disappearance of gold from 1800 onwards. By 1797 Spanish-American eight- and four-reales silver pieces were circulating freely in Britain and were given official status by being countermarked on the obverse with tiny profiles of George III. The dollar or eight-reales may be found with oval or octagonal countermarks, while the half-dollar is known only with the oval mark. In 1804 the Bank of England issued its own dollars. These were eight-reales entirely restruck with dies by Küchler, the obverse portraying George III and the reverse having an upright oval cartouche surmounted by a civic crown. The legend BANK OF ENGLAND and the date appeared round the edge, while the cartouche was inscribed FIVE SHILLINGS and DOLLAR at top and bottom. The vignette in the cartouche was a smaller version of Küchler's Britannia.

The Bank of England also produced smaller denominations, with a portrait of the king (obverse) and BANK TOKEN and the value (reverse). Two values were produced, the three shillings and the eighteenpence (actually inscribed

1796 silver crown, an oval countermark on a Madrid four-reales piece. (*Peter Clayton*)

1804 silver Bank of England dollar, or five-shilling piece. (*Coin Monthly*)

1s6d). A draped bust of the king in Roman armour was used for tokens dated 1811–12, the reverse showing the value in an oak wreath. New designs, adopted in 1812, were used for the majority of the tokens of that date and subsequent years until 1816. In this version a laureated head with truncated neck was used, while the wreath on the reverse was composed of oak and laurel leaves. A ninepence token prepared in 1812 exists only as a pattern. These bank dollars and tokens continued to provide the public with the larger silver denominations until 1816 when the entire coinage system was completely revolutionised.

The Great Recoinage, 1816–20

Robert Jenkinson, Earl of Liverpool, became prime minister on 11 May 1812 on the assassination of Spencer Perceval and held this office for fifteen years. He succeeded his father in the earldom in 1801. The first earl had a long political career but is best remembered for his book *Coins of the Realm*, published in the form of an open letter to the king (1805). He was chairman of the Coin Committee established by the Privy Council in 1797 to examine the problems facing the British currency. His son, the future prime minister, was actually Master of the Mint (1799–1801) and thus had a first-hand knowledge of the working of the Royal Mint.

One of the problems facing the mint was the purely physical one of overcrowding in the Tower of London where inadequate premises were uneasily shared with the army. The expansion of minting activity since the installation of machinery in 1662 had led to the gradual outhousing of several departments, resulting in loss of efficiency and breaches of security. New premises were designed by James Johnson and erected by the leading architect of the day, Sir Robert Smirke, on the site of an old tobacco ware-house on Little Tower Hill. Construction took more than a decade but by 1810 it was sufficiently advanced for personnel to be transferred to it from the Tower, though it was not fully operational until 1816. Steam-powered machinery was installed in 1807 and Mint technicians sent to Birmingham to learn the new technology from Boulton and Watt though eleven years elapsed before this equipment was actually utilised.

The reason for the inordinate delay seems to have been the reluctance of the government to accept the recommendations of the Coin Committee, and it was four years after Lord Liverpool's accession to the premiership that parliament finally accepted the report, enabling the new Royal Mint to make sweeping changes in the coinage. In 1812 Wellesley Pole was appointed Master Worker of the Mint and it was during his tenure of office that the most momentous changes took place. He was a brother of Marquess Wellesley and the Duke of Wellington, and succeeded to the family's Irish peerage as Earl of Mornington in 1821. His aristocratic background is reflected in his often high-handed conduct of the Mint but in fairness to him it needed a man of his autocratic calibre to force through the reforms so long overdue.

Lewis Pingo retired in 1815 and his place was taken by the Roman gemengraver, Benedetto Pistrucci, whose work was greatly admired by the Prince Regent. Pole was prevented by the Statute of Limitations from employing a foreigner in a crown office, but circumvented this by leaving the appointment vacant, while paying Pistrucci £500 per annum for doing the actual work. Pistrucci did well out of the arrangement; in addition to his salary, which was princely by nineteenth-century standards, he was given every facility for the pursuance of his own private work – a situation which he fully exploited. None the less the failure of Pole to implement verbal promises of the chief engravership continued to rankle with Pistrucci and was the subject of much carping on his part.

Following the acceptance by parliament of the recommendations of the Coin Committee in 1816, Britain adopted the gold standard which was to affect monetary policy for over a century. Henceforward gold was treated as the absolute standard of value, and silver was relegated to a subsidiary role in no fixed-value relationship to gold, thus abandoning bimetallism. There was a tremendous outcry at the scrapping of the guinea, then tariffed at 21 shillings, and its replacement by the slightly lighter sovereign of 20 shillings, but the new coin soon proved immensely popular. The guinea survived for a further 150 years as money of account, until decimalisation in 1971

Gold 1820 sovereign – an absolute standard of value after Britain's adoption of the gold standard in 1816. (*Christie's*)

rendered it impractical. Of even greater significance was the decision to revalue silver from 62 shillings to 66 shillings the pound troy, with a corresponding reduction in the size and weight of the new silver coins which thereafter had only fiduciary or token value. Silver ceased to be legal tender in unlimited amounts – the maximum now set being 40 shillings. This made silver more competitive as a monetary medium and freed from its ties to gold. The drastic reduction in the size of the coins also eliminated the age-old problem of coins disappearing from circulation almost as fast as they could be minted. Thereafter a plentiful supply of both gold and silver coins circulated freely, at a time when the need for coin increased enormously in the wake of the Industrial Revolution and the rapid expansion of the British economy.

Production of gold coins was delayed until 1817, and then only sovereigns and half-sovereigns were minted. Pistrucci designed the 'bull head' profiles of the king used for both obverses, as well as the splendid St George and Dragon reverse of the sovereign, while William Wyon designed and engraved the crowned shield reverse of the half-sovereign. It is said that a waiter from Brunet's Hotel, Leicester Square served as the model for St George. A novelty of this issue, for British coins at least, was the insertion of the date below the truncation of the neck on the obverse. At the same time the obverse legend was inscribed BRITANNIAR REX (*King of the British Isles*). In place of the usual Latin legend on the reverse appeared the French motto from the Garter: HONI SOIT QUI MAL Y PENSE (*Evil to him who evil thinks*). It is often stated that this made its debut on the George III coinage, although it can also be found, in very tiny lettering, on the Combe Martin half-crowns of the Civil War and on the Garter star forming the centrepiece of the reverses of the silver coins of Charles II. The half-sovereign followed the style of the half-guineas of 1804–13, but omitted the French motto from the reverse and shortened the Latin for 'Defender of the Faith'. The crown and shield on the reverse were larger than those on the half-guinea. Both sovereigns and half-sovereigns were minted in 1817–18 and 1820, but in 1819 only a relatively small quantity of sovereigns was struck. There were no higher denominations, though Pistrucci produced patterns for two- and five-pound coins in 1820, both showing St George and the Dragon without any inscription, thus creating a medallic appearance of great beauty.

The first of the new lightweight silver coins appeared in 1816 and comprised sixpence, shilling and half-crown, with obverses by Pistrucci and reverses by Thomas Wyon, Junior, showing the arms surrounded by the Garter and surmounted by a crown. Pistrucci's 'bull head' profile of the aged king raised a storm of controversy; it was confined to the half-crowns of 1816 and some early in 1817 before Pistrucci heeded the criticism and engraved a 'small head' profile. Wyon modified Pistrucci's profiles for the shilling and sixpence and worked on a new profile for the half-crown but in the end it was Pistrucci himself who designed and engraved new obverse and reverse dies for the half-crowns of 1817–20. In this version the king's head was greatly reduced and the lettering and date correspondingly enlarged.

Controversial silver 'bull head' half-crown, designed by Pistrucci. (*Coin Monthly*)

Pistrucci omitted the collar and badge of the Order of the Garter from the reverse, which Wyon had originally used to encompass the Garter itself. Only one version exists of both the shilling and sixpence, both having Wyon's reverse showing the shield surrounded by the Garter. A subtle change in the arms was a crown surmounting the escutcheon of Brunswick, Luneberg and Hanover in the centre, alluding to the fact that George III had been elevated by Congress of Vienna from Elector to King of Hanover. Both coins were minted annually from 1816 to 1820.

Silver shilling with king's head by William Wyon. (*Coin Monthly*)

Silver 'small head' half-crown. (*Coin Monthly*)

The Maundy series appeared in 1817 after a gap of sixteen years. The designs of the obverses were by Pistrucci but the dies were engraved by Thomas and William Wyon, while Thomas Junior both designed and engraved the dies for the reverses. The crowns surmounting the numerals

1819 silver crown. (*Coin Monthly*)

were much larger and broader than previously. These coins were minted in 1817–18 and 1820. The last of the silver coins to appear was the crown which was not released until 1818. Pistrucci excelled himself with the noble proportions of the profile on the obverse, and the St George and Dragon within the Garter on the reverse. Whereas all of the other issued coins associated with this artist merely had his initials engraved on them, his surname appears in full beneath the truncation on the obverse of the crown and in the exergue on the reverse – a feature present also in the high-value gold patterns. The crown was struck in 1818–20, but a novel feature was the appearance of the regnal year in Roman numerals as an edge inscription. As the date of George's accession was 25 October coins struck in the first ten months of 1818 and 1819 bore the numerals LVIII and LIX respectively, while those minted in the last two months were inscribed LIX and LX respectively. As the king died on 29 January 1820 all of the crowns minted that year bore the numerals LX.

CHAPTER SEVENTEEN

George IV (1820–1830)

For 58 of his 68 years George Augustus Frederick, Prince of Wales, lived in the shadow of his father and, in the best Hanoverian tradition, was constantly at odds with his parents. When the king's insanity became permanent in 1811 the prince became regent, and ascended the throne nine years later. Due to the scandals of his private life the standing of the monarchy reached its nadir and his shameful treatment of Queen Caroline sparked off nationwide rioting in the summer of 1821. The personal popularity, or lack of it, of George IV had little or no bearing on the political situation. For most of this reign Lord Liverpool was prime minister, succeeded in 1827 by George Canning, Lord Goderich and the Duke of Wellington in quick succession. It fell to the Iron Duke to promote the bill which, in 1829, led to the emancipation of Catholics from the political restrictions which had hitherto made them second-class citizens. Economically the reign opened with widespread depression in the aftermath of the Napoleonic Wars, but by its close the economy was booming. Steam revolutionised industry, technology and communications, giving Britain an impressive lead over all other countries and heralded half a century in which Britain was the most outstanding world power.

The coinage of this reign is surprisingly varied, reflecting the struggle within the Mint between Pistrucci and the Wyon family. Caught in the middle was Jean Baptiste Merlen, a Frenchman employed on a temporary basis (which lasted a quarter of a century!) as Pistrucci's assistant. The first gold coins followed the pattern set in the Regency, the sovereigns featuring St George and the Dragon and the halves showing the coat of arms. Both obverses had a left-facing profile of the king, sculpted by Pistrucci, who contrived to make George IV look like Nero – gross features topped with a riot of curls crowned with laurel leaves in the Roman fashion. The king heartily detested this portrayal and it says much for Pistrucci's tenacity that it endured on the coinage as long as it did. The lettering on both coins was

Gold sovereign by Pistrucci, a design detested by the king. (*Peter Clayton*)

greatly reduced, allowing the profile more space, and the date was transferred from the obverse to the exergue beneath St George (sovereign) or the right of the shield (half-sovereign). The new sovereign was bereft of inscription on the reverse. Pistrucci's initials appeared on both sides of the sovereign and on the obverse of the half-sovereign, while his assistant's initials, J.B.M., were placed on the reverse of the latter coin. Pistrucci's laureated profile was used for sovereigns dated each year from 1821 to 1825. Two versions of the half-sovereign exist with the Pistrucci obverse. In the original version (1821) Merlen's reverse showed the shield extravagantly garnished with the heraldic flowers of the United Kingdom. The legend on this coin consisted of ANNO 1821 at the sides, the lettering pointing inwards. A new reverse was used in 1823–25 with a severely plain shield, a discreet spray of heraldic flowers at the foot and the lettering of ANNO pointing towards the rim.

George IV continually pressurised the Mint to replace the coinage profile with something less insulting. He preferred the bust sculpted by Sir Francis Chantrey and as early as 1821 suggested it should be used. Pistrucci's Latin pride and artistic temperament would not allow him to copy the work of another sculptor and he doggedly refused, almost to the point of being dismissed. At this time, however, he was working on the grandiose Waterloo medal and used this as a bargaining factor to ensure his continued employment. Merlen went ahead and produced a profile based on the Chantrey bust, and this was used for the two-pound piece issued in 1823. George was shown bare-headed and it was, indeed, a truer likeness than Pistrucci's laureated profile. This coin had St George and the Dragon on the reverse and was issued in 1823 alone. The dispute with Pistrucci came to a head in 1824 when William Wyon was appointed chief engraver (though Pistrucci

Gold two-pound piece of 1823 with truer likeness of King George IV. (*Christie's*)

continued to draw his inflated salary). Wyon produced excellent obverse dies based on the Chantrey bust and these were used for sovereigns of 1825–30 and half-sovereigns of 1826–28. Wyon also produced splendid patterns for two- and five-pound pieces in 1826, with a mantled shield reverse. The sovereign and half-sovereign with the Wyon profile had reverses by Merlen showing a garnished shield. By now Pistrucci was in eclipse and the St George and Dragon motif associated so closely with him had been abandoned in favour of something more traditionally British and less Italianate. The crowned shield sovereigns and half-sovereigns were struck in proof versions in 1826 to accompany the pattern two- and five-pound pieces.

The silver coins follow a somewhat similar pattern to the gold. Pistrucci sculpted the laureated profiles for the crown, half-crown, shilling and six-pence as well as the Maundy series. First of the silver coins to appear was the half-crown which was released in 1820. Merlen's reverse had an ornate shield with thistle and shamrock sprays at the sides and a rose at the foot, and the date including ANNO as on the gold coins. Half-crowns of this type were issued in 1820–21 and 1823. In the latter year a new reverse was used for the majority of half-crowns and showed a plain shield surrounded by the Garter and the collar of the Order. This type was minted in 1823–24, yet another type being introduced in the latter year. This had Wyon's bare-headed profile on the obverse and an elaborate shield, surmounted by an armorial helmet and decorated with a ribbon inscribed DIEU ET MON DROIT (*God and my Right*) at the foot. Few half-crowns of this type were struck in 1824 but plentiful supplies were minted in 1825–26 and 1828–29.

Silver 1820 half-crown, design by Merlen. (*Coin Monthly*)

Crowns were issued in 1821–22 with Pistrucci's laureated profile and his St George and Dragon reverse. The previous practice including the regnal year on the edge was followed and crowns of 1822 may be found with SECUNDO (*second*) or TERTIO (*third*). No further crowns were minted, though a proof with Wyon's bare-headed profile and a garnished and crested shield was included in the proof set of 1826.

In contrast with earlier periods the shilling was no longer the mainstay of the silver series and was struck only intermittently. A large quantity was struck in 1821 and this sufficed for two years. The 1821 shillings had Pistrucci's profile and a garnished shield by Merlen on the reverse. Shillings

Silver shilling of George IV, struck only intermittently. (*Peter Clayton*)

of 1823–25 had a new reverse, also by Merlen, with a plain shield in the Garter. The Wyon bare-headed design was adopted in the latter part of 1825 and a new reverse, showing a crown surmounted by a lion, with a spray of heraldic flowers beneath. This type was minted in 1825–26 in large numbers, fewer in 1827 and none in 1828, and only sparingly in 1829. The sixpence was also minted sporadically from 1821, following the same pattern as the shilling in obverse and reverse designs. No more sixpences appeared until 1824 when the Pistrucci obverse and a new Merlen reverse, with Garter shield, were used. This type was minted in 1824–26 and then superseded by a new type with the Wyon profile and lion on crown reverse. Thereafter sixpences were struck annually until 1829. Proof versions of the shilling and sixpence were included in the 1826 set. Pistrucci's laureated profile survived longest on the Maundy series, remaining unchanged from 1822 to 1830. The reverses had the crowned numerals but the inscriptions were now replaced by wreaths and the date was placed in the middle, the digits flanking the numeral.

Silver shilling of 1826, design by Wyon. (*Coin Monthly*)

After a gap of fourteen years a subsidiary base-metal coinage was resumed. This time pennies, halfpence and farthings were produced in a really sufficient quantity and ended a two-century period in which the public had seldom been provided with an adequate subsidiary currency. Only the farthing was issued with Pistrucci's laureated profile, in 1821–23 and 1825–26. On the reverse, Britannia was now shown facing right instead of left. As in the previous copper coins, she was shown with an olive branch in her right hand and a trident in the left, but instead of extending the branch as previously, it now rested almost carelessly on top of the shield, and it was the trident, symbol of maritime power, that was thrust out aggressively. Additionally, Britannia now wore a crested Roman helmet.

Copper penny of 1826; base-metal coinage at last being produced in sufficient quantity for public need. (*Coin Monthly*)

The second issue of coppers was made in 1825, when pennies and half-pence were added to the range. They had a laureated version of the Wyon profile and the new, more warlike Britannia on the reverse. Whereas the date on the earlier farthings had appeared in the exergue on the reverse, it appeared on the higher denominations below the profile and a spray of heraldic flowers was placed in the exergue. Both coins were minted only in 1825–27, proofs being struck in 1826. Farthings with the Wyon obverse and modified Britannia reverse were introduced in 1826 and minted regularly until 1830. Proofs of this type were included in the 1826 set. In addition, half-farthings (1828 and 1830) and third-farthings (1827) of a similar type were minted for circulation in Ceylon and Malta respectively. By now the term BRITANNIAR (*of the Britains*) was coming to mean more than the British Isles, and increasingly referred to the British dominions, colonies and protectorates beyond the seas, many of which used British coinage. For much of the nineteenth century small coins in the British style were provided to fill gaps in various colonial currency systems.

CHAPTER EIGHTEEN

William IV (1830–1837)

The death of George IV on 26 June 1830 brought his brother William to the throne. Posterity has conferred on him two nicknames – the Sailor King and, less flatteringly, Silly Billy. Genial, frank and warm-hearted, he could be blundering and stupid and also meddled in parliamentary matters. For most of his brief reign the Whigs or Liberals were in power and they engineered the greatest political revolution in British history. The reform of parliament was long overdue and the franchise no longer truly representative. The Reform Act of 1832 redistributed seats to the rising industrial towns and cities and laid the foundations for a true parliamentary democracy, which was achieved over the ensuing century by a series of acts extending the suffrage to all classes of society and, finally, to women (1918–28). Nevertheless, much remained to be achieved before a just society was attained. As late as 1834 the men of Tolpuddle who combined to form a friendly society were sentenced to transportation for their efforts, while the infamous Corn Laws protected the farmer against cheap imported cereals and kept up the price of bread, at the expense of the working classes. In this atmosphere a new urban proletariat developed and the seeds of working class radicalism were sown. Dissatisfaction with the mildness of the Reform Act led to the rise of the Chartist movement which demanded adult suffrage and the secret ballot – things taken for granted today but regarded as subversive and dangerously revolutionary by the government of the 1830s.

When William came to the throne it was William Wyon who had the responsibility for engraving the coinage dies, though Pistrucci continued to hang on at the Mint, enjoying official recognition at last as chief medallist. Merlen engraved the reverse dies for the coins from the sovereign to the sixpence, as well as the Maundy series. Wyon executed all the obverse dies, using a right-facing profile of the king taken from a bust by Chantrey, and also engraved the reverse dies for the Britannia groat and the copper coins.

Though two-pound pieces and half-sovereigns were included in the 1831 proof set, the sovereign was the only gold coin put into general circulation that year. All three proof coins had a bare-headed profile on the obverse, while the reverse featured a crowned shield. That on the two-pounds was elaborately mantled, while those on the other coins had rococo scrollwork, with the date and ANNO at the foot. Some confusion had arisen over the size of the sixpence and the half-sovereign, and the armorial reverse on the sixpence of George IV had encouraged unscrupulous individuals to give them a gold wash and pass them off as half-sovereigns. To overcome this it was decided to reduce the size of the half-sovereign and the 1831 proof was, in fact, struck on a smaller flan. No halves were issued until 1834 but there was an immediate outcry from the public at the small size, so the original size was reintroduced the following year and minted again in 1836–37. The sovereign was struck each year except 1834.

The proof set of 1831 included the silver crown, half-crown, shilling, sixpence and the four Maundy coins. In practice, however, no crowns were released for general circulation in this reign. The 1831 crown had a very elegant reverse, with the shield resting on a finely draped mantle, surmounted by a crown and encircled by the collar and badge of the Garter. A similar reverse was used for the half-crown, which did not appear as a general circulating coin until 1834 but was issued annually thereafter. The shilling and sixpence had reverses which were close to the Maundy series in inspiration, the value being expressed in words instead of figures, within a crowned wreath, the object being to prevent confusion between these coins and their gold counterparts, the sovereign and half-sovereign. The sixpence alone appeared in a circulating version in 1831 but no further coins were released until 1834 when both shilling and sixpence were produced and minted regularly from then onwards. Although a fourpenny piece had been a feature of the Maundy series for generations no silver coin of this value had actually circulated since 1729. The need for a circulating coin between the sixpence and the penny had, however, become acute, especially since the Truck Acts abolished the barter system and meant that the working classes now made greater use of coined money. The groat reappeared in 1836 and was distinguished from the Maundy fourpence by having as its reverse the

William IV silver half-crown of 1837. (*Coin Monthly*)

William IV silver shilling of 1836. (*Coin Monthly*)

seated figure of Britannia, a miniature version of that gracing the copper coins. The words FOUR PENCE flanked Britannia and the date appeared in the exergue. These coins were minted in 1836–37.

Just as sub-divisions of the farthing were required for circulation in some of the new colonial territories which Britain acquired as a result of the Napoleonic wars, so also two smaller silver coins were required. A silver threepence was introduced in 1834 for circulation in the West Indies. It was identical in every respect to the Maundy coin but had a dull surface. A silver threehalfpence, for use in Ceylon, the Ionian Islands and other overseas possessions, conformed to the Maundy pattern, with the value 1½ on the reverse. Both of these colonial coins were struck annually from 1834 to 1837. The Maundy series were the only silver coins minted in each year of William's reign, with the crowned numeral motif on the reverse.

William IV copper penny of 1831. (*Coin Monthly*)

The base-metal coinage of this reign is quite straightforward. Both proof and circulating versions of the penny, halfpenny and farthing were produced in 1831, but no further issue of coppers was made until 1834. Pennies and halfpence were not released thereafter until 1837, but farthings were minted in 1835–36 as well. These coins had the right-facing profile of the king on the obverse and the standard Britannia reverse. Two varieties exist of the 1831 penny, with or without the initials of William Wyon on the truncation of the neck. Third-farthings, for use in Malta, were issued in 1835, and half-farthings, for use in Ceylon, were struck in 1837.

CHAPTER NINETEEN

Victoria (1837–1901)

The death of Princess Charlotte, only legitimate child of the Prince Regent, in 1817 seemingly brought the Hanoverian dynasty to its close, for she was the only legitimate offspring produced by the thirteen sons and daughters of George III. By that time the Prince Regent, long estranged from his wife, Caroline of Anspach, was past fatherhood. The solution lay with this three surviving younger brothers. Though all well advanced into middle age, the Dukes of Clarence, Kent and Cambridge abandoned their long-cherished bachelorhood and got married in 1818. The two children of the Duke of Clarence (later William IV) died in infancy. The youngest brother, the Duke of Cambridge, produced a son who succeeded him in the title and was Commander in Chief of the British army for 40 years. The middle brother, Edward, Duke of Kent, however, had a daughter, born on 24 May 1819, and she became heir to the throne in the reign of her uncle William.

Alexandrina Victoria was in her eighteenth year when she succeeded her uncle on 10 June 1837. An immediate political repercussion of her accession was the separation of Hanover from the United Kingdom. Under Salic law a woman was debarred from the succession, and the throne now passed to Ernest Augustus, Duke of Cumberland, William's next surviving brother. He was unpopular in Britain for his outspoken opposition to parliamentary reform and his departure from England was satirised in a well-known medalet, the Cumberland Jack, which parodied Pistrucci's sovereign and showed the Duke on horseback, with the caption 'To Hanover', instead of St George and the Dragon.

Victoria was destined to rule over the United Kingdom for sixty-four years – longer than any of her predecessors and surpassed among her contemporaries only by Kaiser Franz Josef of Austria (1848–1916). Incredible changes were wrought in every aspect of British life, political, social and economic, during that long period. The Steam age was still in its infancy at her accession; by the time of her death it had been overtaken by electricity and petroleum. In science, engineering, technology, medicine and the arts the Victorian age witnessed enormous changes. Colonial expansion in the wake of missionary endeavour was phenomenal, while the British navy, more powerful than all the other navies of the world combined, guarded the important trade routes and policed the less-developed parts of the world. Apart from the Crimean War (1853–6) Britain was not embroiled in any European conflict for a century (1815–1914), but fought countless colonial campaigns in every other continent.

It is inevitable that these sweeping changes should have left their mark on the coinage. Indeed, it is remarkable that the coinage changed as little as it did. Coins reflected the innate conservatism in such public expressions of the applied arts. They did at least move with the times, unlike the postage stamps (invented in 1840) which continued to portray Victoria as a girl in her teens right down to the time of her death at the venerable age of eighty-one. Changes in the coinage were not made so abruptly as in previous reigns, and there tended to be a considerable overlap of gold, silver and base-metal changes in the period before the Golden Jubilee in 1887, and some of the silver designs survived as late as that date.

Early coinage, 1838–87

At the beginning of the reign the battle between Pistrucci and William Wyon was at its height. Pistrucci engraved the dies for the official Coronation medal of 1838, yet it is Wyon's Guildhall medal of the same year which has endured, since it was adapted for the postage stamps of 1840–1901 and in this manner has become something of a symbol of the Victorian age. For the coinage, however, Wyon engraved a most appealing profile of the queen. Numismatists know this as the young head, while the general public nicknamed it the 'bun' portrait, because of the prominent chignon in which the queen's hair was drawn at the back. This elegant profile, with the slightest hint of *embonpoint* about the cheeks and chin, was used for the sovereigns and half-sovereigns throughout the first fifty years of the reign.

No higher denomination was struck for general circulation, but Wyon engraved dies in 1839 for a five-pound which exists only in proof form. The outstanding reverse was the perfect complement to Pistrucci's St George and the Dragon since it depicted Una and the Lion, from the same legend, the young queen being thinly disguised as Una. In her left hand she carried the orb of state and in her right she guided the British lion with her sceptre. The Latin legend around the top was DIRIGE DEUS GRESSUS MEOS (*Direct, Oh Lord, my steps*). In the exergue the date was rendered in Roman numerals and, like Pistrucci's largest coins, the designer had his name in full – W. WYON, R. A – the initials signifying his elevation as Academician in 1838.

On the issued sovereigns and halfsovereigns, however, Wyon's signature was confined to a discreet W. W. on the truncation of the neck. On these coins

Pattern five-pound piece with Una and the Lion reverse. (*Peter Clayton*)

the obverse legend was reduced to VICTORIA DEI GRATIA with the date at the foot, while the reverse was inscribed BRITTANIARUM REGINA FID DEF. The reverses retained the heraldic shield, in a plain wreathed frame (sovereign) or a rococo garnished frame (half-sovereign). The crown was heightened and the Hanoverian heraldic elements were omitted. These designs remained in use until 1887. A technical innovation was the introduction of die numbers in 1863 to test the wear on the dies. They were struck in abundant quantities in most years, both for general circulation as the level of prosperity rose, and also as a convenient form of handling bullion in international transactions, reflecting the status of the British currency overseas. Moreover, the discovery of gold in vast quantities in Australia in 1851 provided a sufficiency of the yellow metal at a time when its requirement as coinage was beginning to escalate. The die numbers from 1863 to 1874 appeared beneath the wreath on the reverse.

1862 gold sovereign. (*Peter Clayton*)

After almost half a century in limbo, Pistrucci's St George and Dragon reverse was revived for the sovereigns in 1871 and thereafter this type was issued most years (except 1875 and 1882–83) in vast quantities. To facilitate the handling of Australian gold, subsidiary mints were established at Sydney, New South Wales (1871) and Melbourne, Victoria (1872). Shield sovereigns were struck at Sydney in 1871–87 (except 1874), and at Melbourne in 1872, 1874 and 1880–87, with s or m mintmarks below the wreath on the reverse. St George sovereigns were also struck at Sydney in 1871–87 (except

1871 gold sovereign. (*Christie's*)

1877–78) and at Melbourne (1872–87), with the mintmarks on the truncation of the queen's neck.

Half-sovereigns followed a similar pattern, with die numbers from 1863 to 1880 (except 1868). A new obverse die was employed for halves struck in 1880 and 1883–85, differing from the earlier version in having a less prominent relief. They were also struck at Sydney from 1871 to 1887 (except 1873–74, 1876–78 and 1884–85) and Melbourne in 1873, 1877, 1881–82 and 1884–87, with the mintmark beneath the wreath of the shield on the reverse.

By contrast with the gold, the silver coins of the period are quite complex, reflecting the first tentative essays in decimalisation which preoccupied the currency reformers in the mid-nineteenth century. As in the immediately preceding reigns, there was little enthusiasm for the crown, which was only struck for general circulation in a relatively few years. The first crowns, dated 1839, were proofs with a modified sovereign reverse, but in 1844 crowns were generally issued in large quantities, with a smaller edition in 1845 and an even smaller number in 1847. In 1846 Wyon engraved dies for a crown of an entirely new design, known as the Gothic crown, from its unusual portrait of Victoria in the manner of the Gothic Revival and in its use of Old English lettering. The crowns dated 1846 had a plain edge and are regarded as patterns or proofs, though some 8,000 are believed to have been struck for allocation to the London banking houses. Gothic crowns were issued for general use in 1847 but are scarcer than the previous design used

1853 silver 'Gothic' crown. (*Coin Monthly*)

in the same year. Wyon designed both obverse and reverse, the latter returning to the cruciform arrangement of heraldic shields, with the star of the Garter in the centre and the floral emblems of the United Kingdom in the angles. The medieval quality of the coin was emphasised by the Latin motto on the reverse TUEATUR UNITA DEUS (*May God protect the united*) – expression borrowed from the unites of James I. This motto was balanced, at the foot, by the date expression in the same script – 'anno dom mdcccxlvii'. Gothic crowns dated mdccliii were produced for the proof set of 1853.

Half-crowns were struck for general circulation in 1839–50 (except 1847). The usual version has two plain fillets or head-bands and Wyon's initials incuse, but a variant has one ornamented fillet and initials in relief. Though generally discontinued in 1850 half-crowns were struck as proofs in 1853 for inclusion in the year set. The temporary suspension of the half-crown in the mid-nineteenth century was caused by the emergence of an entirely new denomination, the florin or tenth of a pound (as proclaimed on the reverse). It was introduced in 1849 as the first step towards decimal currency. The advocates of a decimal system were divided between those who favoured the pound of 100 pence and those who favoured the pound of 1000 milles. The spending power of the pound being very much greater in the 1840s than it is today it is not surprising that the pound-mille system found greater support. Pattern silver centums exist, with the reverse inscribed '100 milles – one centum – one-tenth of a pound'. The term 'centum' was abandoned because it was liable to confusion with the American cent, then on par with the British halfpenny, and the Continental term 'florin' was adopted instead – yet another example of the Victorian predilection for anything medieval. It followed the design of the Gothic crown in both profile and heraldic elements, but in its original version was inscribed in block lettering. The observe was simply inscribed VICTORIA REGINA and the absence of any reference to the grace of God led to the epithets 'graceless' or (much more commonly 'Godless'). A few florins were struck in 1851 in connection with the Great Exhibition, but none was minted again for general circulation until 1852. These florins used Old English script on both sides, the obverse legend being modified to include 'd. g. brit. reg. mdcccli'. With the exception of 1861, florins

1844 silver half-crown. (*Coin Monthly*)

Silver 'Godless' florin of 1849 – first experiment in decimal coinage, two shillings being one-tenth of a pound. (*Coin Monthly*)

were minted each year until 1863 without die numbers. From 1864 to 1867 the original type had die numbers, and from 1868 to 1887 (except 1878 and 1882) the abbreviation for Britain was rendered as 'brit:'. There are several variants, differing in the number of arcs in the border and the presence or absence of the die numbers and Wyon's initials.

The first shillings were issued in 1838, with Wyon's initials on the truncation. This feature appeared on the proofs of 1839, but was omitted from the ordinary shillings of that and subsequent years. Coins without die numbers were struck in 1839–63 (except 1847–48). A few shillings exist with the date 1848 overstruck on 1846 but these are very scarce. The adoption of die numbers in 1864 coincided with a new profile of the queen used in 1864–67. A second profile was employed in 1867–79. A third profile, confined to shillings of 1867, is comparatively elusive. A fourth head was used, in conjunction with an unnumbered reverse, in 1879–87. These shillings were minted in substantial quantities, only those dated 1882 being scarce. Sixpences without die numbers were struck in 1838–66, except 1847, 1861 and 1864–65, and followed the same pattern as the shilling. The first head was used with a numbered reverse in 1864–66, a second with numbered reverse in 1867–79 and a third with unnumbered reverse in 1880–87. Second head sixpences with unnumbered reverses were also issued in some quantity in 1871, 1877 and 1879–80.

Groats with the Britannia reverse were produced in 1838–55 (except 1850). Threepences, in the same design as the Maundy series but with a dull surface, were issued in 1838–87, those down to 1844 being intended for colonial use. This was the only coin in general circulation which exhibited no variation throughout a very long life ending in 1887. None was issued

Victorian silver groat. (*Coin Monthly*)

in 1847–48 and 1852, while those dated 1869, intended for colonial circulation, are fairly elusive. Silver threehalfpence, inscribed $1\frac{1}{2}$ on the reverse, were struck in 1838–43, 1860 and 1862 solely for colonial use. The Maundy series also remained unchanged from 1838 to 1887. These sets appeared annually in steadily increasing numbers as the queen advanced in years, since the distribution was made to men and women in numbers equal to the years in the queen's age. Proof versions of all the silver coins were included in the sets of 1839 and 1853.

After a gap of more than two decades the half-crown was resuscitated in 1874 and issued annually thereafter without interruption until 1887. These coins were similar to the half-crowns of 1841–53 but were generally inferior in finish.

The seated Britannia reverse was retained for the copper coins issued in 1838–60. In this series the date appeared on the obverse, while the exergue on the reverse was occupied by a spray of heraldic flowers. Proofs of the penny, halfpenny and farthing with a bronzed surface were included in the presentation set of 1839, but the proof versions of 1853 did not have the treated surface. The most widely used denomination was the farthing, a handy little coin which had real spending power in the mid-nineteenth century, especially after the repeal of the Corn Laws in 1846 dramatically brought down the price of bread. Farthings were minted annually from 1838 to 1860, though those of 1860 are extremely rare. Halfpence were minted in most years, but were omitted in 1839–40, 1842 and 1850 and are exceedingly rare dated 1860. Apart from the bronzed proofs of 1839 no pennies were struck until 1841. Thereafter they were minted spasmodically and in some years, such as 1843, 1849 and 1860, were produced in very small quantities only. Third-farthings with the Britannia reverse were issued in 1844 for circulation in Malta. Half-farthings, which circulated in Britain as well as the colonies, were issued in 1839, 1842–44, 1847, 1851–54 and 1856, and had the value in words, surmounted by a crown, on the reverse. Quarter-farthings in a similar design were struck in 1839 and 1851–53 for use in Ceylon. Proofs of these lesser denominations were included in the 1853 set.

Victorian fractional farthings. (*Coin Monthly*)

Bronze coinage, 1860–94

An obscure and indirect outcome of the Australian gold rush of the 1850s was an embarrassing, if temporary, shortage of copper. Miners in their thousands abandoned the more prosaic copper mines of South Australia to flock to the goldfields. As Australia was at that time the principal source of copper used in Britain this had the effect of raising the price of this commodity – at a time when it was felt that the subsidiary coinage was too cumbersome anyway. The result was the decision, taken in 1859, to abandon the pure copper coinage and to adopt the cheaper alloy of bronze, in which the copper was compounded with tin. The first of the new bronze coinage, in reduced weights and sizes, appeared in December 1860.

The opportunity was taken to update the queen's portrait on the obverse, a task that fell to Leonard Charles Wyon, son of William, whom he had succeeded as chief engraver at the age of 24 in 1851. L. C. Wyon's 'bun head' shows the queen as a still-youthful personality (then in her forty-first year). Previous profiles had depicted her with a head-band or a crown, but she was now shown in the Roman fashion, with a laurel wreath. The seated Britannia on the reverse remained unchanged, but the date now replaced the flowers in the exergue, and after a gap of half a century the maritime symbols were restored. Now a lighthouse was added to the left of Britannia to balance the man o' war on the right. The lighthouse appears to have been a fairly accurate rendition of the third Eddystone tower, built by John Smeaton in 1756–59. If this is so, then the lighthouse survived longer on the coin than it did in reality, for it was undermined in 1877 and totally replaced by the present structure in 1878–82.

Bronze penny of 1860, portrait by Leonard Charles Wyon, son of William Wyon. (*Coin Monthly*)

Ordinary bun pennies were struck at the Royal Mint, without any distinguishing marks, in 1860–94 except for 1876 and 1882. Pennies were, indeed, minted in both these years, but only by the Mint's sub-contractor, Ralph Heaton & Sons of Birmingham, successors to Boulton and Watt. These coins may be recognised by the H mintmark which appears below the date in the exergue. Heaton pennies were also struck in 1874–75 and 1881.

The halfpenny followed a similar pattern, being struck annually at the Royal Mint except in 1876 and 1882. Coins with the Heaton mintmark may be found with the same five dates – 1874–6 and 1881–82. The humble farthing was the longest lived of the bun series, continuing to appear in 1895. Farthings appeared without mintmark in most years, except 1870–71, 1874, 1876–77 and 1882 and with the Heaton mintmark in the same five years as the penny and halfpenny. It should be noted that the absence of Royal Mint bronze in 1876 was due to a breakdown in the, by now, antiquated machinery which shut down production completely for five months and led to the farming out of the bronze coinage to Heatons. An entirely new Royal Mint was constructed in 1882 and the upheavals of rehousing plant and machinery led to Heatons being given sole responsibility for the bronze coins that year also. Diminutive third-farthings, for use in Malta, were struck intermittently between 1866 and 1885 and differed from the other bun coins by having the profile truncated at the neck.

Jubilee coinage, 1887

By the time of Queen Victoria's Golden Jubilee in 1887 the country she ruled over bore little resemblance to the kingdom at her accession. The Whigs and Tories had given way to the efficient party machines of the Liberals and Conservatives. The franchise was considerably extended by the Reform Act of 1885 but the working classes were now becoming disenchanted with the Liberals and realising that they needed a party of their own. This was advocated by Keir Hardie in 1887 but did not come to fruition until his election to parliament in 1892, when the Independent Labour Party was founded. The great Dock Strike of 1889 over the docker's tanner – an extra sixpence a day – led to a tremendous extension of trade unionism and thereafter socialism became less of an intellectual exercise and more concerned with organising the class struggle along political and industrial lines. In the general election of 1895, however, all of the ILP candidates were defeated. Rising prosperity and full employment, after the depression of the 1880s, booming industry and rapidly expanding overseas markets all combined to raise standards of living in all levels of society.

It was in this atmosphere, beginning with the promise of happier times around the corner and continuing with the mounting euphoria of the 1890s, that the two jubilees of Queen Victoria should be seen. In retrospect the 'Jubilee period' came to be seen as an era of unprecedented material prosperity and progress, a golden age at the close of a very long reign. The crown had come to Victoria as a symbol of political ineptitude and moral degradation; by the time of her Golden Jubilee she had made it a unique symbol of national honour. Her rigid devotion to duty and unflagging industry were qualities which the Victorians prized and respected. To be sure, in the period immediately before her Jubilee, the queen was still somewhat remote from her people, the Widow of Windsor, grieving for her beloved Albert who had died in 1861. On her rare appearances in public she was seen as a small, rather dumpy figure of forbidding mien, severely clad in black. For formal occasions she favoured a tiny crown which may have been more comfortable than the traditional crowns but tended to create a ludicrous effect, especially when viewed in profile. This was taken as the model for a new coinage effigy, sculpted by Sir Joseph Edgar Boehm RA. L. C. Wyon had the unenviable task of translating this into the dies engraved for an entirely new series of gold and silver coins. It is difficult to apportion blame for the results, since, to a large extent, the engraving of dies had become mechanical, thanks to the use of the pantographic reducing machine. Moreover, it should be remembered that the great outcry that greeted the issue of the coins was provoked largely by the shock of seeing the queen as she really was, and not the somewhat idealised teenager as she was portrayed on stamps and the smaller silver coins.

What was so remarkable about the Jubilee series was the inclusion of five-and two-pound coins. No two-pound coin had circulated since 1823 and no circulating coin of comparable value to the five-pounds since the five-guinea of George II in 1753. Now both of these high values were struck in circulating and proof versions. Another feature of the Jubilee series was the extension of the George and Dragon motif to the two largest gold coins as well as the sovereign. The issue of these high-value coins was confined to Jubilee Year itself, but sovereigns with the Boehm profile and George and Dragon reverse were issued until 1892 (Royal Mint) and 1893 (Sydney and Melbourne). The half-sovereign retained a heraldic reverse, though the shield was redesigned and the Victorian small crown substituted for the imperial crown previously used. The date was also transferred from the obverse to the reverse and placed below the point of the shield. Half-sovereigns were not minted again until 1890–93 (Royal Mint), but were also struck at Sydney (1889 and 1891) and Melbourne (1893).

The same spirit of nostalgia that inspired the high-value gold coins probably tipped the balance in favour of the inclusion of a crown in the Jubilee series. This cumbersome coin had not been issued for general circulation since 1847, though a proof crown had been included in the 1853 set. For the Jubilee crown the Mint went back to Pistrucci's St George and Dragon,

Silver double florin – 'the barmaid's grief' as it could easily be mistaken for a crown. (*Coin Monthly*)

last used for a crown in 1822. They were struck in circulating as well as proof versions, the former continuing annually until 1892. As yet another round in the battle for decimalisation, a coin tariffed at four shillings was introduced at this time. The double florin was soon dubbed the 'barmaid's grief' on the grounds that barmaids were frequently confused into regarding this coin as a crown and giving drinks or change equivalent to 5 shillings. It is hard to imagine Victorian barmaids being any less astute than their modern counterparts, and this tale ignores the fact that no confusion ever seems to have been associated with the half-crown and its slightly smaller partner, the florin. Moreover, the double florin had a totally different reverse from the crown, with a cruciform arrangement of heraldic shields. The truth of the matter is that the public, while ready to accept crowns which had existed in the past, were ever hostile to an entirely new denomination. Two versions of this coin exist, with Arabic or Roman numeral (1 or I) in the date. The Arabic version was used for proofs and retained for the double florins of 1888–90. Significantly, far fewer double florins were minted in these three years and the experiment was then abandoned.

The Jubilee half-crown followed the pattern of its predecessor and had a crowned shield on the reverse, though this, too, harked back to the reign of George IV and closely resembled the design used in 1823–4, the shield being surrounded by the insignia of the Garter, though the crown was modernised. Jubilee half-crowns were minted each year until 1892. The florin was like a scaled-down version of the double florin, with the same cruciform shields on the reverse, with sceptres crossing the angles. Two of these sceptres had the usual royal top, while the others were topped by a harp and thistle respectively, and the star of the Garter appeared in the centre. The florin was struck annually until 1892.

The shilling and sixpence abandoned the wreathed value concept and returned to the shield in Garter motif used in the 1820s, with suitable modifications to update the details. The inclusion of the queen's titles in full cramped the effigy on the shillings of 1887–89 but a new obverse, with a larger portrait and smaller lettering, was adopted in 1889 and continued until 1892. No sooner had the Garter shield version of the sixpence been released than dishonest people began gilding them and passing them off as half-sovereigns. The authorities promptly reverted to the wreathed value reverse employed since 1838 but this was updated with the new Victorian

Jubilee half-sovereign and sixpence – the latter often gilded to pass as the former. (*Coin Monthly*)

crown at the top. Sixpences of this type were struck until 1893, though the mintage decreased each year from 1891.

Since the Maundy ceremony of 1887 took place before the Jubilee festivities commenced, the Maundy money that year had been in the style of the young head coinage. The Jubilee profile was not adopted for the Maundy series until 1888 and, thereafter, the four smallest silver coins with Victorian crown surmounting the numerals were struck until 1892. There was, however, a threepence, intended for general circulation, and this appeared as part of the Jubilee set in 1887, in both proof and circulating versions. The circulating version in subsequent years can be distinguished from the Maundy coin by its relatively dull surface. Groats, last minted in 1836, were fleetingly revived in 1888 for use in British Guiana. They had the Jubilee obverse and Britannia reverse.

Jubilee head silver Maundy set. (*Coin Monthly*)

Old head coinage, 1893–1901

In 1876 Queen Victoria was proclaimed Empress of India but sixteen years elapsed before this title was included in the British coinage. This coincided with the scrapping of the unsatisfactory Jubilee effigy and the adoption of a more dignified portrait, known as the old or veiled head. Although India had the distinction of being the only overseas possession to be singled out for mention on the coins the legend BRITTANORUM REGINA (*Queen of the British*) was held to signify the British dominions beyond the seas. The legend on the old head obverses was (with the curious exception of the half-crown) the longest since the time of Charles II: VICTORIA DEI GRA. BRITT. REGINA FID. DEF. IND. IMP. (or, in full, Dei Gratia Brittanorum Regina Fidei Defensor Indiae Imperatrix' – *By the Grace of God Queen of the Britains, Defender of the Faith and Empress of India*). With such a lengthy inscription it would not have been surprising if the profile had been sacrificed, but in fact it was skilfully proportioned so as to fill the available space without any appearance of being cramped. Credit for surmounting the problems of balancing the profile with such a lengthy inscription goes to Sir Thomas Brock RA whose initials (T.B.) may be found below the queen's shoulder. The portrait shows the queen aged seventy-four; wearing a coronet over which is draped a veil. On her left breast is the ribbon and star of the Order of the Garter, but the necklace incorporates the badge of the Most Eminent Order of the Indian Empire, which Victoria instituted in 1878.

Five- and two-pound coins were issued in both proof and circulating versions in 1893 alone. Proof and circulating versions of the sovereign and half-sovereign were also minted in 1893. Pistrucci's splendid St George and Dragon motif, which had fought a long and hard struggle against heraldic reverses, finally triumphed. Since then it has been used exclusively for the reverse of all British gold coins and has come to be regarded virtually as a trademark. Sovereigns were minted for general circulation every year from 1893 until 1901 with the curious exception of 1897 – the year of the Diamond Jubilee when one might reasonably have expected a proof set, let alone circulating coins. Old head sovereigns are among the commonest of the 'bullion' sovereigns and were minted in such vast quantities that even today they are worth little more than their intrinsic value. Old head sovereigns were also struck at the subsidiary mints in Australia and it is significant that there was no gap in the date sequence of either Melbourne or Sydney sovereigns. Production was extended to Perth in 1899 to take advantage of the rich deposits of precious metal which resulted from the Coolgardie and Kalgoorlie gold rush of 1893. By the end of the century gold production in Western Australia had overtaken that of New South Wales. Sovereigns struck at the Perth Mint in 1899–1901 bore a letter P in the ground on the reverse, above the third digit of the date.

Half-sovereigns were struck annually at the Royal Mint 1893–1901 without any gap, but production at the three Australian mints was sporadic. The Melbourne half of 1893 is extremely rare, the bulk of production that year being confined to Sydney. No halves were struck in Australia again until 1896 and thereafter Melbourne and Sydney took turns in producing them. All three branch mints struck half-sovereigns in 1900 but none was minted in 1901.

Having made such a triumphant come-back in the Jubilee series, the crown was a prominent component of the old head series, with Pistrucci's reverse. Whereas the Jubilee crowns had a grained edge, the old head crowns reintroduced a feature which had last appeared in 1821–22 – a regnal date on the rim. Since Victoria had come to the throne in the month of June it followed that the regnal year straddled two calendar years and, conversely, each calendar year contained parts of two regnal years. The first of the old head crowns bore the regnal date in Roman numerals LVI and it was this which also appeared on the proof version. Crowns of 1893 with regnal date LVII are much scarcer, but thereafter each pair of crowns, struck down to the end of 1900, was minted in more or less equal numbers, with a few exceptions (1896 – LIX and 1898 – LXI).

Sir Thomas Brock designed the reverse of the half-crown, the only coin in the series which he designed in its entirety. This explains why the queen's titles were split between the two sides. The lettering was, in fact, the same size as that on the crown and for that reason the inscription on the obverse was shortened to VICTORIA DEI GRA. BRITT. REG. while FID. DEF. IND. IMP. occupied the upper half of the reverse, with the words of the value flanking the date at the foot. The centre of the reverse was occupied by a 'spade' version of the royal

1901 silver half-crown. (*Coin Monthly*)

arms, surmounted by a Victorian crown and surrounded by the collar of the Garter, with St. George at the foot. Proof and circulating versions were minted in 1893 and the latter also appeared annually until 1901.

Sir Edward Poynter RA designed the reverse which was used for both the florin and shilling. This consisted basically of an entirely new approach to the heraldic elements. Traditionally the quarterings had included the English badge twice but now this was reduced to equal status with the arms of Scotland and Ireland. The result was three shields arranged in Y-form, the English and Scottish shields above the Irish. The spaces between the upper shields and at the sides of the lower shield were occupied by the rose, thistle and shamrock and, on the florin, the whole was surmounted by a crown, flatter and broader than that usually associated with late-Victorian coinage. The crown was flanked by crossed sceptres on which the shields were imposed, and the Garter encompassed the heraldic elements. The value on the florin was rendered as ONE FLORIN and TWO SHILLINGS, to left and right of the crown and marked a return to the Gothic series where the value had been expressed also as a tenth of a pound. The Jubilee florin had borne no denomination, but now it was expressed in shillings to avoid any lingering uncertainty as to its value. The shilling was similar to the florin but lacked the crown and the value appeared, without interruption, round the top. To compensate for the omission of the large crown each of the shields was surmounted by a tiny crown and the two sceptres were left out. Both florin and shilling were minted annually from 1893 to 1901, as well as proofs in

1893 silver florin. (*Peter Clayton*)

1893. No change was made to the reverses of the sixpence, threepence or Maundy series, all of which were issued each year until 1901. As usual, the circulating threepence was similar to the Maundy coin except for its dull surface. In each case, of course, proofs were minted in 1893 for inclusion in the presentation set.

The bun pennies and their sub-divisions survived a further two years but in 1895 the bronze coinage was brought into line with the gold and silver. L. C. Wyon's version of Britannia, as shown on the bun coinage, was considerably modified, probably by George William de Saulles who engraved most of the dies for the old head coinage (John Pinches is thought to have engraved the reverse die for the shilling). In the 1895 version Britannia was smartened up; she sits more upright and has a firm grip on her shield rather than resting languidly against it. The helmet doubtless explained her drooping appearance and this was now better proportioned. The heavily beaded border was lightened almost to the point of non-existence and the lettering increased in size. The most startling difference, however, was the omission of the maritime background; sea, ship and lighthouse now vanished from the scene, though subsequently the dies were retouched in order to restore some hint of the sea.

1897 bronze penny – some still circulating until the late 1960s. (*Coin Monthly*)

All of the old head bronze coins were struck annually until 1901 and many of them were still in circulation in the late 1960s when decimalisation was imminent.

Apart from minor variants, such as variations in the position of the trident on the penny, the farthing alone yielded a major type difference. Just as confusion between the armorial sixpence and the half-sovereign had led to a change in the design of the former, so also the appearance of the farthing had to be altered in 1897. Bright new farthings, with the brilliant golden red lustre of freshly minted bronze, were liable to confusion with half-sovereigns, so the bulk of the farthings released in 1897 were treated with a dark finish prior to release. Bright farthings of that date, with original lustre, therefore command a premium. Dark-finish farthings were released annually until 1901, the last year being by far the commonest.

CHAPTER TWENTY

Edward VII (1901–1910)

Albert Edward, Prince of Wales, succeeded his mother on 22 January 1901. In his sixtieth year, he was the oldest heir the British throne ever had and most of his life had been spent understudying his mother who was so paranoid in her jealousy of him that she never allowed him access to the red dispatch boxes of government papers until he was well into his fifties. Although he is often seen, in retrospect, as a playboy with gargantuan appetites for the good life, the fact remains that he was always exemplary in his discharge of his public duties, especially in the long years when the Widow of Windsor was a virtual recluse. He had immense personal popularity. A great patron of the theatre and the turf, he won the Derby three times and also excelled as a yachtsman. Abroad, Edward had great charisma which served him in good stead when he had the task of bringing the Boer War to a reasonably successful conclusion in May 1902. World opinion was ranged against Britain in this war, in which the mightiest power on earth was seen to be engaged in the suppression of two small farming republics in South Africa. Realising Britain's dangerous isolation Edward worked hard to create the Anglo-French and Anglo-Russian ententes and the Anglo-Japanese treaty and to strengthen ties with Scandinavia and the Iberian countries by intermarriage with the British royal family. King Edward and Queen Alexandra were the first British sovereigns to travel extensively on goodwill, public relations and quasi-diplomatic missions and his genial personality and immense natural charm earned for him the title of Edward the Peacemaker. In 1909 the king and queen visited Berlin and dispelled the animosities which had developed between Britain and Germany.

In the same year, however, the domestic political situation escalated into an acute political crisis. The return of a Liberal government in 1909, with a clear mandate for widespread social and political reforms, culminated in Lloyd George's famous budget introducing old age pensions, national insurance contributions and other measures which laid the foundations of the modern Welfare State, at the cost of increased taxation on the upper and middle classes. The budget was rejected by the House of Lords, which had a built-in Conservative majority, and the impasse was only resolved by the threat of abolishing the peers' veto. Fresh general elections in January 1910 merely reinforced the Liberal standpoint and the country was in a turmoil. Never before had Edward been called on to exercise his tact and diplomacy to solve the grave difficulties facing the government and the country. This proved too much for him and a prolonged bout of bronchitis led to his death on 6 May. Unprecedented crowds attended his lying-in-state and his funeral, graced by nine kings and a galaxy of international figures, was the last great royal showpiece.

The old head coinage of Queen Victoria had been in use for a very short period when it became necessary to change the obverses at least. Inevitably, the Edwardian coinage made as few changes as possible in the interests of expediency and economy. Much of the work on the old head series had been entrusted to George de Saulles and he was now responsible for the design of all the Edwardian obverses, distinguished by the skilful placing of the lettering which was even more copious than that on the old head coins.

Shortly after Edward's accession his son and daughter-in-law, the Duke and Duchess of York, visited Canada, South Africa, New Zealand and Australia, inaugurating the newly formed Commonwealth of Australia. The stress laid by the king in his overseas dominions was also reflected in the enlargement of the royal titles at the opening of parliament in November 1901, in which he was styled 'Edward VII, by the Grace of God, of the United Kingdom of Great Britain and Ireland, *and of all the British Dominions beyond the Seas*, King, Defender of the Faith, Emperor of India'. The inclusion of the phrase italicised led to the insertion of the Latin abbreviation OMN (omnium = *all*) after BRITT in the obverse legend to signify '*all* the Britons' wherever they might be.

The right-facing profile of the king, engraved by De Saulles was, in turn, derived from a drawing by Emil Fuchs, the Austrian-born court painter. The initials DE S. appear below the truncation of the neck. In contrast with the changes in the obverse, the reverse of the gold coins remained exactly as before. Five- and two-pound pieces were issued for general circulation only in 1902, while the sovereign and half-sovereign were minted annually from 1902 until 1910. Not only were these 'bullion' coins struck in astronomic numbers in London, but they were abundantly produced by the three Australian branch mints. In 1908, taking advantage of the gold which had been discovered in large quantities in the Klondike, production of gold coins began at the branch mint in Ottawa. In the first year only 633 sovereigns were struck with the C (*Canada*) mintmark but more substantial quantities were minted in 1909–10. Half-sovereigns were struck in 1902–10 at the Royal Mint but, apart from the first year, production was lower than for the sovereign. Production at the branch mints was sporadic and none at all was minted in Ottawa. Proof versions of the four gold coins, struck at the Royal Mint, were included in the presentation sets celebrating the coronation in

Edward VII silver crown, design by De Saulles. (*Peter Clayton*)

1902. Whereas previous proofs had an overall brilliant finish, the 1902 coins had a distinctive matt surface.

De Saulles designed the reverses of the half-crown, florin and shilling as well as all the obverses. Pistrucci's St George and Dragon motif was retained for the crown, and the modified Merlen reverses remained on the sixpence, threepence and Maundy coins. The sole concession to the times, in respect of the smaller silver coins, was the change from the crown of St Edward the Confessor, surmounting the value, to the Tudor crown with its distinctive single convex arch. An armorial theme was retained for the half-crown, but the 'spade' shield with its florid surroundings was now superseded by a much rounder shield with sinuous curves in keeping with the spirit of Art Nouveau, and a surround composed of the collar of the Garter reminiscent

Edwardian silver sixpence, showing Tudor crown. (*Coin Monthly*)

Edwardian silver half-crown with Art Nouveau shield. (*Coin Monthly*)

Edwardian silver shilling with lion on crown motif. (*Peter Clayton*)

of the coins designed by Merlen 80 years earlier. The custom of dividing the royal titles between obverse and reverse was continued on the Edwardian half-crown and also extended to the shilling. The lion on crown motif of the shilling was clearly derived from Merlen's design for the shilling of 1825 but, once again, the influence of Art Nouveau can be seen in the inclusion of curved lines with plant-like finials on either side. It was, however, in the design of the florin that De Saulles excelled himself and he is deservedly remembered largely on account of this coin. Complaints about the previous florin being confused with the half-crown led to an entirely new reverse which replaced the clutter of armorial devices with an elegant standing figure of Britannia, her windswept robe and flag giving free rein to those writhing lines so beloved of the Art Nouveau school. The base on which Britannia stood was the foredeck and prow of a Roman galley, symbol of British naval might. The design was clearly based on the Trade Dollar which had been introduced in 1895 for circulation in the Far East.

New florin design in effort to distinguish more clearly from half-crown. (*Coin Monthly*)

The crown had an ordinary grained edge instead of the regnal date inscription previously used. The practicality of this large coin had been far outweighed by its inconvenient size and no further issues were made in this reign. All of the other silver coins were minted regularly from 1902 to 1910. The threepence can be distinguished from its Maundy counterpart by its matt surface, whereas all the Maundy coins had a brilliant finish.

For the bronze coins the De Saulles obverse was used in conjunction with the modified L. C. Wyon reverse, showing Britannia without the ship or

'High tide' and 'low tide' pennies of Edward VII. (*Peter Clayton*)

lighthouse which had graced the Victorian bronze of 1860–94. All three denominations – penny, halfpenny and farthing – were produced for general circulation each year from 1902 until 1910 but no proof versions appeared in 1902. Two versions of the penny and halfpenny, however, were minted that year, differing in the level of the horizon line on the reverse, the so-called 'low horizon' type being the scarcer in each case. After a gap of seventeen years third-farthings were struck in 1902 for colonial use, the reverse showing the value in words within a crowned wreath.

CHAPTER TWENTY-ONE

George V (1910–1936)

Politically the monarch now exerted little or no influence on the momentous events of his reign, beginning with the budget crisis of 1910 and culminating in the General Strike of 1926, but George V, a career naval officer in his earlier years, played an active part throughout the First World War and was indefatigable in his tours of the battlefront, as well as the numerous morale-boosting visits to hospitals, factories and dockyards on the home front. In July 1917 he renounced his German titles, ranks and honours and changed the family name from Saxe-Coburg-Gotha to Windsor. George V has often been portrayed as a rather gruff martinet of forbidding mien, but this belies the essential kindliness and humanity of the man. At his accession it is significant that, on his personal insistence, the anti-Catholic formula in the proclamation was deleted. A sympathetic profile of the king was sculpted by the Australian artist, Bertram Mackennal, and used for the obverse of the Coronation Medal, the 1912 series of postage stamps and the full range of coinage introduced in 1911. The designer's initials, B. M., may be found on the truncation of the neck. Since the death of De Saulles in 1903 the post of chief engraver to the Mint had fallen into abeyance. It had been more or less redundant following the introduction of more sophisticated die-cutting and reducing equipment. Henceforward it became customary to obtain designs for coins and medals by open competition.

In the George V series the reverses followed the De Saulles Edwardian patterns with some modifications, hearkened back to the more traditional designs by Pistrucci and L. C. Wyon, or introduced new elements by Kruger Gray and Percy Metcalfe. Inevitably, in a reign spanning more than a quarter of a century there were changes, adaptations and modifications of the coinage at various times, including the first actual change in the composition of the coinage metal in sixty years – in fact, since bronze replaced pure copper in the subsidiary coinage in 1860. The stupendous socio-economic upheavals brought about by the First World War and its aftermath had their reverberations on the coinage, driving gold out of general circulation and drastically debasing the silver.

Large head coinage, 1911–27

The fiction of circulating five- and two-pound pieces was not maintained at the outset of this reign and only proof versions were struck for inclusion in the coronation souvenir presentation sets. Both coins recited the king's Latinised name and titles on the obverse while the reverse featured Pistrucci's George and Dragon. On both sovereign and half-sovereign, however, the smaller formats precluded the use of full inscriptions and Defender of the Faith and the Grace of God were denoted merely by initials. Significantly BRITT. OMN. REX. and IND. IMP. – titles by which the king set great store – were left without further abbreviation. Both denominations also depicted the George and Dragon reverse. Sovereigns and half-sovereigns were struck annually until 1915, but production of sovereigns dropped sharply in 1914 and the bulk of the 20 million minted in 1915 was destined for overseas used and doubtless ended up mainly in the coffers of the Arab sheikhs whose support was so vital to Britain's war effort in the Middle East. Over 7 million halves were struck in 1914 but less than one-third of that quantity the following year. As part of the package of emergency measures hastily rushed through over the prolonged August Bank Holiday of 1914 at the outbreak of the First World War, specie payments were suspended and the first Treasury £1 and 10 shilling notes were introduced as a substitute for gold. Thereafter gold coins disappeared from general circulation, though they continued to be minted for overseas bullion transactions. The Royal Mint struck sovereigns in 1916, and a handful in 1917, but no more were minted in London, except a consignment for overseas use in 1925.

Though production of gold coins in London was severely curtailed, the overseas branch mints struck considerable quantities. Both Perth and Melbourne struck sovereigns continuously from 1911 until 1928, though some dates are scarce and it is doubtful whether Melbourne actually struck any in 1927. Sydney minted a sufficiency of sovereigns between 1911 and 1919 but thereafter smaller quantities were minted until 1926, except 1925 when something approaching pre-war output was attained. Sovereigns with the c mintmark of the Ottawa mint were produced intermittently from 1911 to 1919 (none being struck in 1912 and 1915). Sovereigns were also struck at the Calcutta Mint in 1918 and may be identified by the letter I (*India*). In the immediate post-war years, however, South Africa emerged as one of the world's leading producers of gold and in 1923 it was decided that the Pretoria Mint should strike sovereigns with the letters SA (*South Africa*). Only a handful were struck that year for general circulation, but proofs were also produced. Production rose slowly in 1924 and was in full swing by 1925. Large head sovereigns were struck in increasing abundance from then until 1928.

A break with tradition was the omission of a crown from the coronation souvenir sets, even in a proof version. The largest denomination in circulation for all practical purposes was the half-crown. Basically the De Saulles design was retained but the opportunity was taken to improve it in minor details. The circular beaded border was now removed, the pellets at the sides were reduced in size and the cross pattee in the crown was modified. Proofs of the 1911 half-crown were included in the presentation set, and circulating versions were minted annually until 1919 in sterling silver.

Regrettably De Saulles's standing Britannia was dropped from the reverse of the florin in favour of a cruciform arrangement of the heraldic symbols of the United Kingdom. This reverse was apparently designed by a committee within the Royal Mint itself and was clearly derived from the Jubilee florin, though presenting a marked improvement over its Victorian forebear. By confining the royal titles to the obverse and omitting the equivalent value in shillings from the inscription the reverse now permitted a larger and more elaborate treatment of the heraldic devices, with the star of the Garter in the centre and sceptres in the interstices. Tudor crowns surmounted each shield, carrying the motif up to the rim of the coin. De Saulles's shilling reverse of the lion standing on the crown was obviously quite acceptable as it was, since no modifications were made in its design. Indeed, this motif was now extended also to the sixpence, replacing the Merlen-inspired verbal motif. The threepence continued the crowned numeral design and can be distinguished from the Maundy coins by its dull finish. Proofs of the silver coins down to the tiny Maundy penny were included in the 1911 set, and circulating versions of all values from the half-crown to the threepence were produced annually until 1919, both sixpence and threepence also appearing in the original fineness in 1920.

Georgian florin abandoning De Saulles's reverse design. (*Coin Monthly*)

Considering that many of the other countries involved in the First World War had been forced to abandon silver, and even base-metal coins in some cases, it is a measure of Britain's economic resilience, plus the vast resources of the colonial empire, that silver coins continued to circulate freely and unabated throughout that period. In the aftermath of war, however, the world price of silver rose sharply, and this posed a severe problem for the

Royal Mint which suddenly found itself faced with a situation in which sterling silver coins possessed a scrap value appreciably greater than their face value. Although legislation made it a felony to melt silver coins, the point had clearly been reached when more drastic measures were needed. Although it was possible to continue striking the smaller denominations − sixpence, threepence and Maundy money − in sterling silver in 1920, the larger coins were issued that year in 0.500 fine silver, the other main constituent being copper.

The decision to debase the silver coinage was a sound one, since it permitted the Royal Mint to make a plentiful issue of all denominations, in the original designs, from the threepence to the half-crown, every year from 1920 until 1926. The design of the sixpence was altered slightly in 1925, resulting in a broader rim with more prominent beading. Sixpences issued that year may be found in both versions. The Maundy set was likewise debased to 0.500 fine silver in 1921 and continued with the original effigy until 1927. The Maundy threepence differs from the circulating version in the surfacing, as in previous issues. With the exception of the florin, the circulating silver coins struck in the latter part of 1926 and also in 1927 were produced from new dies in which the detail of the king's profile was more sharply defined, and the position of Mackennal's initials on the truncation altered. No modified effigy threepences were released until 1927.

The bronze coinage during the first part of this reign had quite a chequered history. Both halfpence and farthings were minted annually throughout this period but pennies were produced in such large quantities in 1920−21 that relatively few were required in 1922 and none at all in 1923−25. The passage of the National Insurance Act on 1 July 1911, which compelled employers to pay in 'broken wages', created an unusually heavy demand for small silver and bronze coins and the Royal Mint was forced to sub-contract production of pennies in 1912 to Ralph Heaton of Birmingham. Heaton pennies may be recognised by the H mintmark in the exergue to the left of the date. Towards the end of the war demand for pennies forced the Royal Mint to farm out production again, and in 1918 and 1919 substantial quantities were struck by Heatons and the King's Norton subsidiary of Nobel Metal Industries Ltd, H and KN mintmarks appearing in the exergue respectively.

Halfpence were produced annually from 1911 to 1925 with the original large head. A modified effigy with sharper detail and altered initials was adopted for the penny and halfpenny in the mid-1920s. Very few pennies of this type were minted in 1926 but a large quantity appeared in 1927. The modified effigy was used for halfpence in 1925, worth a small premium over the original version of that date, and for all the halfpence struck in 1926−27. Farthings were issued each year from 1911 to 1918 with the dark finish required to distinguish them from the half-sovereign. By 1918, however, as half-sovereigns had disappeared from circulation, it was no longer necessary to continue with this additional expense and the majority of farthings minted that year had the same brilliant lustre as the larger bronze

Third-farthing for circulation in Malta. (*Coin Monthly*)

coins. Bright-finish farthings were issued in large quantities each year from then until 1925. The modified effigy was adopted the following year and farthings of this type continued to appear without break until the end of the reign. Tiny third-farthings, with the same reverse as the Edwardian coins, were struck in 1913 only, for circulation in Malta.

Small head coinage, 1927–36

At the beginning of this second period of the reign British coinage had reached its zenith, in terms of general circulation. The Irish Free State, which had won its independence in 1921, had continued to use British coins but in 1928 adopted its own series, and though British coins continued to circulate in the twenty-six counties of southern Ireland, demand for them inevitably decreased. Australia had adopted its own coinage in 1910–11 but again British coins continued to circulate for some years thereafter. In New Zealand British silver coins were used until 1933 and bronze coins circulated until the Second World War. British coins were used in South Africa until the mid-1920s, while many of the colonies and protectorates continued to employ British coins until relatively recently.

Britain returned to the gold standard in 1925, after an eleven year gap, and in that year production of sovereigns was resumed. At this time, however, the pound was grossly overvalued and this seriously hampered overseas trade. The Wall Street crash in 1929, followed by widespread depression all over the world, forced Britain to abandon the gold standard in 1931 and the effective value of the pound was cut by one-fifth. This greatly boosted trade and the subsequent economic recovery. By the time of the king's Silver Jubilee in 1935 the nation felt that it really had something worth celebrating, and there were widespread displays of genuine affection which greatly touched the ageing monarch. Against medical advice the king spent the ensuing winter at Sandringham and it was there that he succumbed to a chill on 20 January 1936. The crowds that lined the streets of London at his funeral were the largest ever seen.

During the latter part of the king's reign gold coins were absent from general circulation, though sovereigns continued to be minted in the branch mints and thus may be found with the small effigy introduced in 1929. The small head had the same depth as its predecessor, but was significantly narrower. This, curiously enough, had the effect of making the king look younger. It reduced the cramped effect on the legend and produced a more satisfactory appearance all round. Like the original profile, it was the work of the Australian-born sculptor, now Sir Bertram Mackennal, who had been knighted in 1921. Small head sovereigns were struck at Melbourne and Perth in 1929–31 but none at Sydney, Ottawa or Calcutta in this period. Rand gold production was at its peak, however, and the great majority of sovereigns were struck in 1929–32 at the Pretoria Mint, and bore the SA mintmark. The 1932 South African sovereign was, in fact, the last 'circulating' sovereign to be minted until the present reign.

An entirely new series of designs for the silver coinage was introduced in 1927, the work of George Kruger Gray (1880–1943) who also designed coins for a number of Commonwealth countries. His initials, KG, may be found on the reverses of the silver coins. The most remarkable aspect of the 1927 coinage was the resurrection of the crown. The practicability of this large coin had long fallen into abeyance, but it was now revived primarily as a Christmas gift. The 1927 crown was only issued in a proof version, but the mintage was 15,030 — substantially higher than the subsequent 'circulating' versions. For the first time in many years Pistrucci's noble St George was withdrawn and the Tudor crown became the pincipal motif, as befitted the name of the coin, and it was surrounded by a garland of the floral emblems of the United Kingdom. The king's Latin titles FID. DEF. and IND. IMP. appeared at the top but an infelicitous touch was the inclusion of the word CROWN at the foot, split into two by an English rose. The Kruger Gray's crown appeared every year from 1927 until 1936, with the exception of 1935 when a special Silver Jubilee crown was released. This was designed by Percy Metcalfe and hearkened back to Pistrucci, but the angular St George and Dragon were very much a product of the 1930s, and there is little in this Art Moderne design redolent of the Romanticism associated with the Pistrucci version. On this ocassion all the royal titles were placed on the obverse, and only the legend CROWN 1935 appeared round the top of the reverse. Both proofs and circulating coins were produced with an incuse edge, though some 2,500 proofs were also issued with a raised edge. Demand for the Christmas crowns fell after the initial interest waned, and their fluc-

Silver crown revived primarily as a Christmas gift. (*Coin Monthly*)

Silver Jubilee crown, 1935. (*Coin Monthly*)

tuating mintages reflect the economic state of the country. Only 932 crowns were minted in 1934, making this one of the rarest regular issues of this century.

For the florin Kruger Gray took the cruciform shield arrangement hitherto used and turned it upon its axis by 45 degrees so that the sceptres pointed north and south. The crowns, altered in shape, were placed on top of the sceptres and the slightly enlarged shields had a severely plain outline. The star of the Garter was replaced in the centre by the king's monogram. FID. DEF. IND. IMP. appeared in the upper half, balanced by the date and ONE FLORIN in the lower half. Like the crown and half-crown, only proof versions were issued in 1927 but thereafter circulating versions were produced each year. The half-crown continued with a heraldic shield, but this was now stripped of its crown and the ribbon bearing the Garter motto. The Latin titles appeared at the top of the reverse, as before, but the denomination and date were rearranged at the foot, and the digits of the date were no longer separated. Tiny heraldic flowers were incorporated in the legend and crowned cyphers flanked the shield, occupying the space now provided by the 'nipped waist' effect. Proofs appeared in 1927 and circulating versions in 1928–36.

Kruger Gray designed florin. (*Peter Clayton*)

The new shilling was a substantial modification of the previous design, but it has to be admitted that Gray's version of the lion on crown theme was less successful than its predecessor. Principally, the removal of the date from the field and incorporation in the legend served to cramp an already crowded

New design shilling. (*Coin Monthly*)

'Weed garden' sixpence. (*Peter Clayton*)

inscription and this, in turn, cribbed and confined the central motif. The shilling was the only silver coin struck in 1927 in a circulating version as well as proof. Thereafter shillings were minted each year until 1936, though relatively few were struck in 1930 and 1934. An entirely new design was adopted for the sixpence and has since been disparagingly referred to as a 'weed garden'. In fact, despite the superficial impression one has of a haphazard jumble of vegetation, the design is quite ingenious and comprises six acorns linked by sprigs of oak leaves. Proofs were struck in 1927 and circulating coins thereafter. Those struck in 1929–31 had a wide-spaced graining, but from 1931 onwards the milling was much more close-grained. The same principle was applied to the threepence, with three acorns and oak leaves on the reverse. Again, proofs were issued in 1927 and ordinary circulating coins in 1928–36. No change was made in the Maundy coins which retained the modified effigy until 1936, the last issue being posthumous.

The reverse of the penny, halfpenny and farthing remained unchanged in this period, but the small head was adopted in 1928 for the two higher denominations. As a rule, the penny was produced in astronomical quantities each year, ranging between 30 and 50 million on average, and reaching a high point in excess of 154 million in 1936. Fewer than 20 million were minted in 1931 and the glut of pennies in circulation meant that little more than 8 million were required in 1932. No pennies were struck for general use in 1933 and only about 14 million the following year. A handful of 1933 pennies, however, was struck mainly for inclusion in year sets interred under the foundation stones of public buildings, and only one or two are believed to be in the hands of private collectors. Halfpence were produced in abundance each year throughout this period. As already noted, the farthing alone continued to use the modified effigy of 1926 right through to the end of the reign.

CHAPTER TWENTY-TWO

Edward VIII (1936)

The reign of Edward VIII was the shortest in British history since the time of his namesake, the boy-king Edward V, smothered in the Tower by order of his uncle, Richard III, in 1483. During the eleven-month reign four postage stamps bearing his profile were issued in Britain but no coins were generally circulated. None the less, the reign of Edward VIII was not without numismatic impact. Had the king not abdicated on 11 December, to marry the woman he loved, his coronation would have taken place in May 1937. As part of the preparations for this a series of coins bearing his profile were designed. These would have been released in 1937 and thus bore that date. More than 200 coinage and medal dies, in fact, had to be scrapped following the abdication, proof of the intensive preparations which had taken place at the Royal Mint. In accordance with established practice, proof sets ranging from the gold five-pound piece to the bronze farthing were to have been issued. An unspecified, but undoubtedly very small, number of proof sets was actually struck and at least one of these sets has come on the market in recent years.

The obverses were designed by Thomas Humphrey Paget, whose initials H. P. were placed beneath the truncation of the king's neck. The obverse inscription read EDWARDVS VIII D:G: BR: OMN: REX F:D: IND: IMP. and the king's profile faced left. The reverse of the gold coins, comprising five- and two-pound pieces and sovereigns, maintained the well-established tradition of Pistrucci's St George and Dragon, with the date in the exergue.

The silver was to comprise the same six denominations as before, namely crown, half-crown, florin, shilling, sixpence and threepence. The reverses for this series were designed by Kruger Gray. The obverses of the silver coins were similar to the gold but the king's titles were split so that FID: DEF: IND: IMP appeared on the reverses, round the upper half of the circumference. The lower part in each case was occupied by the denomination, the three largest coins also including the date. On the shilling the date was split and placed

Edward VIII crown. (*Royal Mint*)

in the field, but on the sixpence and threepence it followed the titles round the top. For the crown Gray produced a new version of the United Kingdom coat of arms, with the lion and unicorn as supporters and the motto of the Garter in a scrolled ribbon on the ground at their feet. The half-crown also

(a)

(b)

(c)

Designs for Edwards VIII (a) half-crown, (b) Florin and (c) shilling. (*Royal mint*) featured the arms of the countries of the United Kingdom, but on this occasion they were rendered as a royal standard, flanked by crowned royal cyphers. The florin had a crowned Tudor rose, flanked by thistle and shamrock with the initials ER (*Edwardus Rex*) underneath. The shilling broke new ground by having a pronounced Scottish flavour. The lion squatting on the crown, with sword and sceptre upraised, had been commonly used in the insignia of government offices in Scotland since the early nineteenth century, and to reinforce its Scottishness the design included a Saltire Cross of St Andrew and the Scottish thistle.

In the design of the smaller silver coins Kruger Gray seems to have been inspired by the coins of Charles II which, it may be remembered, had a motif of interlocking C's, the number of which was determined by the denomination. On this occasion interlocking signet rings were chosen, six being featured on the sixpence and three on the threepence. Gray's initials, KG, were placed prominently on the reverses.

(a)

(b)

Design for (a) Edward VIII sixpence and threepence (*Royal Mint*) with those of (b) Charles II for comparison. (*Coin Monthly*)

Although a silver threepence was included in the series in accordance with previous tradition, serious thought was given to phasing out this tiny coin and replacing it gradually by a more substantial piece in a hitherto untried alloy of nickel brass. Experiments were carried out with pieces which would feel different, and both serrated and polygonal edges were tried. Eventually it was decided that the brass coin should have a twelve-sided flan. The reverse for this coin showed three thrift flowers and was submitted by Madge Kitchener, a freelance designer who had the distinction of being niece to the great field marshal of the First World War. In addition to the normal brass threepence, patterns were produced in which the thrift plant was given a more naturalistic treatment than in the proof version. Moreover, the pattern had a circular line around the thrift plant, separating it from the inscription.

Pattern brass threepence contrasted with normal reverse. (*Royal Mint*)

Whereas the proof had this rendered as THREE PENCE round the top and 1937 at the foot, the pattern had THREE at the top, PENCE at the foot, and the date split into two parts flanking the central motif. A few of these patterns are alleged to have been produced for experimental purposes and, to quote the catalogues, 'a few did get into circulation'. It would appear, however, that Humphrey Paget had a number of these trial pieces in his possession, and from time to time disposed of them to collectors.

Edward VIII penny. (*Royal Mint*)

The Wyon design for the penny was substantially altered by Charles Walter Coombes, and the lighthouse, absent for half a century, was restored. Paget had submitted a design for the half-crown showing the *Golden Hind*, the three-masted sailing ship in which Sir Francis Drake had voyaged round the world. Though rejected for that denomination, it was accepted for the halfpenny and Paget's initials appeared beneath the bowsprit. The infusion

Reverse design of halfpenny, originally submitted for the half-crown. (*Royal Mint*)

Edward VIII farthing – the introduction of the wren. (*Royal Mint*)

of pictorialism into the series was maintained with the humblest denomination of all which depicted the most loved of all British birds, the wren. This design was the work of Harold Wilson Parker and was unusual in having the denomination at the foot and the date at the top, thus reversing the order found on the other bronze coins.

CHAPTER TWENTY-THREE

George VI (1936–1952)

The abdication of Edward VIII was a devastating blow to the country, and escalating political crises in Europe and the Far East with the rise of Fascism did nothing to dispel the gloom. But the royal family closed ranks behind the new king and, despite the ill health and the physical handicap of a stammer, George VI restored the reputation of the monarchy at a time when its effect on the national morale had never been needed so much. The Second World War dominated this reign and had more sweeping and far-reaching effects on the country than any previous conflict. These dramatic events were reflected in the coinage, which underwent more drastic changes in the first decade of the reign than at any other time in English history.

First coinage, 1937–46

The reign commenced in traditional form with the issue of a proof series in 1937 to celebrate the coronation. This consisted of 22 carat gold coins as before – five- and two-pound pieces, sovereigns and half-sovereigns, with Pistrucci's St George and Dragon on the reverse. No circulating gold coins with the king's effigy were minted. The obverse by Humphrey Paget showed a left-facing profile, like his brother and father before him. Whereas Edward VIII was held to have broken tradition by facing left (he looked better when showing the parting of his hair) George VI had merely restored it – a good omen for his reign. The titles in Latin also clung to tradition: GEORGIVS VI D:G: BR: OMN: REX F:D: IND: IMP. signifying that, in 1937 George VI was still, by the Grace of God, King of all the Britains, Defender of the Faith and Emperor of India.

Proofs of the crown, half-crown, florin, shilling, sixpence, threepence and the Maundy series were included in the coronation set, and circulating versions of all eleven coins were also struck in 1937. The number of the silver coins needs some explanation, being the highest number since Victorian times. Kruger Gray was responsible for all the reverses, except the Maundy series which retained the numeral designs.

The reverse of the crown was, in fact, identical to that used in the unissued proof set of Edward VIII. In addition to the proof version, circulating crowns were struck and 418,699 were issued to the public as souvenirs of the coronation rather than as genuinely circulating coins. For the half-crown, however, Gray produced an entirely new reverse. The armorial theme was retained, but in place of the royal standard which would have graced the coin of Edward VIII there was an elegantly waisted tilting-shield, complete with a ring by which it appeared to be suspended from a peg. The nipped waist of the shield permitted the inclusion of crowned monograms and Gray's initials appeared underneath.

George VI half-crown with entirely new reverse. (*Coin Monthly*)

The florin or two shillings retained Gray's design from the Edwardian series, merely substituting a G for an E below the thistle. Both half-crown and florin were minted annually from 1937 to 1946. The fewest were struck in 1938 and the largest mintages occurred during the war years. It is one of the apparent paradoxes of recent times that such an abundance of silver coins should have been possible during such a critical period. In fact, the war turned out to be a tremendous stimulus to the economy, bringing an end to a twenty-year period of high unemployment. Wages soared dramatically, keeping ahead of the inflation which overtook the economy, and the enormous increase in the money supply was reflected in the size of the silver output. In 1942 alone, for example, output of half-crowns more than doubled on the previous year and was five times larger than that of 1938. The issue of florins was hardly less dramatic.

There were two versions of the shilling, both designed by Kruger Gray. The so-called English pattern retained the previous motif of the lion on all fours surmounting the Tudor crown. Gray modified the design he had previously produced for the George V shillings, the digits of the date now flanking the lion in the field and the space thus provided round the circumference being occupied by a pair of English roses. The Scottish shilling used the reverse which had previously been struck for the Edward VIII shilling.

(a)   (b)

(a) English shilling and (b) Scottish shilling. (*Coin Monthly*)

The Scottishness of the design was marred, however, by the fact that the Tudor crown was used instead of the Scottish crown – a defect which was belatedly remedied in 1968 when the shilling's decimal successor appeared. The combined mintage of English and Scottish shillings just about equalled the mintage of florins, so each type is relatively scarcer than the higher denominations. Moreover, fewer Scottish shillings were minted than English in each year, sometimes considerably fewer, and only in 1945–46 were both versions struck in more or less equal quantities. It has been said that the Scottish shilling was a tribute to Queen Elizabeth who, though born in Hertfordshire, was of Scottish descent, but the fact remains that an identical design had been prepared for the Edward VIII series, when no such explanation was given.

(a)   (b)

(a) George VI sixpence and (b) silver threepence. (*Coin Monthly*)

For the smaller circulating silver coins Gray abandoned the interlocking rings motif of the projected Edwardian series and produced distinctive designs for each denomination. In both cases the value appeared in words round the foot, FID: DEF: IND: IMP. appeared at the top and the year flanked the central motif, consisting of the royal monogram GRI in Old English capitals surmounted by a Tudor crown (sixpence) and the shield of St George superimposed on a five-petalled Tudor rose (threepence). Sixpences were

George VI Maundy set, in 0.500 fine silver. (*Coin Monthly*)

minted annually throughout this period in great abundance, but the silver threepence was gradually phased out in 1944. The small mintages of 1942–44 were intended exclusively for colonial consumption. Complaints that this tiny coin was easily lost, together with the rising costs of production and the raw material, led to the decision to replace it by a base-metal coin, noted below. Like all the other silver coins of the 1937–46 period, the Maundy series was struck in 0.500 fine silver. The full range of the king's titles was confined to the obverse and were it not for the infinite versatility of the reducing machines used at the Royal Mint this would have created problems for engravers cutting the dies, especially for the tiny twopence and penny. As it is, the lettering on these coins is so minuscule as to excite the admiration of those who are unaware of the process by which lettering can be reduced to microscopic proportions if need be.

The dodecagonal (twelve-sided) threepence was struck in nickel brass, using Madge Kitchener's thrift motif modified by Percy Metcalfe to give the plant a more stylised appearance. The king's titles were confined to the obverse, leaving the reverse free for the value at the top and the date at the foot. Coins of this type were produced annually from 1937 until 1948, except 1947. The very small mintage of 620,734 in 1946 was, in fact, intended for use in the West Indies and few came into the hands of collectors in uncirculated condition.

Brass threepenny piece. (*Coin Monthly*)

Three designers shared the credit for the bronze coins. Humphrey Paget designed the reverse for the halfpenny, as well as the obverses of all three denominations. The halfpenny used the *Golden Hind* design originally intended for the Edwardian halfpenny. The ship and lighthouse were restored to the Britannia reverse on the penny by Charles Coombes, while Harold Parker's wren motif for the farthing also followed the Edwardian plan; these were fully described in the previous chapter. All three coins continued without change until 1948, but while the halfpenny and farthing were struck every year, no pennies appeared in 1941–43.

Statistics published in 1938 show that in the preceding year there were 4 shillings' worth of bronze coins in circulation for every man, woman and child of the population (approximately 45 million). The London Passenger Transport Board claimed that it handled more than 6,000 tons of bronze coins annually. It should be noted also that in 1937 production at the Royal

Mint exceeded 400 million pieces for the first time ever, though about 100 million were for the dominions and colonies and about 5 million for foreign countries. Moreover, the phenomenal increase in coin production in 1942–43 was probably due to the enormous influx of Allied troops, principally Americans, stationed in Britain in the period before D-Day (6 June 1944). Since there were more than 5 million men in the American Expeditionary Force their spending power in 1942–44 must have had immense repercussions on the coinage of that period.

Later coinage, 1947–52

The Second World War left Britain drained and exhausted. The stress and strain of the war years undermined the health of the king, never a robust man, and undoubtedly hastened his early death on 6 February 1952. The immediate post-war years were a period of austerity, with continuing shortages and rationing of commodities which were not rationed during the war itself. The Labour party had been swept to power in the general election of 1945, with a mandate to nationalise the major industries and implement the measures conceived during the war for the establishment of the Welfare State. Socialist theory was soon confronted with harsh reality, in which a combination of severe winters and summer droughts resulted in fuel cuts and the rationing of bread and potatoes. The workers found that nationalisation was not the panacea they had imagined and out of industrial discontent came strikes, high wage settlements – sometimes as much as sixpence an hour – and consequent inflation. The domestic situation was aggravated by external economic factors. The American economy recovered from the war more rapidly than the British and this precipitated a flood of American imports with precious little trade in the other direction. A valiant attempt was made to encourage export to North America but the dollar gap steadily widened. During the war the United States had made massive loans to Britain in the form of gold and silver bullion and these had to be repaid. Britain made every effort to repay them, with an almost catastrophic effect on the national bullion reserves. Gold was repaid at the official rate of $35 an ounce – at a time when the price on the free market (i.e. southern Africa) had risen to over $40 an ounce. This was a disadvantageous situation, exacerbated by the fact that silver was needed as much for industrial purposes as for repayment of the American loan.

It was in this desperate situation that the Treasury was forced to take drastic measures. The minting of 0.500 fine silver coins in 1946–47 was well below the wartime output – at a time when inflation and higher wages were making greater demands on circulating coinage. Inevitably something had to be done. Early in 1947 parliament sanctioned the striking of 'silver' coins entirely in base metal, using an alloy of 75 per cent copper and 25 per cent nickel. No change was made in the design of the coins which continued at first with the king's titles in full. The coins thus debased were the half-crown, two-shilling, both English and Scottish shillings and sixpence. All five coins were struck in 1947–48 in fairly large quantities. One of the paradoxes of the financial crisis leading to the substitution of cupro-nickel was the revival of sterling (0.925 fine) silver for the Maundy money which appeared in 1947–48 with the king's titles in full. The debasement of the circulating coinage was followed. by a dramatic devaluation of the pound. Hitherto tariffed at $4.80, it was now reduced to $2.80. This desperate move aimed at closing the dollar gap and making British products more competitive in the vital North American market. At the same time, the Sterling area shrank considerably as the British West Indies bowed to the inevitable and abandoned pounds, shillings and pence in favour of dollars and cents. This meant that, from then onwards, British coins were restricted to the mother country and an ever-dwindling band of colonies and protectorates.

The decline of the British Empire had begun during the First World War and the principle of self-determination, to which successive governments paid lip service, was barely implemented in the interwar period. The Westminster Conference of 1931 had transformed the Empire into a Commonwealth whose independent members enjoyed dominion status. The Indian sub-continent, however, did not receive independence at this time, and constitutional talks dragged on for several years before being shelved by the outbreak of war in the Far East in 1941. The Labour government was pledged to grant the Indian sub-continent its freedom, but the situation was complicated by communal strife between Muslims and Hindus. The old Empire of India came to an end in August 1947 amid civil war and massacres on a frightening scale. From this emerged the dominions of India and Pakistan. George VI was the last of the king-emperors and the independence of India and Pakistan was reflected in the coins issued after the dissolution of the Indian Empire. It is possible that the dies for the 1948 coins had been produced before India became independent but it seems strange, at this remove in time, that the obsolete title of Emperor of India continued to grace the British coins minted in 1948.

The inscription IND: IMP. was omitted from the coins struck in 1949. So far as the cupro-nickel coins were concerned this made no difference to the obverses, but in the case of the brass threepence and the three bronze coins it resulted in a more balanced and less cramped legend. The reverses of the

English and Scottish shillings with IND: IMP. omitted. (*Coin Monthly*)

Reverse of sixpence replacing old GRI motif. (*Peter Clayton*)

cupro-nickel coins were revised, placing FID and DEF round the top of the circumference. The value in words and the date continued to appear round the foot as before, but the lettering was more widely spaced, and adroit use was made of pellets to fill the spaces at the sides. The only entirely new design resulting from these political changes was the reverse of the sixpence which replaced the GRI motif by the new G VI R cypher.

Coins portraying George VI, without the IND IMP legend, were minted from 1949 to 1952 but production was confined mainly to the first three years. Since the king died at the beginning of February plans were made soon afterwards for new coin dies and production of coins dated 1952 was confined to those denominations warranted by the demand. Thus farthings and half-pence were struck that year but not pennies, since there was an abundance from the mintings in previous years. Similarly the minting of cupro-nickel coins in 1952 was confined to sixpences. Dies for the higher denominations were probably produced and trial strikes may have been made for internal Royal Mint purposes. During the change-checking mania which preceded decimalisation in the late 1960s a half-crown with the seemingly impossible date of 1952 was discovered by Horace Burrows of Chelmsford, and the fact that the coin was pretty worn testified to its having circulated extensively in the fifteen years before its discovery.

Some 14 million pennies were minted in 1949, the last year this coin was to be struck in any quantity until 1961. Pennies for use in the few remaining colonies within the sterling area were minted in 1950–51 in editions of 240,000 and 120,000 respectively. Halfpence were produced in substantial quantities in all four years, 1952 being by far the commonest, and farthings of this period are likewise plentiful. Maundy coins were struck with the effigy of George VI in all four years also, and the omissions of IND IMP on the obverse merely relieved the strain on the rather cramped lettering of the previous issue.

In the gloomy years of 1950–51, when the Cold War was at its height and the Labour government teetered on the brink of collapse after narrowly winning the general election of 1950 and facing open defiance from the left-wingers led by Aneurin Bevan, there seemed little to celebrate, and yet coins were twice issued as commemorative pieces. The first occasion was something of a non-event. The year 1950 was hailed – somewhat prematurely – as mid-century (1951 would have been more correct as the halfway mark of the twentieth century) and this seemed a good enough reason for the Royal Mint to produce a proof set of nine coins, from the half-crown to the farthing but excluding the Maundy series. This proof set received little publicity at the time and only 17,513 sets were sold. In May 1951 came the Festival of Britain, a brave attempt to show that Britain was not finished and intended also as a centenary tribute to the Great Exhibition of 1851. The king himself spoke of it as 'a symbol of Britain's abiding courage and vitality'. The Festival did more than anything else to lift British applied design out of the Victorian era.

Festival of Britain crown. (*Coin Monthly*)

For the first time ever, a crown was struck purely as a commemorative piece. Previous issues had pertained to jubilees and coronations but this was a people's piece, a feeling reflected in the incuse legend on the rim: CIVIUM INDUSTRIA FLORET CIVITAS (*By the industry of its people the State flourishes*). The rim also bore the dates 1851 and 1951 in Roman numerals, alluding to the centenary of the Great Exhibition. These crowns had Pistrucci's St George and Dragon reverse, but a break with tradition was the inclusion of the value FIVE SHILLINGS below the king's effigy on the obverse. Just under 2 million crowns were struck in an overall prooflike condition and sold to the public in green cardboard cases. Some 20,000 crowns, however, were packaged in proof sets along with the nine denominations in everyday use. Though the Festival of Britain proof sets exceed the mid-century sets in number they are today much more highly rated, even allowing for the fact that they contain the crown.

CHAPTER TWENTY-FOUR

Elizabeth II (1952–   )

As the illnesses of George VI became more frequent and prolonged, his elder daughter, Princess Elizabeth, took on more of his duties. It was in this role that she and her husband Prince Philip, Duke of Edinburgh, set out in January 1952 on a tour of Australasia. The first stage of their journey took them to Kenya where they stayed at the Forest Lodge, Sagana, a wedding present from the people of Kenya. It was here that she received the news of her father's death on 6 February. The tour was immediately cancelled and the new queen and her husband returned to London the following day. The statutory period of court mourning was three months and it was not until 31 May that the queen began the full round of royal duties. This was broken, however, on 10 April when she distributed the Maundy money to pensioners in Westminster Abbey. It is singularly appropriate that her first official engagement as monarch should have had a numismatic connection.

At the time of accession the Conservatives under Winston Churchill had been in power barely three months but were to remain in office until 1964. The accession of a young queen brought a touch of glamour back to the drab existence of the British people and the popular press was quick to seize upon the notion of a new Elizabethan era. The coronation in June 1953 was a spectacular success, despite the cold, drizzly weather, and in the news, that unseasonably wintry morning, that Everest had been conquered there was a euphoric feeling that the old bulldog British spirit would triumph again — ignoring, of course, that the world's highest mountain had been conquered by a New Zealander and a Nepalese!

Pounds, shillings and pence (£sd) coinage, 1953–67

The early years of this reign did, indeed, seem like some kind of golden age. The New Elizabethans were to Britain what the New Frontier was in America about the same time. Inevitably the nostalgic view and the reality were not always the same but a glance at the cold statistics shows that between 1953 and 1963 average incomes rose dramatically in real terms, the numbers of home- and car-owners escalated enormously and that, whereas those who could watch the coronation on their own television sets were still relatively few, by 1963 most householders owned at least one set. The people of Britain had attained a level of material prosperity never dreamed of before the war, there was virtually full employment, a steady growth rate of 5 per cent in the economy and an inflation rate of just over 2 per cent. 'Never had it so good' was a smug but wholly justified pronouncement by Harold Macmillan, prime minister during half of the thirteen-year period of Conservative government. At the same time, however, the old idea of imperial commitment disappeared as one colony or protectorate after another achieved independence. After the Suez expedition in 1956 the British government kept clear of entanglement in foreign wars. Significantly, though both Australia and New Zealand were to become embroiled with the United States in the Vietnam conflict, Britain managed to steer clear. The change from the old Empire to the new Commonwealth of Nations was again neatly summed up by Macmillan in his aphorism 'the wind of change'. The post-Suez colonial policy, like the loss of India ten years earlier, had repercussions on the British coinage. Indeed, the title BRITT. OMN. (*of all the Britains*) was dropped from the obverse of British coins with almost indecent haste as early as 1954.

If the coinage of this reign can be said to have distinguished itself in any way it would be in the variety of metals employed. At one end of the scale the minting of gold sovereigns was resumed and sterling silver continued to be used for the Maundy series; at the other end of the scale, cupro-nickel, nickel–brass and bronze served the needs of the circulating coinage.

It will be remembered that the full range of gold coins, from half-sovereign to five-pound piece, had formed part of the proof sets issued in coronation years. The Exchange Control Order of 1947 effectively killed the domestic market in gold coins and no attempt was made to include gold in the coronation proof set in 1953. Dies were produced, however, and an unspecified number of sets struck for inclusion in the various national museum collections. None was ever made available to private collectors and it is unlikely that the ten or so sets in existence will ever come on the market. These gold coins had Pistrucci's St George and Dragon reverse, while the obverse bore a right-facing effigy of the queen, sculpted by Mrs Mary Gillick. A novel feature was the legend which commenced at the top of the circumference and continued clockwise all the way round to the top again, a simple cross dividing the end from the beginning. The legend proclaimed ELIZABETH II DEI GRATIA BRITT. OMN. REGINA F.D. The effigy was unusual in two respects. The kings who had preceded Elizabeth had been portrayed bare-headed, with truncated neck. The Elizabethan obverse returned to the style of the bun coinage of Queen Victoria, with a laureated head and bust truncation.

Although gold coins had long since disappeared from circulation in Britain they continued to be highly valued in the Near and Middle East where they admirably filled the gap left by a healthy distrust of paper money. The Arab predilection for sovereigns, however, encouraged entrepreneurs in the Lebanon and other parts of the Mediterranean area to supply the demand by counterfeiting them. To be fair to the counterfeiters, they did a passable job and the British government was faced with the embarrassment of sovereigns which weighed more than the genuine article! Of course, even in the 1950s, British sovereigns were being traded in the souks and bazaars well above their notional value which was still more or less tied to the American official price of $35 an ounce of fine gold, so the counterfeiters could afford to be generous.

The only solution to this thorny problem was to resume the minting of sovereigns. Just over 2 million were produced in 1957 – less than half the 1925 mintage but considerably more than the last of the South African sovereigns struck in 1932. This sovereign had the same, relatively fine, grain on the edge as its predecessors, but the sovereigns minted from 1958 onwards have a very distinctive 'coarse' grain which helps to distinguish them from shillings in poor light (as if the weight alone would not be sufficient distinction). In view of the demand for Elizabethan sovereigns the mintage in 1958 was greatly increased, but dropped sharply in 1959 and no more were minted until 1962. Thereafter sovereigns were struck in comparatively large quantities each year until 1968. Though minted for the convenience of the bullion market and overseas traders it was inevitable that these Elizabethan sovereigns should find their way into the hands of collectors, even if this has been subject to more restrictions and regulations than any other collectable in recent times.

Elizabeth II gold sovereign. (*Peter Clayton*)

The queen has continued the annual Maundy ceremony of distributing purses containing the special silver coins to as many pensioners of each sex as there are years in her age, but unlike her predecessors the queen has made this a 'movable feast', the venue being changed from year to year. In the first year of her reign she distributed Maundy money bearing the profile of her late father at Westminster Abbey, but in coronation year the ceremony took place at St Paul's Cathedral. The Maundy coins of 1953 were the only ones in this series to have BRITT. OMN. in the title and this ensures the keen demand for them as a distinct type from the later coins. The Maundy coins have remained unaltered in both obverse and reverse designs down to the

1977 Maundy set. (*Tony Davies*)

present time. Decimalisation in 1971 had no effect on the reverse which merely showed a numeral. Thus those issued since 1971 are deemed to be valued in new (decimal) pence. While the nominal value, therefore, jumped 240 per cent their silver content remained the same. From 1954 until 1970 the Maundy money was distributed at Westminster Abbey in alternate years, but since then only in 1973, 1977 and 1981. In the earlier years distribution took place at Southwark (1955), St Albans (1957), Windsor (1959), Rochester (1961), Chelmsford (1963), Canterbury (1965), Durham (1967) and Selby (1969). Since then the programme has widened to include Tewkesbury (1971), York (1972), Salisbury (1974), Peterborough (1975), Hereford (1976), Chichester (1978) and Winchester (1979). These coins are the only ones of this reign to have been minted consistently in sterling silver with a proof-like surface.

In keeping with established custom, the coins issued in coronation year included a crown. The quatercentenary of this handsome piece had passed in 1951 without recognition, but Gilbert Ledward's design for the obverse was clearly influenced by the silver crowns of 1551 with their equestrian portrait of Edward VI. On this occasion the crown portrayed the queen riding side-saddle on the police horse Winston at the Trooping of the Colour ceremony. This was a bold and imaginative design which captured the hearts of the general public, hence the comparatively large mintage of 6 million. The queen's titles were recited in full, with the exception of the BRITT. OMN., and the value appeared in words FIVE SHILLINGS at the foot. Another nice touch with late-medieval overtones was the use of tiny Tudor roses as a spacing ornament. The overall effect was marred only by the needless inclusion of

1953 Coronation crown. (*Peter Clayton*)

the royal cypher – twice – in the field. The artist's initials, GL, appear to the right of the horse's hindquarters. The reverse was a joint effort by Edgar Fuller and Cecil Thomas and showed the heraldic devices of the United Kingdom in four shields in the form of a cross, with a Tudor crown at the centre and the heraldic flowers in the interstices. The initials of the designers appear below the two lower shields.

1953 half-crown with BRITT. OMN on obverse. (*Peter Clayton*)

Messrs Fuller and Thomas were also responsible for the reverses used for the half-crown, two-shilling piece and sixpence, and one may detect the family likeness between these three coins and the crown. The half-crown, with its crowned scrolled shield flanked by the royal monogram, was clearly inspired by Nicholas Briot's gold pieces of 1631–32. The initials of the designers appear beneath the shield. In the designs for the two-shilling and the sixpence they let their penchant for vegetation run riot. The sixpence is vaguely reminiscent of its counterpart in the last series of George V, but whereas the earlier coins were confined to acorns and oak leaves, the Fuller–Thomas sixpence was a *bouquet garni* of rose, thistle, shamrock and leek, their stems entwined in such a confusing manner that this coin was frequently depicted in the press at the time of its release wrong way up – an error perpetrated in more recent years in coin catalogues. The two-shilling coin is even more confusing since the effect of the heraldic nosegay is so overpowering that the lettering and date are almost smothered. In this instance the date should be at three o'clock to balance the word TWO at nine o'clock, but again, it was often depicted at the wrong angle. Technically this reverse was described as a double rose surrounded by a ring of five thistles,

Fuller–Thomas sixpence. (*Coin Monthly*)

1963 florin. (*Peter Clayton*)

four shamrocks and three leeks, their frequency and position depending on the exigencies of the lettering.

The tradition of two different shillings was continued, but the designs standardised, to show the badges of England (three lions couchant) and Scotland (a lion rampant) surmounted by a Tudor crown – an unfortunate hybrid so far as the Scots were concerned; once again their own distinctive crown was ignored and insult was added to injury by the use of the numeral II in the queen's title. Both shillings were designed by William Gardner whose initials flanked the shields near the foot.

Reverses of Elizabethan English and Scottish shilling. (*Peter Clayton*)

The cupro-nickel coins from 1954 onwards omitted the BRITT OMN. inscription from the obverse. Half-crowns were minted annually from 1954 to 1967 in considerable quantities, and though two-shilling pieces were struck abundantly in the same period they have not survived in the finest grades of condition to the same extent, due largely to their use in slot machines. Minting of both English and Scottish shillings continued annually until 1966, but in fluctuating quantities. Only 1 million Scottish shillings were minted in 1959 and this coin is decidedly elusive in the better grades. Sixpences were struck in astronomical quantities, rising to 240 million in 1967 alone, the last year of production, but because it was so widely used in slot machines, telephone boxes and gas, electricity and parking meters, relatively few have survived in pristine condition.

Crowns were issued twice in this period. In 1960 a coin with FIVE SHILLINGS at the foot of the obverse, and the Fuller–Thomas heraldic reverse previously used for the coronation crown, was released. Because it was not tied to a

1960 New York Exhibition crown. (*Peter Clayton*)

specific occasion this item was rather overlooked at the time and little more than a million were sold in circulating condition. Some 70,000, however, were also struck from specially polished dies, giving an overall brilliant finish, and these were sold at the British Exhibition in New York. These proof-like coins are worth much more than the ordinary version. An interesting precedent. was established in 1965 when a crown was issued as a tribute to Sir Winston Churchill who had died in January of that year. The Gillick obverse was modified to include the date below the bust, while the reverse reproduced a profile of Sir Winston, based on the statue by Oscar Nemon. The only inscription on the reverse was CHURCHILL. Incidentally, this was the first crown since 1902 not to bear any inscription of its value. Over 19 million Churchill crowns were produced in response to the demand from the public and the ordinary version is thus very common. A very few specimens, however, were produced with a satin finish using specially polished dies and these rank among the great rarities of the present reign.

The nickel–brass threepence followed the pattern used for the previous reign, but the Kitchener thrift motif on the reverse was replaced by a crowned portcullis flanked by chains, designed by William Gardner. This revived a favourite Tudor emblem which had formed a prominent part of

Churchill crown. (*Peter Clayton*)

Elizabethan brass threepence. (*Peter Clayton*)

the design of the large gold coins and also appeared as a mintmark in the reign of Henry VIII. The value THREE and PENCE flanked the portcullis and the date appeared at the foot. Gardner's initials appeared between the central prongs of the portcullis. Over 30 million threepences were struck in 1953 with the BRITT. OMN. legend. Later threepences, without the BRITT. OMN. title, were struck in substantial quantities from 1954 until 1967.

All three bronze coins retained the reverses from the previous reign. The penny was not issued in 1953 for general circulation but some 1.3 million were struck for inclusion in the Royal Mint specimen set which contained the nine coins from half-crown to farthing in a plastic envelope. Both halfpenny and farthing were generally circulated that year. In 1954 the BRITT. OMN. title was omitted from the obverse. Evidently dies for the penny were prepared and a few trial strikes made, but only one specimen (formerly in the Peck collection) ever leaked out. No pennies were, in fact, minted for general circulation until 1961 but thereafter large numbers were issued annually until 1967. In its final year the penny went out in a blaze of publicity and as speculators scrambled to acquire mint bags of them the Royal Mint obligingly continued to strike them as long as the demand lasted. Consequently a staggering 654,564,000 pennies were minted – most of which have survived in the hands of investors, with original lustre intact.

With the exception of 1961, halfpence were minted annually until 1967, though production fluctuated from a low around 20 million in 1954–56 to a peak of 146 million in 1967. The 1957 halfpenny may be found with the normal reverse or one in which the waves are much less prominent – hence the 'calm sea' epithet applied to this variety. Some halfpennies of 1967 have a noticeably wider rim than normal, which literally gives them the edge (no pun intended) over the normal version.

Farthings without BRITT. OMN. were struck in 1954–55, averaging 6 million a year, but fewer than 2 million were struck in 1956. As a result of inflation this coin had ceased to have any practical use and, with the minimum of publicity, it was withdrawn and demonetised. One must remember that, at that time, there was no general periodical devoted to coin collecting and the lay press was not so coin conscious as it later became. A decade later, when everyone, it seems, had taken up coin collecting, the scarcity of the 1956 farthing was suddenly apparent and prices leaped dramatically.

Decimal coinage since 1968

Ever since the third century rebellion of Carausius coins had been minted in London, and the Royal Mint, so long associated with the Tower of London, seemed like it to symbolise endurance and reliability. A century and a half after the Mint was moved out of the Tower into nearby premises the need for more space to expand output had become a matter of extreme urgency. In December 1967 it was decided that the Royal Mint should move right out of London altogether. The Labour government, which had come to power under Harold Wilson in 1964, felt it politic to re-establish the Mint in South Wales, an area of growing unemployment due to retrenchment in the iron and coal industries, and thus it was that Llantrisant in Glamorgan was selected. Work on the new Mint proceeded rapidly and within twelve months it had been sufficiently completed for the queen to perform the opening ceremony by setting the presses in motion. A further seven years elapsed before the task of bringing Llantrisant up to full production was completed and during that transitional period minting continued at Tower Hill. The London end of the operation ceased late in 1975, though the Royal Mint still maintains administrative offices in the capital.

Just as the change of premises in 1816 coincided with sweeping currency reforms, so also the move in 1968 brought drastic changes in its wake. For 120 years successive governments had toyed with the idea of adopting a decimal system of coinage and for years the argument had raged back and forth regarding the relative merits of the pound–cent and pound–mil systems. In the end, inflation overtook the argument and the pound–cent system was adopted. Tradition was upheld at the risk of confusion by retaining the good old Anglo-Saxon word 'penny' for a one-hundredth part of the pound. To lessen the confusion, however, it was officially called a 'new penny' – but having become rather stale after more than a decade the adjective 'new' was dropped in 1983.

The changeover to decimal coinage proceeded at a leisurely pace, though bearing in mind that the process of metrication has not become an accomplished fact even now, we must be thankful that the coinage was decimalised in the space of three years. The first phase took place in 1968 when shillings and florins were transformed into five and ten new pence. Conversely the existing shillings and florins were absorbed into the system, and have continued to circulate to this day. Theoretically any shilling since 1816 and any florin since 1849 are legal tender and could turn up in change, though this is now most unlikely, since the silver coins were systematically withdrawn from circulation after the change from 0.500 silver to cupro-nickel in 1946. Even by the time of the change-checkers' mania in the late 1960s it was not uncommon to find a good proportion of pre-1946 silver coins in bank bags and even in one's loose change. All this changed dramatically, however, in November 1967 when the Labour government was forced to devalue the pound sterling by 14 per cent, bringing it down from $2.80

to $2.40. Older readers will doubtless recall ruefully the aphorism about 'the pound in one's pocket remaining the same'. By the end of 1967 the bullion price of silver had risen to the staggering sum of 18 shillings (90 new pence) the Troy ounce which meant that the 0.500 fine silver half-crowns minted up to 1946, containing one-fifth of an ounce each, were worth 3 shillings 7 pence as scrap. Although the Gold and Silver Export Control Act of 1920 expressly forbade the melting down of coins, with a penalty of two years' imprisonment or a fine of £100, the hoarding of silver coins which then ensued rapidly drained them from circulation. The half-crown was demonetised in January 1970, but whether it has since become possible to melt such coins down is largely an academic matter.

The halfpenny was the first victim of decimalisation, being demonetised in August 1969, but not before speculators had hoarded away such astronomical amounts of them as to render the 1967 coin a drug on the market for all time. The penny and the nickel–brass threepence continued until 1971, while the oft-threatened sixpence was continually reprieved until 1980. Although the changeover to decimal coinage did not become effective until 15 February 1971, the designs of the new coins were well publicised long before that date. In 1968 the cupro-nickel five- and ten-pence pieces were put into circulation. At the same time they were made available in specimen wallets, along with bronze half, one and two new pence dated 1971. This is believed to be the first time that any country has issued coins so far in advance of their actually becoming legal tender. The range of circulating coins was completed in 1969 with the introduction of the 50 new pence piece. The lay press, always keen to promote neologisms, suggested that the new coin should be known as a 'wilson'; mercifully that idea fell flat on its obverse! Regrettably, the movement to revive the term 'half-sovereign' also sank without trace. With that singular perversity for which the British are noted, the coin quickly acquired the nickname of a 'ten-bob bit', despite government propaganda for the decimal nomenclature. 'New pence' proved too much of a mouthful and the public, subconsciously distinguishing the new from the old, adopted the term 'pee', which has even acquired the respectability of dictionary status.

The decimal coins were not without controversy for several reasons. The opportunity was taken to replace the Gillick effigy of the queen with a more mature portrait. For this purpose the bust by Arnold Machin RA was selected. This broke with the tradition, whereby Britain led the rest of the Commonwealth, since this bust had been used by Australia since it adopted decimal coinage in 1965, and had since been used by Canada and New Zealand, and some purists felt that it was rather bad form for the mother country to be upstaged by the 'colonies' in this way. But this splendid diademed profile has since won wide acceptance, not only in Britain but in virtually every other country which has the monarch's effigy on its coins. The Machin profile was matched by a rather undignified compression of the royal titles, which caused a great deal of unfavourable comment at the time. ELIZ-ABETH II appeared down the right side, while D.G. REG. F. D. and the date ran up the left side. This arrangement had the merit, so far as the Mint was concerned, of permitting the use of the same master dies to produce secondary obverse dies for other Commonwealth countries, with their name substituted for the royal titles.

The task of designing the reverses was entrusted to Christopher Ironside. Whatever his own fancy, he was limited to a great extent by the brief which insisted that the words NEW PENNY or NEW PENCE should appear around the top in each case, and prominent numerals at the foot. This did not leave much scope for the principal motifs in between, and Ironside was reduced to using fairly basic heraldic elements. The crown of St Edward the Confessor (new halfpenny) had gradually replaced the Tudor crown on all government insignia – right down to the watermark on postage stamps – since 1954. The crowned portcullis (new penny) and Prince of Wales's plumes (two new pence) had both featured as mintmarks in Tudor and Jacobean coinage. In keeping with the tradition since 1937 of issuing a Scottish shilling, the five new pence depicted the Scottish thistle, this time surmounted by the crown of King James IV which forms part of the Honours of Scotland, or regalia, in Edinburgh. The ten new pence showed a crowned lion passant gardant.

At first there were complaints that Britannia should have been allowed to vanish after three centuries, but when the design of the highest denomination was revealed a year later it was seen that the grand old lady had merely switched from the subsidiary coinage. She was now depicted with a lion alongside. The design shows the strong influence of Küchler's cartwheel coinage: Britannia has the trident cradled in repose and extends the olive branch of peace – an appropriately conciliatory stance in view of the government's policy of disengagement east of Suez which had only recently been announced. The most startling feature of the fifty new pence, however, was its size and shape. The age-old policy of having coins related to each other by weight was abandoned. The new coin was only marginally larger and heavier than the ten new pence – one-fifth of its value. The government contended that the shape, a rounded heptagon without any graining or edge inscription, was so distinctive that confusion would not arise. As a compromise, however, the life of the ten-shilling note, which it had been designed to replace, was prolonged for the benefit of elderly and partially-sighted people.

Fifty-pence piece and EEC reverse of 1973. (*Peter Clayton*)

At the other end of the scale the new halfpenny came in for considerable criticism. In particular the legend NEW PENNY at the top was confusing since it had to be read in conjunction with the fraction at the foot; even more annoying was its diminutive size. All the hoary arguments against the silver threepence and the farthing were resurrected, though the Mint was quick to point out that many European countries had even smaller coins in circulation. Although the new halfpenny was worth more than one old penny, its worthlessness in everyday use was soon apparent. It never had any purchasing power on its own – except to purchase a halfpenny stamp which was likewise of no use alone, and tradesmen and shopkeepers soon began rounding prices up when converting from pounds, shillings and pence to new pence. In this manner decimalisation took much of the blame for the price increases of 1971–72. In fact, it merely obscured the fact that the country was in the grip of inflation which rose first to 4 per cent per annum and then to 10 per cent before going into orbit in 1973 at the time of the miners' strike, the three-day week and the industrial chaos of 1974. This time inflation and recession were world-wide. Originally a retaliatory measure for European attitudes towards the Arab–Israeli conflict, the Arab oil increases in 1974 were soon to become a means of earning enhanced revenues for producing less oil – an argument which met with some favour from conservationists. The inflationary spiral which drove the ten-shilling note out of existence has since threatened the existence of the pound note and other relatively low-denomination paper money all round the world. The Isle of Man led the way by introducing a circulating 'round pound' in 1978. The United Kingdom, bedevilled by the old argument of relating the value of coins to their weight, shied away from introducing a pound coin twice the weight of the fifty pence, but the Isle of Man neatly solved the problem by returning to the sovereign size, and using an entirely new coinage metal called virenium, an alloy of copper, nickel and zinc with a magnetic element as an in-built security device.

Continuing demand for gold sovereigns as a convenient method of handling bullion led to the resumption of minting in 1974. Paradoxically, legislation the following year made it illegal for United Kingdom residents to possess these coins. Sovereigns were minted in 1976, 1978 and 1979–81 and one of the first acts of the Conservative government under Margaret Thatcher was to repeal the restrictive legislation of her predecessor. To meet the new-found demand from the indigenous collector market the Royal Mint announced the minting of a proof version of the 1979 sovereign. By the time of its release, however, the price of gold on the free world market had risen sharply from $250 to over $800 an ounce, and in the atmosphere of gold fever this sovereign was heavily oversubscribed. The bullion price subsequently dropped to around half that figure, and the Royal Mint's issue of the full set of gold coins, in denominations of half-sovereign, sovereign, two-pound and five-pound, in 1980 was less successful. A total of 10,000 proof sets was produced but it is significant that only 5,000 five-pound proofs were issued in 1981, and though the number of proof sovereigns remained substantial, neither half-sovereign nor two-pound coin was included that year.

Apart from the Maundy coins, sterling silver was used for proof versions of commemorative crowns, minted on several occasions since 1972. The first of these pieces celebrated the Silver Wedding of Queen Elizabeth and the Duke of Edinburgh. On this occasion the obverse did not include the date, since the dates 1947–1972 were placed on the reverse. The design, by Arnold Machin, was inscribed ELIZABETH AND PHILIP round the top, with the date at the foot and the crowned initials EP in a floral setting in the centre. A circulating version in cupro-nickel was available to the public at 25 new pence – a fine example of a commemorative item which had nobly withstood the onslaughts of inflation.

Silver Wedding crown, 1972. (*Peter Clayton*)

Five years later came the Silver Jubilee crown with no fewer than four different versions. The obverse hearkened back to the coronation crown with an equestrian portrait of the queen and ungainly lettering for the legend which many found disappointing. The reverse featured the ampulla and anointing spoon used in the coronation ceremony, surmounted by the St Edward crown and surrounded by heraldic flowers. The crown was issued in

Silver Jubilee crown, 1977. (*Peter Clayton*)

cupro-nickel with the normal finish at face value of 25 pence, but a second version in cupro-nickel, sold by the Mint in a souvenir folder, had 'specimen' striking, akin to the satin finish of the rare Churchill crown, and a third version in this alloy was proof-struck from specially polished dies and made available only as part of a proof set, mentioned below. A proof version in sterling silver was also released.

Queen Mother crown, 1980. (*Peter Clayton*)

A crown celebrating the eightieth birthday of Queen Elizabeth, the Queen Mother, was issued in 1980 – the first time that a person other than the reigning sovereign had been portrayed on a British coin in their own lifetime. The reverse, by Professor Richard Guyatt, had a tiny profile of the Queen Mother facing left in the centre, surrounded by a radiating pattern of bows and lions, a pun on her family name of Bowes-Lyon. It should be noted that two of her ancestors had served as under-treasurers at the Tower Mint and Durham House and John Bowes had used a bow as his mintmark in 1548–49. The legend round the upper half read QUEEN ELIZABETH THE QUEEN MOTHER, while the date of her birthday was rendered as AUGUST 4th 1980 round the foot. Three versions were struck, in sterling silver proof and both

Royal Wedding crown, 1981. (*Peter Clayton*)

ordinary and proof-like versions in cupro-nickel. Similar versions of a crown celebrating the wedding of Prince Charles and the Lady Diana Spencer were issued in July 1981. For the first time three people were portrayed on a British coin simultaneously, the Machin profile of the queen being on the obverse while conjoined profiles of Lady Diana and the Prince of Wales appeared on the reverse, with their names round the circumference and the date at the foot. The reverse was designed by Philip Nathan, whose initials appear below the truncation of the Prince's neck.

It is somewhat anomalous that the traditional crown size should have survived into the decimal era and continue to be tariffed at 25 new pence – the equivalent of 5 old shillings. This seems all the more incongruous in view of the fact that the fifty-pence coin is an ideal medium for commemorative purposes and was, in fact, thus used in 1973. A decade after President De Gaulle had vetoed British entry into the Common Market, the Conservative government under Edward Heath succeeded in gaining British admission to the European Economic Community (EEC). This was celebrated in 1973 by a fifty-pence coin with the usual Machin obverse and a symbolic design by David Wynne showing nine clasped hands to denote the nine member countries of the EEC. This coin was only produced in cupro-nickel, but both circulating and proof versions were issued.

The pattern of issuance of the circulating coinage has been very erratic compared with the previous series. With the exception of 1972, the new halfpenny and new penny have been minted each year since 1971, but the bronze two new pence did not appear until 1975, after the inaugural issue in 1971. The cupro-nickel five and ten new pence have appeared since 1968 but the five new pence was not minted in 1972–74 or in 1976, while the ten new pence was omitted in 1972. The fifty was struck in 1969–70, but the Britannia design was not used again until 1976 and annually thereafter. Aware of the raggedness of the decimal series, the Royal Mint came up with the brilliant concept of 'the coins that never were'. Retrospective proof sets were produced of the six coins from the half to the fifty, in series dated from 1972 onwards, and this has now become an annual event. The 1973 series contains an EEC fifty new pence, since the Britannia design was omitted in that year, and commemorative proofs have been incorporated in the set for the year in which they were issued. The idea for these proof year sets arose from two commemorative issues made at the time of the changeover to decimal coinage. A proof set containing the eight coins from the halfpenny to the half-crown was issued in 1970, the coins bearing the 'impossible' date of 1970, even though the highest and lowest denominations had been demonetised. This was followed in 1971 by a decimal proof set of six coins, from the new halfpenny to the fifty new pence. These proof year sets include a handsome medallion bearing the Royal Mint emblem.

And what of the future? In line with the more liberal and commercial approach of the Mint's Numismatic Bureau we can expect a steady flow of commemorative coins at annual intervals, though whether the crown size is retained is a matter for conjecture. Enormous fluctuations in the price of silver in 1980–81 emphasised the problem of issuing proof versions of such large coins. Due to the attempts by the Hunt Brothers of Texas to manipulate the world market, the price of silver rose from an average £3 an ounce to almost seven times as much, before dropping again. In 1982 Britain was compelled to introduce a heptagonal 20 pence coin – the same shape as the fifty but no larger than the five. Altering the shape is one way of breaking out of the weight–value trap; another is to alter the composition of the alloy used. Taking a leaf out of the Isle of Man's book, the Royal Mint experimented in 1981 with a golden-coloured alloy for a circulating pound coin issued by Guernsey. To help the partially sighted the Isle of Man had given its coin a distinctive edge of alternating plain and grained sections, but Guernsey's pound was struck on flans of double thickness. The latter concept was adopted for the British pound coin, introduced in April 1983. Slightly smaller than the five-pence coin, it was very much thicker and considerably heavier, while the pale yellow colour simulating gold contrasted with the usual silvery appearance of cupro-nickel. The reverse was designed by Eric Sewell, formerly Chief Engraver of the Royal Mint, and featured the royal coat of arms. In 1984 a new reverse, depicting the English arms, was scheduled, to be followed in successive years by reverses showing the arms of Scotland, Wales and Northern Ireland. In addition to the normal grained edge, the pound coin bears an incuse inscription – DECUS ET TUTAMEN (*an ornament and a safeguard*) – echoing the Latin motto which was a feature of the milled coinage of 1662.

One pound coin with inscription on grained edge introduced in 1983.

In the meantime the Isle of Man went a stage further, adopting a five-pound coin in 1981. This coin has the same diameter as the traditional gold five-pound piece but is minted in the base-metal alloy virenium. At the time of its introduction inflation was still in double figures, but as inflation dropped steadily in 1982 and fell to around four per cent in 1983, it seemed unlikely that the United Kingdom would have to resort to a five-pound coin for general circulation. Since a coin has a life expectancy of 25 years, compared with a few months for a banknote, serious consideration must always be given to the practical advantages of coins, particularly for use in vending equipment. On the other hand, the general public is notoriously conservative and, given a choice between coins and notes, will always tend to prefer the latter. Although the Bank of England·intends to phase the

Twenty-pence piece.

pound note out of circulation the three Scottish banks have announced that they will continue to issue pound notes for the foreseeable future.

The advent of the small twenty pence and pound coins makes a nonsense of the existing cupro-nickel five, ten and fifty-pence coins which are now far too large and cumbersome in relation to their actual spending power. If the opportunity is taken to revise the coinage and scale it down in size, the existing bronze coins will almost certainly disappear. They will either re-emerge in some cheaper alloy, like titanium—zinc or aluminium, or be retained with new values. Even if inflation is curbed the fact remains that the pound in 1983 is worth only a third of its pre-decimal counterpart, and in that context the coinage of 1968—71 now seems both antiquated and impractical.

Select reading list

Bramah, E., *A Guide to the Varieties and Rarity of English Regal Copper Coins, 1671–1860* (Methuen, 1929).

Brooke, G. C., *English Coinage* (revised ed, Spink, 1950).

Craig, Sir John, *The Mint* (Cambridge Univ. Press, 1953).

Feavearyear, A. E., *The Pound Sterling: A History of English Money* (Oxford Univ. Press, 1963).

Gould, J. D., *The Great Debasement: Currency and the Economy in Mid-Tudor England* (Oxford Univ. Press, 1970).

Linecar, H. W. A., *British Coin Designs and Designers* (G. Bell, 1977).

Nelson, P., *The Obsidional Money of the Great Rebellion, 1642–1649* (1905, reprinted 1968)

North, J. J., *English Hammered Coinage* (3 vols) (Spink, 1960–3).

Oman, C., *The Coinage of England* (Oxford Univ. Press, 1931).

Peck, C. W., *English Copper, Tin and Bronze Coins in the British Museum, 1558–1963* (The British Museum, 1964).

Porteous, J., *Coins in History* (Weidenfeld and Nicholson, 1969).

Seaby, H. A. and Rayner, P. A., *English Silver Coinage from 1649* (B. A. Seaby, 1968).

Seaby, P. J., *The Story of the English Coinage* (B. A. Seaby, 1952); *Standard Catalogue of British Coins, Vol. 1: Coins of England and the United Kingdom* P. Seaby and P. F. Purvey (eds) (B. A. Seaby, 1981).

Seaby, P. J. and Bussell, M., *British Copper Coins* (B. A. Seaby, 1970).

Spink and Son Ltd, *The Milled Coinage of England* (Spink, 1950).

Sutherland, C. H. V., *English Coinage, 600–1900* (Batsford, 1973).

Sweeny, J. O., *A Numismatic History of the Birmingham Mint* (Birmingham Mint, 1981).

Index